The Caregiver Helpbook

Powerful Tools for Caregivers

THIRD EDITION

Some materials on pages 12–13 are adapted from *The Arthritis Helpbook,*
Fourth Edition, by Kate Lorig, R.N., Dr.P.H. and James F. Fries, M.D.,
copyright © 1995 by Perseus Books, L.L.C. Reprinted by permission of
Perseus Books Publishers, a member of Perseus Books L.L.C.

ISBN 978-0-615-85610-0

Printed in the United States of America

Cover design by Anita Jones, Another Jones Graphics
Text design and layout by Jonathan Wills Graphic Design and
Mike Staudinger, Legacy Health System Marketing & Creative Services.

∾

Dedicated to
the many hard-working families and friends
who devote time and energy caring for the chronically ill.

∾

AUTHORS

∾

Chapters 1–7

Marilyn Cleland, B.S., R.N.

Vicki L. Schmall, Ph.D.

Marilynn Sturdevant, R.N., M.S.W., L.C.S.W.

∾

Chapters 8–21

Lydia Abrams, MSW, LCSW, C-ASWCM

Leslie Congleton, B.A.

Kay Kirkbride, B.S.N.

Jean McFalls

Stephanie Ross, LCSW

Kathy Shannon, M.A.

Virginia Sponsler, M.S.W.

Howard Turner, M.S.W.

∾

Table of Contents

FOREWORD

Powerful Tools for Caregivers (PTC) is an independent non-profit organization providing training, technical assistance, and materials to help promote the dissemination of the PTC program for family caregivers. The PTC program and all materials were developed over 3 years of pilot testing, refinement, and evaluative research at Legacy Health in Portland, Oregon. Initiated through grant funding from the Meyer Memorial Trust, The Robert Wood Johnson Foundation, the Northwest Health Foundation and the Good Samaritan Foundation, the program has been offered since 1998.

In 2007, PTC received the National Family Caregiver Award for innovation, responsiveness and effectiveness from the National Alliance for Caregiving and the MetLife Foundation. In 2009, PTC received the Network of Multicultural Aging Excellence Award from the American Society on Aging/AARP. In 2012, the program was deemed to have met the highest-level criteria for evidence-based disease prevention and health promotion programs by the Administration on Aging.

Research studies find high rates of depression and anxiety among caregivers and increased vulnerability to health problems. Caregivers frequently cite restriction of personal activities and social life as problems. They often feel they have no control over events – and that feeling of powerlessness has a significant negative impact on caregivers' physical and emotional health.

In the six weekly classes, family caregivers develop a wealth of self-care tools to: reduce personal stress; change negative self-talk; communicate more effectively in challenging situations; manage their emotions; and make tough caregiving decisions. Class participants receive a copy of *The Caregiver Helpbook* when attending the class. *The Caregiver Helpbook* is also an excellent stand-alone resource for family caregivers.

Since the program's inception, a great deal of research, evaluation and revision has been done to ensure its continued value and success. The 6-week PTC class has been shown to have a positive impact on caregiver health for a diverse group of caregivers including rural, ethnic minorities, adult children of aging parents, well-spouses/partners, caregivers at differing stages in their caregiving role, living situations, financial and educational backgrounds.

Data from class participant evaluations indicates the PTC program improves:

◆ Self-Care Behaviors: (increased exercise, use of relaxation techniques and seeking medical care)

◆ Management of Emotions: (reduced guilt, anger, and depression)

◆ Self-efficacy (increased confidence in coping with caregiving demands)

◆ Use of Community Resources: (increased utilization of community services)

PTC is based on the highly successful *Chronic Disease Self-Management Program* developed by Dr. Kate Lorig and her colleagues at Stanford University's Patient Education Research Center.

PTC is a national program sustained by extensive collaborations with community-based organizations including Area

Agencies on Aging, AARP, disease-specific organizations, Cooperative Extension Services, the Veteran's Administration, organizations supporting caregivers of children with special needs, hospitals, healthcare systems, faith-based organizations and hospice programs.

For more Information about *The Caregiver Helpbook* or the curriculum for the class, "Powerful Tools for Caregivers," contact powerfultoolsforcaregivers.org.

ACKNOWLEDGMENTS

Many people made *The Caregiver Helpbook* possible. First, we gratefully acknowledge the work of Dr. Kate Lorig and her colleagues at Stanford University's Patient Education Research Center whose pioneering work in patient education and chronic disease self-management formed the foundation for our work. Dr. Lorig's advice and encouragement were invaluable. We are particularly appreciative that Dr. Lorig and Bull Publishing of Palo Alto gave us permission to use and adapt materials on goal setting, contracting, and problem solving from the book, *Living a Healthy Life with Chronic Conditions.*

We are most indebted to the Meyer Memorial Trust, Portland, Oregon, for the generous grant to support the development of *The Caregiver Helpbook* and the caregiver educational program, "Powerful Tools for Caregivers."

We also appreciate the generosity of the American Society on Aging for allowing us to use photographs from their collection, including photographs by Steven W. Brummel, Faye J. Clark, Lena Sexton, Don Huff Photography and Susan M. Knechtel.

Thanks to Ron Schmall, David Gorsek and Loaves and Fishes for photographs.

We wish to acknowledge the contributions of Linda Boise, PhD, whose research identified the evidenced-based outcomes of the program.

A special thank you goes to the many family caregivers and professionals who helped us to identify the needs and concerns of family caregivers, participated in pilot testing of program materials, and reviewed chapters of *The Caregiver Helpbook.* We could not have reached our goal of developing a book that makes a difference for caregivers without their participation and insights.

CHAPTER ONE

Taking Care of You

Caregiving involves many challenges. You often need to master new skills. You may need to develop new ways of relating to a family member if his or her ability to communicate or remember is compromised by illness. You may have to make tough decisions. But often one of the greatest challenges is taking care of yourself.

Too often caregivers neglect their own health and well-being, and put their own needs "on the back burner." Sometimes caregivers become a second victim of the disease that afflicts their family member. It's sad when someone says, "My mother was the ill person, but her illness destroyed my father." Usually, we cannot stop the impact of a chronic illness on a family member. However, we are responsible for our own self-care.

When you board an airplane, the flight attendant gives several safety instructions. One of them is, "If oxygen masks drop down, put on your oxygen mask first before helping others." This is because if you don't take care of yourself first, you may not be able to help those who need your help. It's the same thing with caregiving. When you take care of yourself, everyone benefits. Ignoring your own needs is not only potentially detrimental to you, but it can also be harmful to the person who depends on you.

THE CAREGIVER HELPBOOK

The Caregiver Helpbook was designed to help you maintain personal well-being while providing quality care to your family member. The first half of the book focuses on several tools to help you to take care of *you*. These tools will help you to:

◆ set goals and make action plans.

◆ identify and reduce personal stress.

◆ make your thoughts and feelings work for you, not against you.

◆ communicate your feelings, needs, and concerns in positive ways.

◆ cope with difficult situations, including asking for help and setting limits.

◆ deal with emotions, especially feelings of anger, guilt, and depression.

◆ make tough caregiving decisions.

Chapters in the second half of the book address special concerns and decisions you may face as a caregiver. These include what to do when a family member is no longer a safe driver, hiring in-home help, using community services, how to communicate with and respond to a family member who is memory impaired, options available when a family member is having problems managing his money, coping with depression, and making a decision about a care facility. You can turn to these chapters for guidance and resources when you face a specific decision or concern.

MANAGING SELF-CARE

Managing our self-care means that as caregivers we:

◆ **Take responsibility.** We realize we are responsible for our personal well-being and for getting our needs met. This includes maintaining activities and relationships that are meaningful to us.

◆ **Have realistic expectations.** We fully understand our family member's medical condition and we are realistic about what our family member can and cannot do.

Ask yourself the following questions about your caregiving:

YesNo

❐ ❐ Do you ever find yourself trying "to do it all?"

❐ ❐ Do you ever say to yourself "I should be able to…," "I can never…," or similar statements?

❐ ❐ Do you ever ignore your feelings or find that they are overwhelming?

❐ ❐ Do you ever get frustrated because of something you can't change or someone who won't change?

❐ ❐ Do you resist seeking, asking for, or accepting help?

❐ ❐ Do you feel that your family or others just don't understand what you are going through as a caregiver?

A "yes" answer to any of these questions indicates an area of self-care you might want to work on.

The more you know about your family member's medical condition, the better you will be able to plan successful caregiving strategies. Knowledge is power.

It's also important to look at your definition of a "good caregiver." Unrealistic expectations can set you up for feelings of failure, resentment, and guilt. Placing burdensome expectations on yourself does not make you a better caregiver. In fact, you are much more likely to become an exhausted, irritable, and resentful caregiver...and then to feel guilty!

◆ **Focus on what we can do.** It's important to be clear about what you can and cannot change. For example, you will not be able to change a person who has always been demanding and inflexible, but you can control how you respond to that person's demands. You can accept—"let go" of—the things you cannot change. Managing your self-care also means you seek solutions to what you can change.

◆ **Communicate effectively with others.** These include family members, friends, health care professionals, and the care receiver. Don't expect others to know what you need. Recognize it is your responsibility to tell others about your needs and concerns. Communicate in ways that are positive and avoid being demanding, manipulative, or guilt-provoking when you make requests.

◆ **Learn from our emotions.** Realize there will be emotional ups and downs. Listen to your emotions and what they are telling you. Don't bottle up your emotions. Repressing or denying feelings decreases

energy; causes irritability, depression, and physical problems; and affects your judgment and ability to make the best decisions. Also, don't strike out at others. You are in control of your emotions; your emotions don't control you.

◆ **Get help when needed.** An important part of self-care is knowing when you need help and how to find it. Help can be from community resources, family and friends, or professionals. Most important is that you do not wait until you are "hanging at the end of your rope" before you get help. Don't wait until you are overwhelmed or exhausted, or your health fails. Reaching out for help, when needed, is a sign of personal strength.

◆ **Set goals and work toward them.** Be realistic in the goals that you set and take steps toward reaching those goals. Seek solutions to the problems that you experience. Changes do not need to be major to make a significant difference.

In summary, self-care means that you seek ways to take better care of yourself. As a caregiver, you don't just survive. You thrive!

Trying To Do It All

One problem that caregivers frequently experience is trying to do it all and doing it all alone. Is it possible to do it all? The answer to the question can be both "yes" and "no." It really depends on you. What is critical is how you define what it means to "do it all." And, whether or not your definition of "doing it all" includes taking care of yourself so that you thrive, and not just survive.

To Maxine, the answer to the question "Is it possible to do it all?" was "no." She says, "Mother's needs are endless and no matter what I do, I can never make her happy." Yet, at the same time, Maxine was trying to do it all. Her mother's care dominated Maxine's life.

Another caregiver, Maria, answered "yes" to the question, "Is it possible to do it all?" She explained that "All that needed to be done for my mother was done."

A major difference between Maxine and Maria was the rules by which they operated. Maxine operated by the rule, "I must do everything for my mother." The rule had

become, "I must help Mama at all costs." As a result, her relationships with other family members suffered and Maxine found herself becoming increasingly resentful. Maxine's feelings of wanting to do everything is legitimate, but the actions associated with her feelings usually are impossible to carry out. As a result, Maxine experiences feelings of failure and lack of success.

Maria was more realistic. She recognized that the things she wanted to be done—whether they were her desires, her mother's desires, or the desires of others—were not the same as the things that needed to be done. Maria's goal was to make her mother as comfortable as possible, without sacrificing herself and the other important relationships in her life. She also got help from family and a community agency in meeting her mother's needs. Maria said:

> To some degree I recognized that caregiving was like a job and my goal was to find the best way to get the job done. A friend also told me that doing any job well—including the job of caregiving—requires four things:
>
> 1. Recognizing you can't do everything yourself—you work with others.
> 2. Taking daily breaks.
> 3. Taking vacations to renew oneself.
> 4. Being realistic about what you can do.

There was another difference between Maxine and Maria. Maxine felt it was selfish to think of herself. Maria, on the other hand, viewed that if she was going to be there for the long haul, she must take care of herself, and make sure that she had pleasurable moments in her life.

As a caregiver, you are more likely to "be there" for your family member who needs your care and to be a more loving and patient caregiver when you meet some of your own needs. It's important to "fill your own cup" and not allow it to "run dry."

It's not being selfish to focus on your own needs and desires when you are a caregiver to a family member who has a chronic or progressive illness. It's important to ask yourself, "If my health deteriorates, or I die, what will happen to the person I provide care for? If I get emotionally drained, become deprived of sleep, or become isolated because I am trying to do it all, how loving am I likely to be to my family member?"

Taking Time for Yourself

Do you value yourself and your personal needs? What do you do for personal renewal? Do you save some time for yourself out of each day? Do you take occasional extended breaks? Or are you so involved with caregiving tasks that you have little or no time for yourself?

What activities do you enjoy? What would you like to do that would give you a lift? When was the last time you gave yourself a treat?

Breaks in caregiving are a must. They are as important to health as diet, sleep, rest, and exercise. It's important not to lose sight of your personal needs and interests. Studies show that sacrificing yourself in the care of another and removing pleasurable events from your life can lead to emotional exhaustion, depression, and physical illness. You have a right—even a responsibility—to take some time away from caregiving.

Regular breaks from the tasks of caregiving are essential. Decide on the time, date, and activity—then follow through. Breaks don't have to be long to make a positive difference. It's important to plan some time for yourself in every day, even if that time is only for 15 minutes or half an hour. Most important is to do something that "fills your cup" and helps you to feel better and thrive.

If you have difficulty taking breaks for yourself, consider taking them for your family member. Care receivers also benefit from caregivers getting breaks.

SETTING GOALS

An important tool in taking care of yourself is setting goals. A goal is something you would like to accomplish in the next three to six months. What would you like to do to take better care of yourself and to help yourself to thrive? This might be to get a break from caregiving for a week, get help with caregiving tasks, be able to walk three miles, or quit feeling guilty.

Goals often are difficult to accomplish because they may seem like dreams or they may be overwhelming. As a result, we may not even try to accomplish them or we may give up shortly after we get started. We will address this problem shortly. For now, take a moment and write your goals here:

Goal 1 _____

_____

_____

Goal 2 _____

_____

_____

Goal 3 _____

_____

_____

Put an asterisk (*) next to the goal you would like to work on first.

After identifying a goal, the first step is to brainstorm all of the different things you might do to reach your goal. Identify and write down all possible options.

Option 1 _____

_____

_____

Option 2 _____

_____

_____

Option 3 _____

_____

_____

Option 4 _____

_____

_____

Option 5 _____

_____

_____

The second step is to evaluate the options you have identified. Which options seem like possibilities to you? It's important not to assume that an option is unworkable or doesn't exist until you have thoroughly investigated it or given it a try. Assumptions are major self-care enemies.

Put an asterisk (*) next to two or three options you would like to try. Select one to try.

The third step is to turn your option into a short-term plan, which we call *making an action plan*.

MAKING ACTION PLANS

An action plan is a specific action that you are confident you can accomplish within the next week. It's an agreement or contract with yourself.

Action plans are one of your most important self-care tools. An action plan is a step toward reaching your long-term goal. It is to be something you want to do. It is *not* to be something you feel you *should* do, *have to* do, or *need to* do. The intent of making an action plan is to help you to feel better and to take better care of yourself. Remember, an action plan is a "want to do."

Here are the five steps for making an action plan:

1. Decide what you want to do.

2. Make your plan behavior-specific.

3. Make a specific plan.

4. Determine your confidence level.

5. Write down your action plan.

Decide What You Want To Do

Think about what is realistic for you to accomplish within the next week. It's important that an action plan is reachable; otherwise, you are likely to experience frustration. An action plan is to help you experience success—not frustration, increased stress, or failure. An action plan starts with the words, "I will…" If you find yourself saying "I will try to…," "I have to…," or "I should…," then re-examine your action plan. It probably is not something that you truly want to do.

Make Your Plan Behavior-Specific

The more specific your action plan, the greater your chances of accomplishing it. For example, "taking better care of myself"

PARTS OF AN ACTION PLAN

1. It's something you want to do.

2. It's reachable (something you believe you will be able to accomplish during the next week).

3. It answers these questions:
   —What?
   —How much?
   —When?
   —How often?

4. It has a high confidence level. (You are certain that you will be able to complete your *entire* action plan during the next week.)

---

is not a specific behavior. However, making an appointment for a physical check-up, walking three times a week, getting a massage on Thursday afternoon, or asking someone to stay with your family member for one morning are all specific behaviors. "I will relax" also is not a specific behavior; however, reading a book, listening to your favorite music, or puttering in the garden are specific behaviors.

Make a Specific Plan

Making a specific plan is often difficult, yet it is the most important part of making an action plan. A specific plan answers these four questions:

1. **What are you going to do?**
   Examples: I will read (*book name*) for pleasure. Or, I will walk.

2. **How much will you do?**
   Examples: Will you read one chapter or will you read for a half hour? Will you walk two blocks or for 20 minutes?

3. **When will you do this?**
   Examples: Will you read the first thing in the morning when you awaken, before you go to bed, when the care receiver is sleeping, or…? If your plan is to walk, when during the day will you do it ?

4. **How often will you do this activity?**
   Example: Three times a week on Monday, Wednesday, and Friday.

A common mistake is to make an action plan that is unreachable within the time frame. For example, if you plan to do something every day, you might fail. Caregiving, and life in general, has its surprises. Although well-intentioned, it's often not possible to do something every day. It's better to plan to do something once or twice a week and

exceed your action plan than to plan to do something every day and fail because you only did it six days, rather than seven. Remember, an action plan is meant to help you to take better care of yourself and to experience success. The last thing you need is additional pressure, disappointment, and stress.

Here are two recommendations for writing an action plan that can help you achieve success.

1. **Start where you are or start slowly.** If there's a book you've been wanting to read, but just haven't found the time, it may not be realistic to expect to read the entire book in the next week. Instead, try reading for a half hour twice during the week. If you haven't been physically

active, it may be unrealistic to make an action plan to start walking three miles. It is better to make your action plan for something that you believe you can accomplish. For example, make your plan for walking three blocks or a half mile, rather than three miles.

2. **Give yourself time off.** We all have days when we don't feel like doing anything. That's the advantage of saying you will do something three days a week, rather than every day. That way, if you don't feel like doing something on one day, or something develops that prevents you from doing it, you can still achieve your action plan.

Determine Your Confidence Level

Once you've made your action plan, ask yourself the following question: On a scale of 0 to 10, with 0 being not at all confident and 10 being totally confident, how confident am I that I can complete my action plan?

If your answer is 7 or above, your action plan is probably realistic and reachable. However, if your answer is 6 or below, it's important to take another look at your action plan. Something probably needs to be adjusted.

Ask yourself, "What makes me uncertain about accomplishing my action plan? What problems do I foresee?" Then, see if you can either find a solution to the problems you identified or change your action plan to one in which you feel greater confidence.

Write Down Your Action Plan

Once you are satisfied with your action plan, write it down. Putting an action plan in writing helps us to remember, keep track of, and accomplish the agreement we have made with ourselves. Keep track of how you are doing. Write down the problems you encounter in carrying out your action plan. Check off activities as you accomplish them. If you made an adjustment in your action plan, make a note of what you did.

At the end of the week, review your action plan. Ask yourself, "Am I nearer to accomplishing my goal?" "How do I feel about what I did?" What obstacles or problems, if any, did I encounter?" Taking stock is important. If you are having problems, this is the time to seek solutions.

See page 12 for a sample action plan. See page 13 for an action plan form that you can duplicate and use to develop your own action plans.

PROBLEM-SOLVING: A SOLUTION-SEEKING APPROACH

Sometimes you may find that your action plan is not workable. You may encounter unusual circumstances that week and need to give the plan a try for at least another week. Or you may need to make adjustments in your original plan. The following solution-seeking approach can help you identify solutions to problems.

◆ **Clearly identify the problem.** This is the first and most important step in the solution-seeking approach. It also can be the most difficult step.

◆ **List ideas to solve the problem.** Family, friends, and others may be helpful in giving ideas. When you ask for ideas, just listen to each suggestion. It's best not to respond as to why an idea is or isn't likely to work. Just focus on getting the ideas.

◆ **Select one to try.** When trying a new idea, give it a fair trial before deciding that it won't work.

◆ **Assess the results.** Ask yourself, "How well did what I chose work?" If all went well, congratulate yourself for finding a solution to the identified problem. If the first idea didn't work, try another idea. Sometimes an idea just needs fine-tuning. It's important not to give up on an idea just because it didn't work the first time.

If you have difficulty finding a solution that works, utilize other resources. Share your problem with family, friends, and professionals and ask them for possible ideas. If you still find that suggested solutions do not work, you may need to accept that the problem is not solvable right now.

Remember, just because there doesn't seem to be a workable solution right now doesn't mean that a problem can't be solved later, or that other problems can't be solved in the same way. It may be helpful to go back to the first step and consider if the problem needs to be redefined. For example, a caregiver had thought that her problem was "I am tired all of the time." However, the real problem was the caregiver's beliefs that "No one can care for John like I can," and "I have to do everything myself." As a result of these beliefs, the caregiver was doing everything herself and getting worn out. When she redefined the problem and focused on changing her beliefs and view of the caregiving situation, she found a workable solution. Sometimes, too, a problem may be easier to work on if you break it down into smaller problems.

Most of the time if you follow these steps, you will find a solution that solves the problem. It's important to avoid making the mistake of jumping from step 1 to step 7 and thinking "nothing can be done."

> ### SUMMARY OF THE SOLUTION-SEEKING APPROACH
>
> 1. Identify the problem.
> 2. List ideas to solve the problem.
> 3. Select one idea to try.
> 4. Assess the results.
> 5. Substitute another idea if the first one didn't work.
> 6. Utilize other resources if your solutions don't work.
> 7. Accept that the problem may not be solvable now.

REWARD YOURSELF

Accomplishing action plans is often a reward in itself. However, it's also important to find healthy pleasures that add enjoyment to your life. Rewards don't have to be fancy or expensive or take a lot of time. One caregiver, for example, regularly goes to a movie or a play as a gift to herself from her husband. She said:

> When my husband was well, he would take me out Friday nights to a movie or a play at least twice a month. Because of his medical condition, he is no longer able to do so. Now a friend and I go to a movie or a play at least once a month. I consider this is a treat that my husband is still giving to me.

Another caregiver said:

> Before my wife's illness, I would go golfing with my buddies on Saturday morning. When Carmela needed more care, I quit golfing. I now treat myself to Saturday golfing, while my daughter or a friend visits with Carmela. This gives me something to look forward to each week and I feel more alive when I return home. I'm also finding I am more patient with Carmela. My daughter says I am always happier and calmer when I return home. So, I look at Saturday golfing as my treat not only to me, but also to Carmela.

SUMMARY

In review, a caregiver who practices self-care does the following:

1. Sets goals.

2. Identifies a variety of options for reaching a goal.

3. Makes an action plan toward accomplishing the goal.

4. Carries out the action plan.

5. Assesses how well the action plan is working.

6. Makes adjustments, as necessary, in the action plan.

7. Rewards himself or herself.

Not all goals are achievable. Sometimes we must accept that what we want to do is not possible at this time, and we must let go of the idea. Be realistic about goals and don't dwell on what can't be done.

Consider what is likely to happen to the caregiver who is driven by a goal to make her mother happy. Given her mother's personality, this goal may be completely unachievable. Such a goal creates a heavy burden and a caregiver is not likely to achieve it. However, an achievable goal might be to provide a pleasurable activity for her mother at least once a week—perhaps taking her to get her hair done, visiting a friend, watching a comedy on television, or working together on a project her mother enjoys.

Remember, what is important in caregiving is not just to survive, but to thrive! This book is designed to give you a set of tools to help you take care of yourself. This in turn will help you provide better care.

MY ACTION PLAN—*Sample*

When writing an action plan, be sure it includes:

1. **What** you are going to do.

2. **How** much you are going to do.

3. **When** you are going to do it (i.e., what time of day).

4. **How often** you are going to do it.

Example: This week I will read a favorite book (what) for a half hour (how much) in the mid-afternoon when my spouse sleeps (when), three times—Monday, Wednesday, and Friday (how often).

This week I will _____*read a book*_____[what]

_____*half an hour*_____[how much]

____*mid-afternoon, when my spouse naps*_____[when]

____*3 days—Monday, Wednesday, Friday*_____[how often]

How confident are you that you will complete your entire action plan during the week?
(*Circle*)   0   1   2   3   4   5   6   ⑦   8   9   10
     not at all confident   *totally confident*

Check off each day you accomplish your plan	**Comments:**
Monday ✓	*Felt good to read for pleasure*
Tuesday ____	
Wednesday ____	*Granddaughter came over. Nice visit!*
Thursday ✓	*Read for an hour—refreshing!*
Friday ✓	*Read for 15 minutes, fell asleep.*
Saturday ✓	*Awakened early; read while drinking coffee — a good way to start the day*
Sunday ____	

MY ACTION PLAN

When writing an action plan, be sure it includes:

1. **What** you are going to do.

2. **How** much you are going to do.

3. **When** you are going to do it (i.e., what time of day).

4. **How often** you are going to do it.

Example: This week I will read a favorite book *(what)* for a half hour *(how much)* in the mid-afternoon when my spouse sleeps *(when)*, three times—Monday, Wednesday, and Friday *(how often)*.

This week I will _____[what]

_____[how much]

_____[when]

_____[how often]

How confident are you that you will complete your entire action plan during the week?
(Circle)　0　　1　　2　　3　　4　　5　　6　　7　　8　　9　　10
　　　　　not at all confident　　　　　　　　　　*totally confident*

Check off each day you accomplish your plan　　**Comments:**

Monday　　_____　　_____

Tuesday　　_____　　_____

Wednesday　　_____　　_____

Thursday　　_____　　_____

Friday　　_____　　_____

Saturday　　_____　　_____

Sunday　　_____　　_____

Overview

Chapter Two

The Stress of Caregiving
Factors That Affect Stress

Steps to Maintain and Avoid Stress
Step 1: Recognize Your Warning Signs of Stress
Step 2: Identify Your Sources of Caregiving Stress
Step 3: Identify What You Can and Cannot Change
Step 4: Take Action to Manage Your Stress

Summary

Reducing Personal Stress

The philosophy of Virginia Satir, noted family therapist, sets the tone for this chapter on the stresses and challenges of caregiving. She reminds us that how we perceive and respond to an event is a significant factor in how we adjust and cope with it.

This chapter explores the stress of caregiving. It will help you identify and understand your particular stressors, challenges, and strengths. You can then plan strategies that help you cope, change, and reduce stress. A basic premise of this chapter is that each of us has a reservoir of strength. The challenge is to identify our strengths and build on them.

Life is not the way it's supposed to be. It's the way it is. The way you cope with it is what makes the difference... I think if I have one message, one thing before I die that most of the world would know, it would be that the event does not determine how to respond to the event.

That is a purely personal matter. The way in which we respond will direct and influence the event more than the event itself.

Virginia Satir

THE STRESS OF CAREGIVING

There has been so much written about stress it has become a household word. Studies show that a certain amount of stress is helpful. It can challenge us to change and motivate us to do things we might not do otherwise. However, when the amount of stress overwhelms our ability to cope with it, we feel "distress" or "burnout."

According to Webster's Dictionary, distress is "suffering of mind or body; severe physical or mental strain." As a caregiver, you no doubt have increased stress in your life, whether you are caring for a mother with early Parkinson's disease, who is still able to care for her personal needs, or a spouse who doesn't recognize you because of advanced Alzheimer's disease.

Each caregiving situation is unique. What is stressful for you may not be stressful for someone else. In his book *The Survivor Personality,* Al Siebert says, "there is no stress until you feel a strain." Since the feeling of stress is subjective and unique to each individual, it is difficult to define objectively. The stress you feel is not only the result of your caregiving situation, it is also your perception of it. Your stress will increase or decrease depending on how you perceive your circumstances. And your perception will affect how you respond.

Factors That Affect Stress

Your level of stress is influenced by many factors, including:

◆ whether your caregiving is voluntary or not.

◆ your relationship with the care receiver.

◆ your coping abilities.

◆ your caregiving situation.

◆ whether support is available.

Whether your caregiving is voluntary or not

Many people become caregivers voluntarily. Others acquire the role because no one else is available. When you become a caregiver voluntarily, you are making a choice. However, if you "inherited" the job and feel you had no choice, the chances are greater for experiencing strain, distress, and resentment. Nancy became a caregiver because no one else was available.

Nancy couldn't have been more surprised when the visiting nurse asked her if she was the primary caregiver for her mother-in-law, Joan. Nancy was fond of Joan. She called and stopped by frequently to see how Joan was managing, but hadn't thought of herself as the primary caregiver. It was apparent that Joan's medical condition was worsening and she was becoming increasingly weak. Nancy realized there were no other children or relatives available, so she agreed, although somewhat reluctantly, to be Joan's caregiver. Nancy felt anxious and uncertain about what it meant to be a primary caregiver and whether she had the necessary skills to perform the role.

Luckily, Nancy and Joan had a good relationship and they were able to communicate openly, minimizing some of the potential for stress. You can't always think about a caregiving relationship in advance, but if you can, it has greater potential for success.

Your relationship with the care receiver

If your relationship with the care receiver has been difficult, becoming a caregiver is more of a challenge. If the care receiver has always been demanding and controlling, you will probably feel more stress, anger, and resentment.

Sometimes people are caregiving with the hope of healing a relationship. The healing may or may not happen. If healing doesn't happen, the caregiver may feel regret, depressed, and discouraged. A professional counselor, spiritual advisor, or trusted friend can help deal with such feelings and emotions.

Your coping abilities

How you have coped with stress in the past predicts how you will cope now. Did you find constructive ways to manage your stress? Perhaps you were able to find time to exercise regularly and generally take care of yourself. Or did you rely on alcohol or drugs to help you cope? Sometimes people rely on medications and alcohol in times of stress, which only makes matters worse.

It is important to identify your current coping strengths and build on them. Learning new coping skills also will help make your caregiving situation less stressful.

The caregiving situation

What does your caregiving situation require of you? Does it require 24-hour-a-day availability? Or do you just need to make an occasional telephone call to check on the person? What disease does the care receiver have? Does he have a mental or physical disability, or both?

Certain caregiving situations are more stressful than others. For example, caring for someone who has a dementia such as Alzheimer's disease is often more stressful than caring for someone with a physical limitation. Also, stress tends to be highest when:

◆ the caregiving situation continues for a long time.

◆ the care receiver's needs gradually increase.

◆ caregivers feel they have limited or no support.

◆ caregivers have their own health/physical problems.

Whether support is available

Caregivers who feel isolated and without adequate support usually experience a higher level of stress. Support may be lacking for several reasons:

◆ The caregiver may resist accepting help, even when he or she needs it.

◆ Others may be willing to help but don't offer because they are uncomfortable around the ill person, frightened of the illness, or don't know what they can do.

◆ Others don't want to interfere, especially if the caregiver seems to have everything under control and has refused help in the past.

Caregiver stress is influenced by many factors, including the need to adapt to ongoing changes and losses caused by the care receiver's illness. These changes cause you to redefine your life. What was normal has changed. You are living with a new reality.

STEPS TO MAINTAIN HEALTH AND AVOID DISTRESS

Whatever causes stress in your life, too much of it can lower your resistance to disease and lead to "burnout." Current research shows that there is a close connection between stress and health. Unrelieved stress is one of many factors that cause illness. Research also shows that thoughts and emotions affect the immune system, which is the first line of defense against disease. It is possible to strengthen the immune system by reducing stress. The following four steps will help you maintain your health and avoid distress:

1. Recognize your warning signs of stress.

2. Identify your sources of stress.

3. Identify what you can and cannot change.

4. Take action to manage your stress.

Each of these steps will be discussed in detail.

Step 1: Recognize Your Warning Signs of Stress

The first step in managing stress is to be aware of how it affects you. What are your warning signs and symptoms of stress?

The following are signs that may occur when you experience an unusual amount of stress. Answering these questions can help you identify your own warning signs.

What is usually your earliest sign of stress? It's important to recognize stress early and do something about it, before it

YesNo

❑ ❑ Do you feel a loss of energy or zest for life?

❑ ❑ Do you feel tired or exhausted much of the time?

❑ ❑ Do you feel out of control, exhibiting uncharacteristic emotions or actions?

❑ ❑ Do you feel tense, nervous, or anxious much of the time?

❑ ❑ Do you lack interest in people or things that were formerly pleasurable?

❑ ❑ Are you becoming increasingly isolated?

❑ ❑ Are you consuming more sleeping pills, medications, alcohol, caffeine, or cigarettes?

❑ ❑ Are you having increased health problems: for example, high blood pressure headaches, ulcers, upset stomach, or other difficulties with digestion?

YesNo

❑ ❑ Do you have sleep problems, such as difficulty falling asleep at night, awakening early, or sleeping excessively?

❑ ❑ Are you experiencing appetite changes?

❑ ❑ Do you have problems with concentration or memory?

❑ ❑ Are you increasingly irritable or impatient with others?

❑ ❑ Do you have feelings of helplessness or hopelessness?

❑ ❑ Are you abusing or neglecting to provide care to the care receiver?

❑ ❑ Do you have thoughts of suicide?

A "yes" answer to even one or two of these questions can indicate stress that has become debilitating.

causes you serious problems. For one caregiver, the early sign might be increased irritability. For another, it might be lying awake for hours before falling asleep. For another, it might be fatigue and a lack of energy.

Sometimes, too, when we are involved in a situation, we may not listen to our early warning signs, but they are voiced in the words of others: "You look so tired," "You get upset so easily lately," "Why are you snapping at me?" If you hear such statements, it is a "red light" warning sign. Just as a flashing red light on your car's dashboard warns you that something is wrong with your car, we also display warning signals. What happens if we ignore the early red flashing light on the car's dashboard? What happens if we ignore our personal early warning signals?

Do you listen to your early warning signals? What are they? And what do you do about them? Warning signs usually mean we need to stop, evaluate what's happening, and make some changes. The earlier warning signals are recognized, the greater the chance of avoiding or reducing the destructive effects of stress.

Step 2: Identify Your Sources of Caregiving Stress

The second step in managing stress is to recognize what causes your stress. Not all stressors are the result of caregiving. Other sources can affect your ability to be a caregiver. The following questions include many common sources of stress. Answering these questions can help you recognize some of your own sources.

Yes No

❏ ❏ Are you experiencing many demands on your time, energy, or money? What are they?

❏ ❏ Do you feel you have conflicting responsibilities? Which ones?

❏ ❏ Are there differences in expectations between your family, your boss, the care receiver, and yourself? What are they?

❏ ❏ Do you feel others don't understand the care receiver's mental or physical condition?

❏ ❏ Do you have difficulty meeting the care receiver's physical or emotional needs?

❏ ❏ Are you pressured by financial decisions and lack of resources?

❏ ❏ Do you feel a loss of freedom, to the point of feeling trapped?

❏ ❏ Is there disagreement among family members?

❏ ❏ Do you feel that other family members aren't doing their share?

❏ ❏ Does the care receiver place unrealistic demands and expectations on you?

❏ ❏ Is there a lack of open communication between you and the care receiver?

❏ ❏ Do other family members have negative attitudes that create difficulty for you?

❏ ❏ Is it painful to watch the care receiver's condition get worse?

❏ ❏ Are there other problems with children, marriage, job, finances, or health? What are they?

Consider your "yes" answers carefully. The sources of stress you have identified are indicators for change. Use the awareness you have gained in the first two steps to make helpful changes.

The following story is an example of a caregiver who recognized the source of her distress and made changes to better manage the situation.

> Ernestine was increasingly fatigued, irritable, and depressed with the responsibility of caring for her husband, Richard, who had Parkinson's disease. Richard's condition was steadily getting worse. He was bedbound and needed help with many functions. Other family members hadn't offered to help, and Ernestine felt abandoned, alone, angry, and overwhelmed. A few friends and neighbors had offered to help but Ernestine refused. When she started having health problems, it became clear that something had to change. She had to have help.
>
> Because Ernestine had difficulty asking for help, she devised a simple plan that would give others an opportunity to help without having to be asked. She made a list of tasks she needed help with and posted it on the refrigerator. The list included such things as vacuuming the living room, grocery shopping, staying with Richard so she could go to church, weeding the garden, picking up audio books at the library, picking up medications at the pharmacy, and preparing food. When visitors offered to help, Ernestine referred them to the list, suggesting they choose a task that suited them. This proved to be a successful plan for everyone.

It's important to identify the causes of your stress before they overwhelm you. Don't wait until you develop health problems, as Ernestine did. Many caregivers keep going until they become ill. You can only be an effective caregiver if you are healthy. Self-sacrifice to the point of illness benefits no one and is not required or recommended.

Step 3: Identify What You Can and Cannot Change

A major challenge of caregiving is to not only survive, but to rebuild your life and thrive. This is possible once you know the sources and signs of your stress. Then you can determine those you can do something about and those that are beyond your control. Step three is to identify what you can and cannot change.

Identifying what you can change gives you a sense of control over events. However, it isn't easy to determine what can and cannot be changed. Too often people try to change things they have no control over. For example, someone who focuses on trying to change another person usually ends up more frustrated. The only person you can change is yourself. You may be able to change a situation, how you respond to it, or your perception of it, but you can't change another person. It wastes valuable time and energy trying to change what is outside of your control.

Some situations can't be changed. However, you may be able to manage them better if you change your outlook about a situation, or decide to "roll with the punches."

The frustration and hopelessness that result from trying to change the unchangeable are self-defeating and can adversely affect a relationship, as in the case of Hal and Sue.

Sue and Hal had been a socially active couple. Sue was diagnosed with early Parkinson's disease and gradually started backing out of social plans because she didn't feel up to it. Since the beginning of the disease Sue has been on a roller coaster of having good days and bad days. Hal encourages Sue to go out when she doesn't feel like it, urging her to "snap out of it." He wants things to remain as they were.

Hal is frustrated in his attempts to change the effect of the disease on their lives. By not accepting Sue's feelings, he is adding stress to their relationship. But recently he has learned more about Parkinson's disease and is trying to be more realistic and flexible about what he can and cannot change. Flexibility is crucial. A Japanese saying is:

In a storm, it is the bamboo, the flexible tree, that can bend with the wind and survive. The rigid tree that resists the wind falls, victim of its own insistence on control.

Bending with the wind is crucial to surviving the winds of change, including those involved in caregiving. At times, both you and the care receiver may feel a loss of control over your lives. While feeling in control is important, sometimes it can become a problem because the more we try to control, the less control we seem to have. Being flexible can help us keep a positive attitude, despite hardships.

Use the following guidelines to look at your situation and to determine what can and cannot be changed:

1. Accept the reality of your caregiving situation.
2. Educate yourself about the care receiver's disease.
3. Identify unrealistic expectations, especially your own.
4. Seek and accept support.
5. Identify what you still have, rather than focus on what is lost.
6. Let go of what cannot be changed.

Accept the reality of your caregiving situation

When making changes it is necessary, but not always easy, to accept reality. We often deny things that hurt, and that can keep us from seeing a situation as it really is.

Jane heard the doctor tell Joe that he had a serious illness. He also told Joe he would need more rest and help with certain daily activities. Still, Jane found herself feeling annoyed when Joe took frequent naps, especially since she was taking on more responsibility for managing things at home. It took time for Jane to stop denying, and start accepting, the full impact of the disease. It was then that she was able to see realistically what could and couldn't be changed.

Jane is coping in a more adaptive way. However, Joe's mother denied the seriousness of the disease long after Jane came to terms with it. Family members may take different lengths of time to accept reality, which can add to the stress of caregiving.

Educate yourself about the care receiver's disease

You will be better able to identify what you can and cannot change when you understand the disease. For example, without knowledge about the communication abilities of someone with Alzheimer's disease, you may try to reason with the person or expect him to tell someone something you consider easy to remember. This will probably frustrate both of you.

There are many sources of information about specific diseases, including your personal physician, medical libraries, and associations related to specific diseases, such as Alzheimer's and Parkinson's disease. If you have access to a computer that is linked to the Internet, you can find a wealth of current information on diseases and disease-related associations.

Identify unrealistic expectations, especially your own

You can make changes successfully only when your expectations are realistic. How realistic are yours? Do you often feel anxious because you expect more of yourself than you can achieve? Many caregivers listen only to the "shoulds" they have been raised with. Women, especially, often believe they "should" be able to do everything themselves, and when that isn't possible, they feel guilty or depressed. If you have unrealistic expectations of yourself, then your expectations of what can be changed probably will be unrealistic also.

The following story is an example of a caregiver, Rosa, who with her husband, Dean, made constructive changes in what was a difficult, stressful situation.

Rosa was devastated when Dean, her husband of 40 years, suffered a sudden, severe stroke that left him partially paralyzed on one side of his body and unable to speak. The stroke was a shock. Rosa's initial response was to become overly protective and do everything for Dean. She was afraid to leave him alone for fear something terrible would happen.

Before the stroke, Rosa and Dean had been making retirement plans, which included extensive travel. Those plans were forsaken as they both felt increasingly overwhelmed, fearful, isolated, and depressed.

Rosa became extremely fatigued and irritable as Dean became increasingly dependent on her. The visiting nurse talked with them about what Dean could and could not do for himself. She emphasized the importance of Dean maintaining as much independence as possible. It became apparent that Dean could do many things for himself, including writing letters to family and friends. Dean felt better as he became more independent. Rosa was able to be more realistic in her expectations. She realized that Dean's dependence on her was detrimental to their relationship.

As Rosa and Dean gradually adapted to living with the stroke, they became less fearful and more hopeful. They began looking at the quality of their remaining life together. They wanted, more than anything, to travel together and decided to take a short trip to see how it would go. The first trip was successful and they felt encouraged to travel more. Rosa found a travel agent who helped them plan trips that accommodated Dean's disabilities. They enjoyed several trips before Dean's death 12 years later.

Rosa and Dean responded to this challenge by gaining an understanding of the disease, accepting reality, setting realistic expectations, and changing what could be changed.

Seek and accept support

Many caregivers find it difficult to ask for help. Rosa initially refused help from friends and neighbors. She did everything herself until she started feeling distressed. The expectations she had for herself were overwhelming and unrealistic. It wasn't until she began seeking support from the visiting nurse, travel agent, and others that she was able to find a way to make changes. Often you can make changes only with the help of others. Seeking and accepting support may be the single most important factor in making constructive changes.

Identify what you still have, rather than focus on what is lost

When Rosa and Dean decided to look for "what remained" in their situation, they hoped that they still had quality in their life together. They looked at what they still had, rather than focusing on what had been lost, and they made changes that were still possible.

They found an unexpected "gift" as they made changes and adapted to the illness. Rosa said, "I never would have asked for the stroke to happen, but it was because of it that Dean and I learned what love was all about. I am a different person than I was. I am more understanding, patient, caring, and sensitive to the pain of others."

Many caregivers, as they learn more about themselves, experience personal growth. That is the "gift" that can often be found in difficult times.

Let go of what cannot be changed

It is natural to want to hold on to things as they were. But letting go of what you cannot change is accepting the situation as it is. It releases you from the need to control what you cannot change. Letting go is a way to cooperate with the inevitable. It releases new energy for accepting reality and seeing new possibilities. Sam is a prime example of someone who is learning to let go.

Sam had always been an intense athletic competitor, and sports had been the driving force in his life. At age 45 he had a slight stroke which left him mildly affected. Sam's problem wasn't that he had a stroke; the problem was that he couldn't let go of wishing that he hadn't had one. He continuously wanted things to be as they had been. This made him feel angry and frustrated. Fortunately, Sam reached a point of wanting to learn to live with the stroke and to let go of wanting life to be as it had been before.

Sam was unable to live in the present until he let go of his desire for things to be as they were. The "if onlys" and "what ifs" were a source of suffering. When Sam let go, he learned to live with the stroke and made changes that helped him develop a satisfying life. What Sam learned also applies to caregivers, as shown in the case of Marsha and Bud.

Marsha was the caregiver for her husband, Bud, who had Parkinson's disease. Bud's condition worsened and he and Marsha were unable to do many of the things they had done in the past. Marsha continually wanted things to be the way they had been. "If only" became her constant thought: "If only Bud could dress himself," "If only we could go dancing like we used to," "If only Bud had more energy," "If only he could still drive us places."

Marsha's unhappiness caused a strain in their relationship. It was only when she and Bud were having a good time playing cards with friends one day that she realized how much valuable time she was wasting by constantly wanting things to be different. She began to let go of "if only" and to accept "what is." In letting go, she found acceptance and peace of mind.

As you reflect on your challenges as a caregiver, consider these questions. What can I change? What must I accept? What can I improve? The challenge is beautifully written in "The Serenity Prayer."

The Serenity Prayer

...grant me Serenity to accept the things I cannot change, Courage to change the things I can, and Wisdom to know the difference.

Reinhold Niebuhr, 1934

Step 4: Take Action to Manage Your Stress

The fourth step points the way for you to manage and reduce your stress. There are many different tools for managing stress. But you must find what is most effective for you. Proven ways to manage and reduce stress include:

- managing your thoughts, beliefs, and perceptions.
- practicing self-care.
- getting social support.
- using techniques that lower stress.
- developing plans of action.
- finding hope and meaning.

Managing your thoughts, beliefs, and perceptions

Thoughts and beliefs are the foundation of experience. They are not only reactions to events but our thoughts and beliefs can also influence events. What we think and believe affects what happens. Managing our thoughts means we have control over how we view things. As a caregiver, there may be times when the only thing you can change is how you view a situation.

There are several tools for managing thoughts, beliefs, and perceptions. Two that can be helpful are reframing and self-talk.

Reframing. Your frame of reference is the window through which you view the world. It gives meaning to your world. You see things one way, but someone else sees the same circumstances differently. Situations become more stressful when you view them in a negative way.

Reframing is learning to look at things in a different way, for example, finding something

positive about a difficult situation. Some examples of reframing include:

◆ A caregiver who views the behavior of someone with Alzheimer's disease as "purposefully behaving that way to get to me" versus taking the view that "the behavior is a part of the disease."

◆ A caregiver who is angry at her brother for helping only once a month versus taking the view that "any help, no matter how little, will lighten my load."

◆ A caregiver who puts the situation into a religious or philosophical framework, such as "This is happening because God is angry with me" versus taking the view that "God is giving me an opportunity to learn and grow."

People who are able to reframe difficult situations generally feel less burden and more in control. Feeling a greater degree of control often leads to acting in control. Clara is a good example.

Clara had difficulty taking breaks from caregiving. Before becoming a caregiver, she had worked in a demanding position and had realized the importance of taking weekends off and vacations to refresh herself and cope better with work demands. When she started to view caregiving as a job, it made a difference in how she viewed breaks in caregiving. They became not only more acceptable, but a necessity.

Julie also found that reframing a difficult situation reduced her stress and helped her act in new ways.

Julie felt resentful and burdened with the increasing demands of caring for her mother. She had no help, feeling that as a good, dutiful daughter she should do it all. A social worker told her about available resources and suggested she think of herself as a personal care manager as a way to find help in caregiving. Julie gained a sense of control over the situation once she realized she didn't have to provide all of the care herself, but could oversee her mother's care.

As a caregiver, you may feel overwhelmed and burned out, especially if you are assuming responsibility for most of the caregiving. Changing your perception of your role from a caregiver to care manager is a way of reframing. As a care manager you still get the job done, but you don't have to provide all the care yourself. The role of care manager means that you:

◆ coordinate and supervise another's care needs. This includes using available support.

◆ are aware of available community resources.

◆ plan and prioritize care.

◆ understand the disease of the care receiver and what to expect.

◆ participate as an equal partner with other health care professionals.

◆ are knowledgeable about the health care system.

As a care manager you assume an active role and reach beyond giving hands-on care, to planning and coordinating care and using available resources. You will feel an increased sense of mastery as a successful care manager.

Self-talk. Most stress management courses include learning how to use self-talk to promote health. Self-talk is what we say to ourselves. As Ralph Waldo Emerson said, "A man is what he thinks about all day long."

What do you think about all day long? What do you say to yourself? It's especially important to notice your self-talk when you suffer setbacks and when you feel anxious, angry, discouraged, or distressed. Negative self-talk statements often begin with the following phrases:

◆ I just can't do…

◆ If only I could (or didn't) do…

◆ I could never…

◆ I shouldn't have done…

◆ I should have…

Negative self-talk is defeating. It can lead to depression and a sense of failure, because with negative self-talk we tend to focus on:

◆ what we did *not* do versus what we have done.

◆ what we *can't* do versus what we *can* do.

◆ Our mistakes and failures versus our successes.

You want your self-talk to work *for* you, not against you. If your self-talk is negative or unhelpful, challenge it. Learn to change the negative things you say to yourself into positive statements, such as affirmations.

Affirmations are positive, supportive statements that counteract the effects of negative thinking. When positive statements are repeated several times a day, they begin to replace negative thoughts. This helps to change one's attitude, promote relaxation, and reduce stress. Karen's story is an example of changing negative self-talk to positive self-talk with the use of affirmations:

Karen felt angry and discouraged when her mother didn't eat the tasty, nutritious meals she prepared for her. She didn't accept the fact that her mother's lack of appetite was caused by the illness. Karen constantly told herself, "No matter what I cook, it is never good enough for mother."

This is an example of negative self-talk. Karen became aware that she often thought she was not doing good enough, especially in caring for her mother. These thoughts made her feel like a failure.

With determination, patience, and practice, you can change your self-talk from negative to positive. The following steps lead to change:

1. Identify your negative thoughts. Listen to what you say to yourself, especially during difficult times.

2. Write your negative thoughts down on paper. This helps to identify and clarify them.

3. Challenge your negative thoughts. Give them a good argument.

4. Write a simple, positive statement for each thought you want to change.

5. Memorize and repeat the chosen statements. This helps establish the habit of positive self-talk.

6. Put your written statements where you see them frequently. This is a helpful visual reminder.

Karen chose the affirmation, "I am preparing nutritious food. That is enough." In fact, the statements, "I am doing my best. It is good enough," became her frequent affirmation and counteracted her negative thoughts of "not doing good enough."

These statements have the dual purpose of affirming what Karen is doing and helping her let go of the idea that she has control over her mother's appetite. Accepting that was important. Telling herself that she is doing her best and it is enough is a positive way of saying she is changing what she can and letting go of what she cannot change. Karen's expectations for herself have become more realistic.

Practice over time will change negative, habitual thinking. Repeat this activity frequently to identify other negative self-talk. Remember, thoughts and attitudes create your reality. Changing your negative thoughts will help you focus on the positive things in your life, rather than on what you don't have.

CHALLENGING YOUR SELF-TALK

Identify an example of your negative self-talk and the situation when it is most likely to occur. Be as clear and as detailed as possible. Write it down.

1. My negative statement:

3. I will replace the negative thought with this positive statement:

2. I say this to myself when:

4. Repeat the chosen affirmation whenever the above situation occurs.

There will be times when you will find it hard to shake off negative thoughts. This is normal. However, paying attention to the frequency and content of these thoughts is the beginning of self-awareness and the possibility of change.

Practicing self-care

To be an effective caregiver you need to maintain your own health and spirit, and to nurture yourself. All too often caregivers put their own needs last. Studies show that sacrificing yourself in giving care to another can lead to emotional exhaustion, depression, and illness.

Maintaining your health and spirit can reduce your level of stress. It is critical to find activities that help you to stay healthy and nurture yourself. These activities are different for each individual. What works for one person may not work for another. You must find stress-reducing methods that work best for you.

We can learn a lot from a self-care program in Florida called "Getting Well." This is a group of people who are supporting each other in learning to live and feel better. They take part in life-affirming activities such as "laughing, juggling, playing, meditating, painting, journal writing, exercising, and eating nutritiously." They demonstrate the necessity of associating with others who help you maintain your spirit and help you feel loved and supported.

To manage stress, it is essential to take breaks from caregiving. Plan them into your schedule, starting immediately, if you have not done so already. Studies show that caregivers often don't take breaks until they are at the "end of their rope" or "burned out."

ARE YOU TAKING CARE OF YOURSELF?
YesNo

☐ ☐ Are you uncomfortable putting yourself first at times?

☐ ☐ Do you think you should always meet the needs of other people before your own?

☐ ☐ Do you feel you should be a "perfect caregiver"?

☐ ☐ Do you minimize or deny that you have needs?

If you answered "yes" to any of these questions, you may be ignoring your own needs.

This serves no one's best interest as your ability to function can be seriously affected. To avoid problems, it is your responsibility to take time off from caregiving to refresh yourself.

It is important to the well-being of care receivers that you take breaks. If you don't, they may become increasingly dependent on you. If you take breaks, they will be less isolated and will benefit from having contact with other people. They also need breaks from you. (This is an example of reframing your perception of a situation.)

You are responsible for your own self-care. Practicing self-care means that you:

- learn and use stress reduction techniques.
- attend to your own health care needs.
- get proper rest and nutrition.
- exercise regularly.
- take time off without feeling guilty.
- participate in pleasant, nurturing activities.

◆ reward yourself.

◆ seek and accept the support of others.

◆ seek supportive counseling when you need to, or talk with a trusted counselor, religious advisor, or friend.

◆ identify and acknowledge your feelings.

◆ tell others what you need. Don't assume "they should know."

◆ change the negative ways you view situations.

◆ set goals and prioritize.

Reflect on what it means to practice self-care. Consider the items above. How do you fare? Are you caring for yourself as well as you are caring for another? Remember, it is only when we love and nurture ourselves that we are able to love and nurture another.

As a caregiver, appreciation and "thank yous" for what you do may be lacking. For example, a person with Alzheimer's disease may be unable to show appreciation for what is done. Everyone has a need for approval. It motivates us to keep going. If you don't receive appreciation from other people, find a way to give it to yourself.

What would be helpful for you? Consider the following suggestions:

◆ Acknowledge and take satisfaction in those things you do well.

◆ Reward yourself on a regular basis.

◆ Involve yourself in an activity that will provide positive feedback.

Carol found a creative way to reward herself for a job well done when her mother could no longer express appreciation.

Carol's mother, Irene, had Alzheimer's disease. Irene often expressed frustration and anger at Carol, in spite of the fact that Carol was her mainstay. Carol understood the disease process and successfully avoided taking her mother's attacks personally. To give herself a gift of appreciation, Carol bought flowers regularly. She said, "I considered the flowers a gift from Mom to me. It's something she would have done for me if she were well."

Memories of past generosity and love from her mother sustained Carol. In buying herself flowers she reminded herself weekly that the gift of love and caring she gave to her mother had first been given to her. At a difficult time she found a way to nurture herself.

What are you doing to nurture yourself? Are you choosing healthy activities? Or are you relying on drugs, alcohol, cigarettes, and tranquilizers to handle the emotional and physical burdens of caregiving? According to the National Institute on Drug Abuse, millions of people abuse these drugs to reduce tension and to relax. It is in your best interest to choose healthy, nurturing ways of coping with the difficulties of caregiving.

Getting social support

Caregiving can be a lonely experience. According to the National Family Caregivers Association, caregivers often report that they feel alone and isolated.

Support from family, friends, and others is an important stress buffer. Something as simple as a two-minute telephone call can make you feel cared about and supported. It helps to share your experiences and burdens with a person you trust—a friend, family member, counselor, religious advisor, or support group member—who will listen and understand.

Support groups can be helpful when you're going through a difficult time. Sharing with others who are going through similar experiences is a way to give and receive support, and take time out from caregiving duties. You can learn new ways of coping from others in the group, which may include learning to look at the light side of difficult situations with a bit of humor. Sharing lightens the load. A support group is a place to express thoughts and feelings in a confidential setting. Most important, you learn that you are not alone. This can be a wonderful relief.

Support groups are available for caregivers and for people with various chronic illnesses. Local hospitals and disease-related associations often have groups available.

Using techniques that lower stress

It is of little help to identify your stressors if you don't take action early to reduce them. Recognize obstacles to taking action. These may include:

◆ Not giving yourself permission to take care of yourself.

◆ Lacking awareness of stress-reduction techniques.

◆ Choosing unrealistic stress-reduction techniques for example, those that are too complicated, lengthy, or difficult for you.

◆ Delaying or postponing a stress-reduction activity. For example, planning a break or trip too far into the future to be of help now, when you need it.

Take care of yourself daily. Use "tried and true" stress reduction tools that work for you. In addition, learn and incorporate new stress-reducing techniques into your life. There are many worthwhile techniques available. We offer some quick and easy ones that you can fit into your busy life.

Basic wellness practices. It is vital to maintain your health and well-being. Ask yourself the questions in the box below.

Yes No

☐ ☐ Do you participate in physical activity at least three times a week?

☐ ☐ Do you get enough sleep daily so that you feel rested in the morning?

☐ ☐ Do you eat balanced, nutritious meals?

☐ ☐ Do you take time to sit down and eat your meals?

☐ ☐ Do you take care of your own physical health (e.g., get regular medical check-ups and take care of yourself when you are ill)?

☐ ☐ Do you participate regularly in recreational/leisure activities?

☐ ☐ Do you drink at least eight glasses of water or other liquid daily?

☐ ☐ Do you limit alcoholic beverages to no more than two drinks a day? (One drink is 1.5 oz. of hard liquor, 12 oz. of beer, or 4 oz. of wine.)

☐ ☐ Do you avoid using alcohol, medications/drugs, or cigarettes to calm your nerves?

☐ ☐ Do you maintain a healthy weight?

If you answered "yes" to all of these questions, congratulate yourself. A "no" response reflects areas to work on for better health.

Proper diet, adequate sleep, and regular exercise are necessary for all of us, and even more so when we are caregivers. These lifestyle factors increase our resistance to illness and our ability to cope with stressful situations.

Exercise promotes better sleep, reduces tension and depression, and increases energy and alertness. If finding time to exercise is a problem, try to incorporate it into your usual day. Perhaps the person receiving care can walk or do stretching exercises with you. If necessary, do frequent short exercises instead of using large blocks of time. Find activities you enjoy.

Walking is considered one of the best and easiest exercises. It helps to reduce psychological tension as well as having physical benefits. Walking 20 minutes a day, three times a week, is very beneficial. If you can't be away 20 minutes, 10-minute walks twice a day or even a five-minute walk are beneficial.

Work walking into your life. Walk whenever and wherever you can. Perhaps it is easiest to walk around your block, at the mall, or a nearby park. The next time a friend or family member comes to visit, take time for a short walk. When the care receiver is getting therapy, take a walk around the medical facility.

Breathing for relaxation. Stressful situations or memories of those situations can cause changes in our breathing. Often the more tense we feel, the more shallow our breathing becomes.

Stress management tools usually include a focus on breathing. The following breathing exercise takes only one or two minutes and you can easily do it anywhere. Use it often to lower stress.

BREATHING FOR RELAXATION

Follow these steps:

1. Close your eyes. If that isn't possible, quietly become aware of your breathing.

2. Inhale to the count of seven, slowly and deeply. Exhale to the count of seven, slowly and deeply. Exhaling is "letting go."

3. Repeat—without forcing your breathing in any way. If your mind becomes distracted, refocus on your breathing.

4. Continue for one to two minutes or longer if you want. Notice how relaxed you feel overall.

Meditation. The word "meditation" comes from the Sanskrit word *medha* which, when taken literally, means "doing the wisdom." Meditation aids in relaxation and in achieving physical and mental well-being. Meditation is keeping your attention focused in the moment to quiet the mind and hear your body's inner wisdom. You, too, can learn to meditate. See the "Process of Meditation" box on the next page.

Meditation

The more faithfully you listen to the voice within you, the better you will hear what is sounding outside.

Dag Hammarskjold

Music. Music is another tool for reducing stress. It can alter the body and the mind. It can induce deep relaxation, act as a stimulant, and take you into other states of consciousness. Music is often used specifically for healing and decreasing stress and tension. Use the following steps as a guideline.

1. Choose soothing music you like.

2. Relax and close your eyes.

3. Breathe deeply and easily.

4. Lose yourself in the music, listening with your body, not your mind.

5. After the music is finished, open your eyes and notice how you feel.

Music is a universal language. Listening to music can be healing for both you and the care receiver, either together or alone. People with dementia, especially, respond to music when they may respond to little else.

Humor. Caregivers who maintain and foster their sense of humor do better. It is often hard to find much that is humorous in caregiving, but the secret to succeeding as a caregiver is to find humor in your daily routine. Finding humor does not deny the fact that, at times, your heart is heavy with the pain and sadness of caregiving. Those times will exist, but they can coexist with laughter and humor.

Tears and laughter are closely related. They each offer a release of tension and are often intermingled. Humor does not minimize the seriousness of a situation; rather, it helps you embrace it.

Humor can be a helpful tool in many ways, from making us laugh at our shortcomings and impossible situations, to reducing anxiety and stress. Laughter relaxes and helps calm emotions, allowing us to regain emotional balance and think more clearly. If you want to laugh, or want someone else to laugh, you may have to find a reason, as George and Alma do.

George and Alma watch their favorite comedy show on television every week-night at 7 P.M. They look forward to it and anticipate laughing together. In addition, Alma and George look for humorous cartoons and jokes to share with each other. The fact that Alma has a disabling medical condition doesn't mean they can't appreciate laughter.

In his book *Anatomy of an Illness*, Norman Cousins wrote of his fight against a crippling disease. He credited his recovery to the use of laughter. He intentionally sought healing through watching videotapes of comedies, reading joke books, and listening to people tell jokes. He had read about the effects of stress and emotions on illness. He understood that disease was caused by chemical changes in the body, due to the stress of strong emotions such as fear and anger. He concluded that perhaps love, laughter, hope, and the will to live would counteract those effects. He was right in his

PROCESS OF MEDITATION

1. Choose a quiet spot where you will not be disturbed. Ten to 20 minutes should suffice.

2. Sit in a comfortable position.

3. Close your eyes to better concentrate.

4. Relax your body by tightening, then relaxing, each of your major muscles from head to toe. This need not take long, only a minute or two.

5. Be aware of your breathing without trying to change it. Your breathing may get slower as meditation proceeds, because of relaxation and your body's metabolism slowing down. Breathe naturally in and out.

6. If you like, choose a word for focus. This is sometimes called a mantra. It can be any word or words that mean something to you. Many people find that words like "love," "let go," and "peace" work well. Others may use a phrase from a favorite prayer. Repeat the chosen word or phrase silently with your breathing, on the in- and out-breaths. One

caregiver's focus words are "I," on the in-breath and "AM," on the out-breath, "I AM." Together the breathing and words anchor the mind.

7. Don't judge your performance or wonder how you are doing. You will have distracting thoughts which you can let go of by returning to awareness of your breathing and focus. With repetition, awareness will continue to develop and carry over into the rest of your life, inducing a peaceful state of mind.

8. Practice a minimum of once a day for 10 to 20 minutes. Twice a day is even better. The best times to meditate are often in the early morning, after exercise and a shower but before breakfast, or before dinner. Since meditation is an exercise in concentration, avoid meditating when you're tired or you might fall asleep. However, if you have difficulty falling asleep at night, meditate while lying down to facilitate relaxation and sleep.

belief. Recent studies show that laughter helps to stimulate breathing, muscular activity, and heart rate. This serves to reduce stress and strengthen the immune system.

Humor is important to health. It lifts the spirit and provides a way to connect with others. The following suggestions can help you make laughter and humor a larger part of your life:

◆ Seek out humor. Humorous tapes and books can be found at video stores and libraries. Spend time with friends or family members you enjoy and can laugh with.

◆ Surround yourself with humor. Put jokes, cartoons, funny pictures, and humorous sayings on the refrigerator or bulletin board where others can enjoy them with you.

◆ Laugh at yourself. Don't take yourself too seriously. Poke fun at yourself by making light of your shortcomings (which we all have).

Developing action plans

Action plans are tools for change. They can be a useful way to identify and plan specific activities for reducing stress and making change. Feelings of accomplishment are necessary for thriving as a caregiver. Action plans can help you achieve these feelings. Even the smallest action can make a big difference. This was true for Evelyn.

Evelyn needed more time for herself during the day. She made a plan to take a leisurely, warm tub bath four times a week instead of the always-hurried shower. Evelyn settled her father to watch the news on TV when she took her baths. This worked well for both of them and became an accepted part of their routine. Accomplishing the action plan encouraged Evelyn to make other action plans that made a big difference to her.

See pages 7–9 for more information on action plans.

Feelings of mastery and confidence are usually the result of developing new ways of coping. Use the information presented in this chapter to help you identify your stressors, and improve coping skills. The activity in the box on the next page can be a useful tool for managing stress.

This activity can be useful on a regular basis. It will help you assess and cope with current stressors. Since your caregiving situation and stressors continually change, it is important to be aware of when you feel stress and to use stress-reducing tools that work for you. Most important, build stress reduction and nurturing activities into your daily life to prevent distress. Be proactive. And remember, what is good for you is good for the person receiving care!

Finding hope and meaning

The ability to find hope and meaning in the caregiving situation enables you not only to survive, but to thrive. Finding meaning and hope are what keeps us going. It is a way to make sense of our circumstances.

In his book *Man's Search For Meaning,* psychiatrist Viktor Frankl tells of his experience as a long-time prisoner in a prisoner of war camp during World War II. Many of his family members died in the camps. In spite of the fact that he faced

---

REFRAMING YOUR STRESS

Make a list of those things that you find most difficult or stressful. Be specific. Write at least two (more if you can).
1.

2.

Answer the following questions in relation to each item on your list.
Can I ignore this? Or can I let it go?
1.

2.

Can I change anything about this? If so, how can I change it?
1.

2.

If it can't be changed, can I change my perception of it? If so, how? What is a more helpful perception?
1.

2.

Select one stressor from your list to work on first. The stressor is:

Develop an action plan for addressing this stressor. Be specific and realistic. (See pages 7–9 for more information.)

death constantly and suffered severe punishment, Dr. Frankl was able to find meaning and hope in his life. He noted that the prisoners who were able to sustain even a flicker of hope were better able to survive the terrible circumstances than those who felt hopeless. He concluded that what did remain, when all else was taken away, was "the last of the human freedoms," the ability to "choose one's attitude in a given set of circumstances." Out of that experience, Frankl's guiding philosophy was born: "To live is to suffer, to survive is to find meaning in the suffering." He also believed that man's need for meaning is universal.

The need to find hope and meaning is also important when you are a caregiver for a person with a chronic illness. Uncertainty, loss, and suffering may shake your foundation. After all, you have much at stake. Your world, as you have known it, has changed drastically and you may be left with questions such as, "Why me?" and perhaps, "Where is God?" Questioning often leads to a search for meaning. No one else can tell you what the meaning is for you. It can be a lonely journey.

> *A sense of hope is knowing that your present moment has meaning.*
>
> Robert Randall

A search for meaning can be a conscious choice. There are ways to stimulate your search. The following can be helpful:

1. **Ask yourself questions like "What am I to learn from this?"** What good can come from this? Am I a better person now? These types of questions can help you open up to possibilities for finding meaning.

2. **Reflect.** Periods of quiet reflection, especially after a difficult time, are important and offer opportunities to learn from the experience.

3. **Talk with a trusted person.** Whether this person is a counselor, religious advisor, or friend, sharing can help clarify your thoughts and feelings. As you tell your story, it often takes on meaning.

4. **Write.** This is also a way to clarify your thinking. Writing is a way to bring out your thoughts and feelings. Write freely and spontaneously. Don't concern yourself with proper sentence structure or punctuation. Writing is a way to talk to yourself.

   Re-reading your journal over time provides an understanding of where you were when you started and where you are now. You will probably see changes and find new understanding and meaning.

5. **Seek spiritual renewal.** This is especially important when you are facing difficult times. Many caregivers report that faith and prayer help them find comfort, purpose, and meaning. It may be that even when you feel anger because of suffering and sorrow, your need for meaning is greatest.

Like Frankl, it is hopeful to believe that meaning can be found in difficult and painful experiences. Hope and meaning play a large part in the following story of Margaret and Tim.

Tim's frequent visits to his elderly mother, Margaret, in the nursing home, were meaningful to him. Years ago, when Margaret was healthy, she shared some of her beliefs with Tim. She had told him, "If there comes a time when I am not able to recognize you because of Alzheimer's

disease, or for any other reason, I want you to know what I believe to be true. I believe that my true essence, my spirit, will always be present, even though my physical body and mind may not be the person you remember. Please know that I am with you. We may not be able to talk with each other as we did in the past, but if you play my favorite music, read poetry, hold my hand, or just be with me, I will feel your love and you will feel mine for you."

In sharing her beliefs, Margaret gave Tim the gift of finding meaning in what can be a most difficult and challenging situation. Meaning is all around us. It is the "stuff" of life. Meaning is personal. It is up to each person to find his or her own meaning.

SUMMARY

Are you better acquainted with your stress? Have you identified what you can do to reduce at least one stressor? Do you realize the potential strength in considering your needs and in practicing self-care? Can you find meaning in difficult experiences? Have you learned that often the compassion and care you give to another comes back to you as a gift of meaning?

Remember that your response to a situation will affect the situation itself. As much as possible, make it be what you want it to be. Reflect again on the words of Virginia Satir:

> *Life is not the way it's supposed to be. It's the way it is. The way you cope with it is what makes the difference... I think if I have one message, one thing before I die that most of the world would know, it would be that the event does not determine how to respond to the event. That is a purely personal matter. The way in which we respond will direct and influence the event more than the event itself.*

Communicating Effectively with Others

Many caregivers say that a lack of communication is the underlying problem in misunderstandings and poor relationships with family members, friends, and health care professionals. It doesn't have to be this way. Although we cannot cure chronic illness, we can do something about how effectively we communicate with others.

> *The greatest problem in communication is the illusion that it has been accomplished.*
>
> George Bernard Shaw

Good communication skills are critical in caregiving. Over the course of long-term illness we must rely on our communication skills to obtain and share information, to adapt to change, to ask for what we need, and to stay connected to others. Our effectiveness as communicators depends on:

◆ how well we listen and what we think and feel.

◆ how we come across to others.

◆ what we choose not to say.

◆ whether others feel we respect their rights and feelings.

This chapter will review tools to enhance the communication process. It will discuss listening skills, positive ways to express yourself using "I" statements, and two communication styles—assertiveness and aikido.

LISTENING: THE HEART OF COMMUNICATION

Effective listening skills are more important than many of us realize. In her book *Communicate With Confidence* Dianna Booher claims that mindful listening is important because it keeps us "informed, up-to-date, and out of trouble." Also, how well we listen is an important sign we care.

> *One of the best ways to persuade others is with your ears—by listening to them.*
>
> Dean Rusk

To be good listeners we need more than just ears. If ears were all that we needed, then we would only need feet to run the Boston Marathon. Good listeners also have an open mind—they respect differences of opinion, and they try to understand the perspectives and feelings of the other person.

The challenge of being a good listener is greater if you provide care. Fatigue may be a problem. Worry is another. At times your worries might completely occupy your thoughts; you may hear people speaking to you without actually listening to a word they say. This unintentionally sends the message that you don't care enough to listen.

Barriers to Being a Good Listener

Marge stood in front of us and introduced herself and her husband. We were all part of a tour group. We were gathered at a meeting to get acquainted. In a kind but serious manner, she gave us a short lesson about listening. She said:

My name is Marge and this is my husband, Norm. I have his permission to talk to you tonight. My husband had a stroke a year ago and because of it he has some trouble communicating. He understands what you say to him but he has difficulty speaking. Because of this, I would like to ask two very special favors of you.

Please give Norm an extra ounce of attention when he talks to you. You may be able to pick up clues from his gestures and the expressions on his face that will help you understand. It is so much less stressful for him when he doesn't have to struggle to be heard. Also, if he feels listening to him is too difficult for you, he won't join in the fun. Norm needs extra time to respond because it takes him a while to put his thoughts into words. If you would give him a little extra attention and time, it will mean more than I can say to both of us. Thank you for listening.

We were touched and we were educated. Without her words, we wouldn't have realized that we, not Norm's stroke, would be his biggest barrier to being heard, to taking part, to feeling important enough for people to listen to him.

A good place to start working on listening skills is to figure out why we may not listen sometimes. Our preconceived ideas about strokes might have been our reason for not listening to Norm. In addition to preconceived ideas, fatigue, and worry, other personal and environmental barriers can interfere with listening.

Personal listening barriers

We all have personal listening barriers we bring to every conversation with another person. These barriers change depending on the situation and the people involved. They include:

◆ personal needs

◆ emotions and moods

◆ attitudes

Personal needs. Our personal needs play a huge role in how well we listen. Anything we need at a given time (food, rest, peace of mind) can reduce our ability to listen. For instance, to meet our need for peace of mind, many of us develop ways to tune out whatever is bothersome to us and unwelcome news.

Tuning out allows us to hear only what we want to hear; it saves mental energy, helps us concentrate, and protects us from problems we can't face yet. Tuning out may help us ignore the repetitive questions of a family member who is memory-impaired. In other words, it works. After a while we may tune out even when listening is important. We have to make an effort to catch ourselves tuning out and to concentrate on paying attention.

Emotions and moods. Living with chronic illness means you sometimes feel strong emotions. These may include feelings of anger, sadness, or "down in the dumps." You may be in no mood to listen. If you can't listen because of your mood, postpone your conversation to a time when you're in a better frame of mind.

Attitudes. Your attitudes and beliefs about a person's behavior, motives, age, race, religion, appearance, education, and lifestyle play a large role in whether you listen with an open or a closed mind. You can change an unfavorable attitude by changing the way you look at a person or situation. In the following story, think about how a different view of a care receiver's behavior would affect a caregiver's attitude.

Sally was convinced Roger was eating his mashed potatoes with his hands just to get on her nerves. Then she remembered what Lena said at an Alzheimer's support group meeting:

"When my husband starts annoying me, I try to change the way I think about him. Instead of thinking he's just trying to 'get my goat,' I look at him and say to myself, 'He has forgotten his memory of good manners and he's doing the best he can.' My whole attitude toward him changes when I do this."

Being a good listener does not mean abandoning your values and beliefs. Rather, it means being aware of how they affect how well you listen.

Identify someone you have trouble listening to. Check the statement below that most closely describes your personal listening barrier or add your own barriers.

I find it difficult to listen because this person:

❐ has a different education level than me.

❐ smokes or drinks.

❐ is offensive to me because of his or her appearance.

❐ has different religious beliefs than mine.

❐ always seems to say the same thing.

❐ is like _____, whom I don't respect.

❐ _____

❐ _____

Sensory barriers

We need to be aware of and correct changes in our own vision and hearing that interfere with our ability to listen. Adequate lighting and quieter surroundings, perhaps a hearing aid or glasses, can make it easier for others to communicate with us.

Environmental barriers

Activities and noise can disrupt our ability to listen and the speaker's ability to focus. Remember, the other person may be bothered by noise and activity you don't notice anymore. As you read the list in the box below, check off the distractions that apply to your surroundings. Add your ideas to the list.

You may have no control over some distracting noises and activities. However, reducing the ones you can control will improve your effectiveness as a listener.

Environmental distractions that affect my ability to listen:

❐ Outside noise, ranging from barking dogs to power mowers, trains, cars, and wind chimes

❐ Background music, radio, or TV that is either too loud or barely audible

❐ Household noises, from electrical appliances to ticking clocks

❐ Interruptions from ringing telephones or people coming and going or needing attention

❐ Poorly lighted rooms

❐ A room that is too warm or too cold

❐ Uncomfortable or overly comfortable seating

❐ Mouth-watering cooking smells or unpleasant odors

❐ Pets and small children in the room

❐ _____

❐ _____

Setting the Stage to Listen

With listening barriers noted, there are still some listening challenges to overcome. One challenge is listening with an open mind to opposing opinions about emotional issues. The following suggestions will help you meet this challenge.

Prepare yourself

In a highly emotional situation, it can seem impossible to listen objectively. However, you can prepare yourself by asking, "What if…?" and thinking about how you would respond. For example, "What if Dad refuses to give up the car keys?" Feeling prepared reduces anxiety and increases your ability to listen. It also helps to be at your physical best, rested and fed.

Help others prepare for an exchange with you

Prepare people in advance for a discussion with you. For example, tell them, "I want to hear your point of view about…" Advance notice gives people time to think things over. It's crucial to planning and decision-making. People who feel prepared and who believe they will be heard are more likely to participate in making caregiving plans and decisions.

Create an atmosphere of trust and confidentiality

Some people won't speak openly until they are assured, in advance, that you won't reject them or get angry over differences of opinion. They must hear you say something like, "I won't get mad, and I will keep our discussion just between us."

Building trusting relationships is a gradual process. People need time to confirm that it's safe to speak openly, especially if this hasn't been true in the past. Ruth will vouch for this.

When they were children, Ruth, being the oldest, bullied her younger sister, Cynthia. Even as adults Ruth let little secrets "slip out" that embarrassed her sister. Now their mother is ill and Ruth needs her sister's help. She knows she has to earn her sister's trust if they are going to work together to provide care for their mother.

Ruth called Cynthia to arrange a time to discuss their mother's memory problems. She said, "I would like to hear your ideas about Mom and what you think we should be doing to help. I'll come to your place if it's okay. When would be a good time for you?" Cynthia agreed to meet. However, she suspected her sister had already reached a decision and the meeting was simply to divide up the tasks.

Ruth set the stage. She knew Cynthia felt intimidated by her so she arranged to meet where Cynthia felt strongest, in her own home. She told Cynthia her intentions in advance so Cynthia could prepare her thoughts. Ruth said, "I want to hear your ideas…" to reassure Cynthia that she was coming to listen. Ruth recognized it would take time for Cynthia to trust her.

If people feel apprehensive about speaking honestly, chances are they won't reveal why they feel that way. We have to assume their trust must be won by listening to them with an open mind. If you wanted to reassure someone they could speak openly with you, what would you say?

How the Best Listeners Listen

Ellen considered herself a good listener. She said proudly, "People just seem to open up to me." She considered her listening skills a matter of being polite. Actually, people talked to Ellen about their personal matters because she listened without judging, interrupting, or arguing, and she never betrayed a confidence.

Ellen was a skillful listener because she knew how to make people comfortable. People talked to her because they felt she cared and they trusted her. Ellen also knew how to end a conversation without "cutting people off." She knew if they felt "cut off" they wouldn't reach out to her again.

Although each situation varies, you will be a better listener if you do the following:

◆ Give the speaker your full attention

◆ Encourage people to speak

◆ Confirm what the person said

◆ Acknowledge spoken and unspoken feelings

◆ Fit your voice, tone, and mood to that of the person speaking

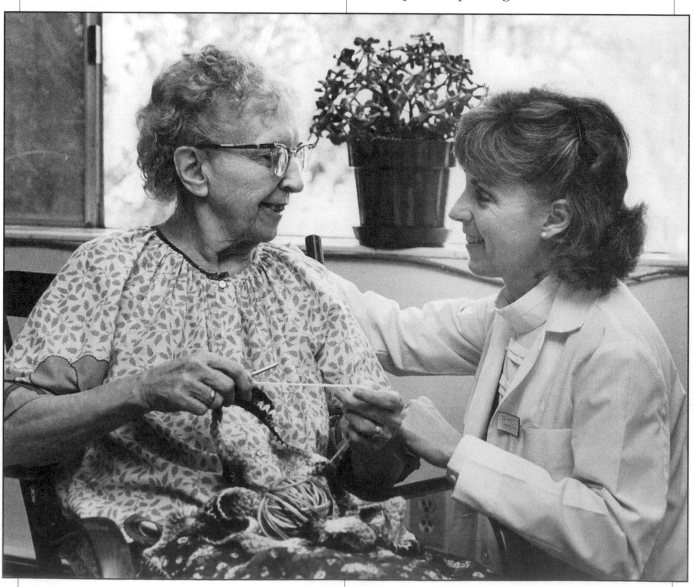

◆ Use the words the speaker uses

◆ Make certain all concerns have been heard

◆ Be aware of disclaimers

Give the speaker your full attention

Attentive listeners act interested. They stop what they are doing and reduce distractions. They use good eye contact. They don't read the paper or walk away with the comment, "Go on, I'm listening."

Encourage people to speak

Sometimes people are reluctant to speak, especially about sensitive issues. Signals like nodding, maintaining gentle eye contact, and making short comments like "I see," "really," "um-hum," or "how interesting," are cues that encourage people to share with you. Comments like these are especially helpful during telephone conversations.

Confirm what the person said

Confirming what you heard eliminates guessing, making incorrect assumptions, and jumping to conclusions. Two ways to make certain you understand the speaker's meaning are (1) asking open-ended questions and (2) paraphrasing.

Open-ended questions. The purpose of the open-ended question is to check out your understanding of the speaker's feelings or to request more information to improve your understanding. The other person is not limited to a one-word answer such as "yes" or "no." The open-ended question encourages people to talk about their thoughts, feelings, fears, and concerns and it gives them control over how much they want to say. The following are examples of open-ended questions:

◆ "I am not sure I understand. Could you tell me more about your situation to make it clearer to me?"

◆ "Would you give me an example?"

◆ "Could you tell me more about how you feel about this?"

Paraphrasing. If you feel you have missed the point, you can check whether you have understood by paraphrasing. To paraphrase, you restate what the speaker said using your own words. Paraphrasing shows the speaker you are listening and lets the speaker know if you need further explanation. It also helps you focus on the important parts of a conversation, particularly when the speaker tends to ramble.

You can paraphrase on different levels: words, feelings, and hinted words and hinted feelings. The following are suggested ways to paraphrase (reflect) on these levels:

◆ "So, as you see it…"

◆ "Let me make sure I understand. Are you saying that…?"

◆ "So, to sum this up, is it that you feel…?"

◆ "Do you mean that…?"

Acknowledge spoken and unspoken feelings

Problems related to changing care needs are usually emotionally laden. Tone of voice and how loudly, softly, quickly, or slowly a person speaks often reveal his true feelings. If you reflect the person's feelings with statements like, "Are you feeling…," you communicate understanding, acknowledgment, and acceptance. Once you deal with a person's emotions it is then easier to discuss the facts and details of a problem.

Fit your voice, tone, and mood to that of the person speaking

This sends an indirect message that you are "in sync" with him. For instance, if the person is sad and talking in hushed tones, reflect his mood by being serious and quiet-spoken.

Fitting the mood doesn't mean matching it. Fitting means using an appropriate response to convey understanding. This means you wouldn't match anger with anger nor would you laugh at an angry person. Because anger is a serious emotion, your mood should be serious. There are times when you can use humor to lighten a conversation, but be careful that it doesn't demean the person, situation or someone's feelings.

Use words the speaker uses

Using the same language as the speaker tells the person you hear, understand, and respect his words. If the person uses "down in the dumps" to describe feeling sad or depressed, you should do so to.

Make certain all concerns have been heard

The sensitive nature of many caregiving problems may prevent them from being raised and resolved. You can try to bring these issues out in the open by asking, "What troubles you that we haven't touched on?"

Be aware of disclaimers

Listen for words such as "may," "might," "perhaps," "maybe," "probably," "ordinarily," "usually," and "I'll try." These words are disclaimers, and are like the "small print" of a contract. Be sure you understand them. When you hear disclaimers, especially during discussions with health care professionals, ask for explanations. For example, ask: "What do you mean by 'the treatment may help'?"

Listen for other qualifiers that imply that the word "but" belongs at the end of the sentence. Notice how the implied word "but" changes the meaning of the following sentence. "For the most part, the diagnosis is correct, (but)…" When someone uses qualifiers, politely repeat the important words in a question: "What do you mean by 'for the most part'?" Other "qualified" sentences begin with "of course," "essentially," "basically," "all in all," and "most."

Good listening tools include keeping an open mind, reducing listening barriers, creating a safe haven for openness, using appropriate eye contact, confirming what you hear, and giving your undivided attention. Listening well is at the heart of good communication and it takes conscious effort.

To become a more effective listener, apply "The Golden Rule of Listening." It says, "Listen to others as you would have them listen to you." If you do this, your listening effectiveness will take a giant leap forward.

> **Listening in a nutshell**
> Listen as you want others to listen to you.

EXPRESSING YOURSELF EFFECTIVELY

Communication is a two-way street. It involves both listening carefully and expressing yourself clearly. Caregiving offers enough challenges without having to struggle to be heard and understood. Often the words we choose to say—or choose not to say—can have a major impact on our relationships.

> *Please fill my mouth with worthwhile stuff and nudge me when I've said enough.*
>
> H. H. Brackenridge

For many caregivers, a big hurdle is getting needed information from health care providers and help from family members. Some caregivers are afraid they may lose valuable support from friends and family if they ask for help or set limits. They don't want to risk upsetting and losing the people they love and need. As you read the following statements, check the box that reflects how you feel at times.

YesNo

❐ ❐ I hesitate to ask for help for fear of being a burden and risk losing the help I do receive.

❐ ❐ I shouldn't have to ask for help. People should see what I need and offer to help.

❐ ❐ I rarely set limits because I feel guilty saying no.

❐ ❐ I feel like I'm letting people down and disappointing them.

❐ ❐ I rarely express feelings such as anger or frustration because I don't want people to think less of me.

If you answered "yes" to any of these statements, you have plenty of company. Speaking up is a daunting task for many of us; sometimes it may seem easier or safer to say nothing. But eventually issues need attention and decisions must be made.

How to Best Express Yourself

Learning to express ourselves more effectively takes time and practice. Sometimes we have to unlearn old habits. The best way to begin is by practicing the following tools for expressing yourself.

1. Use "I" messages.
2. Respect the rights or feelings of other people by what you say or do.
3. Be clear and specific.
4. Speak directly to the person(s) involved.
5. Be a good listener.

If you keep these tools in mind and use a positive speaking style, people are more likely to listen to you. They will better understand what you are saying, how you are feeling, and what you need. Next we will discuss the importance of using "I" statements and positive styles of communication.

"I" Messages: The Backbone of Expressing Yourself Effectively

Bill is 75 years old. He has been a caregiver to his wife, Mary, since she was diagnosed with Parkinson's disease years ago. Several weeks ago Mary fell and broke her hip. In addition to the in-home nursing services Mary receives, Bill hired a housekeeper to help him with housework and cooking. Ellen, his daughter, has dropped by for a visit, but Bill doesn't have much to say to her.

Ellen: "What's wrong Dad? Why are you so quiet?"

Bill: "Nothing's wrong. Everything is just fine."

Ellen: "From your tone of voice, I have a feeling you're upset about something? Is it something I did?"

Bill: "No, it's something you didn't do."

Ellen: "What didn't I do? "

Bill: "If you really cared you would know. You didn't bother to look around here and see what you could do to lend a hand when your mother came home from the hospital. I had to hire a stranger to help me with the housework. Apparently, you can't even pick up a few groceries for us."

Ellen: "Not that it matters to you, Dad, but I have a family and a job. I barely have time to clean my own house."

You can see where this conversation is headed. Upset and tired, Bill indirectly accused Ellen of not caring. He also expected her to read his mind. His words put his daughter on the defensive because they contained "you" messages: "If you really cared you would know…" and "You didn't bother…"

When people hear "you" statements they feel attacked; they either fight back or withdraw in silence from the situation. "You" messages also tend to increase anger and frustration in a situation. Ellen felt attacked and fought back with her own "you" messages.

Relationships face many tests during the course of chronic illness. Knowing this, some caregivers hesitate to ask for help or express their feelings. They fear getting too emotional and "opening the flood gates." Others feel that when they speak up, their frankness creates hard feelings. What they said was heard as blaming and they aren't sure why. If they had voiced their concerns by using "I" statements, they would have greatly increased their chances of being heard.

"I" statements: A powerful communication tool

Speaking for yourself from the "I" position is one of your most effective communication tools. With "I" statements, you take ownership for your feelings, thoughts, and concerns. By saying "I feel…," "I need…," "I am frustrated…," or "I am worried about…" you are expressing your own feelings, motives, and needs. You are not blaming someone else for the way you feel.

How might you feel about or respond to the following "you" messages versus the "I" messages?

"You" message: "Apparently, you can't even pick up a few groceries for us."

"I" message: "I have a short list of groceries we need. I wonder if you could pick them up the next time you go grocery shopping?"

"You" message: "You didn't call back yesterday. You made me wait all day to hear from you."

"I" message: "I was hoping to hear from you yesterday, Doctor."

Like any new skill, "I" messages take practice. The trick is to catch a "you" statement before you say it. You can begin by simply taking the "oops" challenge. Every time you are about to say "you," think "oops," and take a moment to change the "you" to "I." Then, in a matter-of-fact manner, say what is on your mind. Take the "oops" challenge for a week or so and you'll notice a difference in how people respond.

Watch out for hidden "you" statements

Sometimes "I" statements carry a blaming tone because they contain hidden "you" messages. They are not true "I" statements because they are subtle accusations. "I" is usually followed by the words "when you" in a sentence. You can sense the implied blame in the following statement:

Hidden "you" message: "I feel badly when you treat Mother like a child."

"You" message: "You treat Mother like a child."

"I" message: "I feel badly because I think Mother feels like she's being treated like a child."

Other uses for "I" statements

Besides expressing feelings and needs, "I" statements can be used to raise concerns, return problems to the person who raised them, and to state your intentions. They also are an effective way to express positive feelings and compliments. For instance:

◆ Raise a concern: "I am concerned about your living alone."

◆ Return a problem to the person who raised it: "I need to know how you will deal with this."

◆ State your intentions: "I want to work this out with you. I'm here to learn, not to criticize."

◆ Express praise and appreciation: "I really like the way you fixed Mom's hair."

Changing "You" to "I" statements

Consider the following examples. How would you change them into "I" statements?

Stating feelings: "I know it doesn't matter to you, but I get depressed."

_____

_____

Stating needs and desires: "You always give me advice, but you never help me take care of Mom."

_____

_____

Stating expectations: "You're always late picking up Dad, and you worry him. You should be on time."

_____

_____

Take a moment to re-read the statements. Do you feel any different with the "I" messages you have written versus the "you" messages? Look over your "I" messages. Are there any hidden "you" messages in them?

Speaking for yourself from the "I" position increases the chances people will hear you out. When done correctly, "I" messages come across as "speaking from the heart." They make it more difficult for people to argue with your feelings and perceptions, and they leave room for others to express their point of view and to use their own "I" statements.

If your "I" messages don't seem to work at first, keep trying. People who are used to hearing "you" messages may automatically hear them for awhile. Eventually, your "I" messages will make a positive difference and you will be heard.

Remember: The purpose of "I" messages is to express your personal needs, feelings, and concerns in a positive way. It is not to get others to do what you want them to do. When "I" messages are used as a means to manipulate another person, problems can get worse.

The ability to communicate effectively is a powerful caregiving tool. It helps you build and maintain supportive networks of family, friends, and health care professionals.

Positive communication skills also allow others, such as the care receiver, to express needs and wishes that differ from your own. This give-and-take philosophy strengthens caregiving relationships and reduces stress caused by unresolved misunderstandings. Two effective communication styles are assertiveness and aikido.

ASSERTIVE STYLE OF COMMUNICATION

Some caregivers hope and hint rather than ask for help or set limits. They hope that people will anticipate what they want and need. It is unrealistic to expect others to know how we feel or what we want. To avoid feeling hurt and to be fair to others, we have to communicate directly.

Assertiveness is a specific, direct communication tool for expressing ourselves. The goal of assertiveness is honest, open communication. Being assertive means that you:

◆ express your thoughts and feelings honestly and fairly.

◆ respect the rights and feelings of others, including their right to be assertive.

◆ listen attentively and validate what you are hearing.

Assertive communication is used to settle problems, not to win contests.

Assertiveness is not a form of aggression. People who are aggressive do express their feelings, wishes, and thoughts, but they do so at the expense of another person's rights and feelings. They often verbally attack, intimidate, raise their voice, use sarcasm, or put down someone else to get what they want. Statements often begin with "you" and contain absolutes such as "always" and "never."

To use assertiveness effectively, you may have to erase a few lessons you learned as a child, such as "children are seen and not heard." Or perhaps you were told that standing up for yourself was rude and asking for things was selfish. As an adult you have to speak up or lose control by default. Your responses to the following statements can help you decide if you need to work on being more assertive.

Yes	No	
❐	❐	I sometimes look back and wished I'd expressed myself more strongly.
❐	❐	I tend to brood about something a person said rather than talk about it.
❐	❐	I sometimes blame others for my feelings.
❐	❐	I have trouble setting limits.
❐	❐	I can't prevent situations in which people take advantage of me.
❐	❐	I rarely get all the information I need from the doctor.
❐	❐	I tend to accuse others when I criticize.
❐	❐	I sometimes regret something I said.
❐	❐	I often find it difficult to disagree without getting upset.
❐	❐	I have trouble asking for help.

Your responses to these statements will help you decide if you need to work on being more assertive. If you answered "yes" to any of these questions, assertiveness will help you express yourself more effectively.

"I" statements and assertiveness

"I" statements are the foundation of assertiveness. Using "I" says, "These are my feelings, needs, and motives; I own them." "I am…," "I feel…," "I need…," "I will…," and "I expect…" clarify where you stand

and what you want. At the same time you respect the rights of others to disagree and to express themselves. Being assertive means:

◆ you are clear, direct, and fair.

◆ there is no mind-reading or second-guessing.

◆ you do not blame or accuse others.

The Four Steps of Assertiveness

In her book *Assert Yourself*, Sharon Bower breaks down assertiveness into four manageable steps. She calls them DESC for describe, express, specify, and consequences. It's important to do them in the following order.

1. DESCRIBE: Use "I" statements to describe an observable behavior or problem. Describe what happened or what is bothering you without emotion, evaluation, or exaggeration (as if you were giving a report).

Example: "I received a call from Dad's doctor yesterday. He missed his appointment. I'm wondering what happened."

2. EXPRESS: Using an "I" statement, express how you feel. Identify your feelings without blaming the other person for making you feel that way. ("I feel _____ __ about what happened.")

Example: "I am concerned Dad won't make the appointment that has been rescheduled for next Thursday."

3. SPECIFY: Using an "I" statement, tell the other person specifically what needs to happen or what needs to be done.

"I want/need _____."

Example: "I need to know if you can pick Dad up and take him to the doctor next Thursday morning. He has to be there by 10 a.m."

4. CONSEQUENCES: Close with an "I" statement explaining the consequences of the behavior. The consequences include what you will do or what will happen if the person doesn't follow through. Avoid blaming, bluffing, or threatening. The consequences also can include what you will do or what will happen if the person does follow through.

The use of the word "consequence" may seem negative. But consequences are the result of an action or condition and can be positive and rewarding. ("Because of ____, this happened or will happen.")

Example: "I'll be glad to take Dad to his appointment next time if I can count on you to take Dad to his appointment this week."

Example: "If you cannot take Dad to his appointment, he will have to pay for a cab. This will put a strain on his budget."

Example: "If you can't take Dad, please make other arrangements for his transportation."

Give it a try. How would you change the following statements to assertive responses?

Describe: "Everybody says they'll help but nobody does."

Describe: _____

_____

_____

Example: "I would like the family to meet so we can divide up the housekeeping and transportation responsibilities."

Express: "Nobody knows what it's like to be the only one responsible for the folks."

Express: _____

_____

_____

Example: "I feel totally responsible for the folks being able to live at home."

Specify: "Any help is better than nothing."

Specify: _____

_____

_____

Example: "I'm concerned about the handrail on the porch at the folks' place. I'm afraid it will give way. Will you help me see that it gets fixed?"

Consequences: "The folks may have to move into a care facility because nobody else helps them and I can't do it all anymore."

Consequences:_____

_____

_____

Example: "I can't provide all the help the folks need to stay in their own home. I would be able to continue with some help."

Limits to assertiveness

Like all things, assertiveness has its limits. It won't change other people and it doesn't guarantee happiness or fair treatment. There are times when the assertive style is not appropriate, for example, when the other person:

◆ is already trying to do what you want.

◆ is unstable medically or emotionally.

◆ has the power to penalize you or cause you harm.

Timing and letting go

Someone said "timing is everything." Dealing with issues and problems in a "timely" manner means that what we say is appropriate and beneficial. For instance, we correct an in-home helper as soon as we can do so privately, not a month later or when other people are present.

Knowing when to say nothing and let go of an issue is also important. After considering the situation and the consequences, you might decide to drop the matter if:

◆ your personal safety is in jeopardy.

◆ you are wrong.

◆ the issue is much more important to the other person than to you.

◆ the outcome would unnecessarily hurt someone.

◆ maintaining harmony is more important than solving the problem.

◆ the situation is temporary.

◆ you don't have time to deal with the consequences of pursuing the issue.

During times of conflict we can lose sight of what we have in common. Sometimes letting go may be in our best interest because it helps us reach common goals. Being flexible and deciding to let go of an issue, when letting go makes sense, doesn't weaken effectiveness; it strengthens it. Remember, assertiveness is about settling problems, not winning disputes.

You may find situations where you feel uncomfortable being assertive. If so, there is another positive, less direct style you can use to express yourself effectively. It is called the aikido or alignment style.

Assertiveness in a nutshell

◆ Use "I" statements.

◆ Apply the tools for best expressing yourself.

◆ Follow the DESC steps.

◆ Use assertiveness with the knowledge of its limits.

AIKIDO STYLE OF COMMUNICATION

The aikido style of communication is patterned after the principles of the aikido style of martial arts. These principles state that instead of fighting with another person, you try to move with the person's energy. This is called alignment, and it is the key to the practice of aikido.

The aikido style of expressing yourself is disarming and somewhat less direct. It is a particularly effective tool when emotions are running high. Many caregiving issues involve strong feelings and differences of opinion. In an emotionally charged situation you may find "you" blaming messages directed at you. These can be very hard to hear.

Your gut response may be to fight back or withdraw from the situation. Neither of these responses will solve the problem. Using the aikido style of communication helps neutralize the attack so you can redirect the conversation to the problem and look at ways to solve it.

Aikido regards anyone who behaves aggressively as "not balanced." Based on this belief, the aikido style involves recognizing and understanding the other person's needs or motives. The goal in using aikido is to help the person regain balance by meeting some of his needs. You use your energy to look at the situation from his perspective, not to fight back or give in. You try to help the other person feel heard so he has no more reason to argue or resist.

Aikido focuses on building harmony. It has two goals:

◆ Maintain your own peace by not giving in to emotion.

◆ Help the other person maintain his equilibrium and peace.

Getting started

To use the aikido style, follow these steps.
1. Align.
2. Agree; find areas of common ground.
3. Redirect energies.
4. Resolve problems.

Align

To align with a person you put yourself in his place. It is the same as empathizing with the person to build rapport with him. You have to try to relax and stay physically and emotionally balanced. This is not easy in situations involving strong emotions. However, staying in control is necessary because you need to pay close attention to what is being said and done around you. (The deep breathing and relaxation exercises in Chapter 2 will help you do this.)

When you feel relaxed, put yourself in the aikido frame of mind by asking these questions:

◆ How would I feel in this person's place?

◆ What does this person need from me to feel better? Does the person need understanding? Sympathy? Praise? Recognition? Control?

The following statements are suggestions to help you develop aligning statements that fit your style and situation:

◆ "If I could do one thing to help you feel better, what would that be?"

◆ "I don't know exactly what you need. I need an example of something I can do."

◆ "I want to understand your point of view about_____."

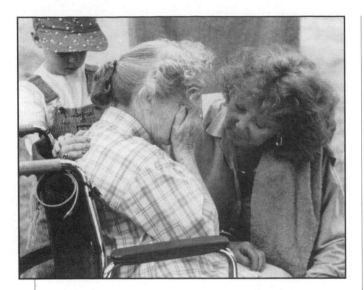

In addition to putting yourself in the other person's place, you align with the person in speaking style and mood. For instance, you are direct with people who are direct with you. You carefully reflect the serious nature of anger and sadness with genuine seriousness. The opposite of aikido is to be indifferent to the person's feelings or to make light of his problems.

Agree

Find concerns you agree upon. Look for areas of common ground to support alignment. Listen for goals, feelings, needs, and motives that you share with the person. For instance, "I share your concern about Mom's driving." Listen for opinions and suggestions you can agree with such as, "I agree we have to do something before she has an accident." Other statements that foster alignment include:

◆ "If that happened to me, I'd be upset too."

◆ "If I were you I'd feel the same way."

◆ "I share your concerns about_____."

Redirect

Once you discover what concerns or goals you share, you can redirect the exchange and focus your discussion on those areas. You might use statements like:

◆ "We both want to do what is best. Now all we have to do is _____."

◆ "I believe we agree we have a problem. What do we need to begin working on it?"

Resolve

Using "I" messages, try to settle issues and solve the problems you agreed upon. You may do this by working together on the problem or meeting the other person halfway. Or you may "agree to disagree" about this specific issue. An aikido-style statement to start the problem-solving process might be:

◆ "I can learn from your experience. What would you do about_____?"

In the following conversation, Mark heard many "you" messages. Even though he felt under attack, he responded to his mother using the aikido style.

Marge: "You never talk to Dad since his stroke and he can't talk about sports with you. You ignore him and it hurts him. You should know that. I think you take his crying jags personally and you shouldn't. The doctor said some people cry for no apparent reason after they've had a stroke."

Mark: (Aligning: How would I feel in Mom's shoes? What does Mom need from me to feel less troubled?) "I do take Dad's crying jags personally. I'm sorry that it looked like I was ignoring him. I just don't know how to act when he cries."

Marge: "Your Dad won't be around forever, you know."

Mark: (Agreeing) "You're right. I worry about losing Dad too. (Redirecting.) What do you do when Dad cries? What do other people do? (Resolving.) Maybe we could go to a stroke support group and ask other people how they handle tearfulness."

Mark heard many "you" blaming statements: "You never…," "You ignore…," and "You should…" Mark purposely overlooked the "you" messages. He showed compassion. He found a problem he and his mother shared (common ground) and found ways to work on it.

Other purposes for alignment

You also can use alignment as a tool to encourage people to cooperate with a treatment or to accept help. Aligning tells people you want to understand how they feel and what they need so you can address those needs. Once people feel heard, they are more likely to listen. Take Mary, for example:

Mary doesn't want to try walking since she broke her hip and had hip replacement surgery. Her doctor wants her to exercise. Bob gets frustrated with his wife and tells her she is her "own worst enemy." Finally, he asked Ellen, their daughter, to talk her mother into using the walker.

AIKIDO IN A NUTSHELL

Align. As you listen and observe, put yourself in the other person's place and then ask: What does this person need from me to feel better?

Agree. Look for areas of agreement or common ground.

Redirect. Redirect the exchange to those areas of agreement.

Resolve. Seek to resolve by finding a middle ground you can live with, working together on areas of common concern, or agreeing to disagree.

Ellen: "Walking must seem scary after all you've been through, Mom."

Mary: "It is. What if I fell and broke the other hip? I'd probably end up in a nursing home if that happened."

Ellen: "If I was worried about that I'd be afraid to use the walker too. Keeping up your strength is important though. What would make you feel safe using the walker?"

Mary aligned with her mother by asking herself the following questions:

◆ How would I feel if I was in my mother's place?

◆ What does Mom need from me to feel better?

Reaching people who are hard to reach

The aikido style works well in emotionally charged situations with people who are verbally aggressive. But how can you align with someone who communicates with sighs, sulking, and silence?

If you believe the person who is sulking feels unable to express his feelings outwardly, you can try to draw the person out with soft-spoken statements like, "I want to understand what is troubling you. I'd like to talk it over." If you don't get a response, give the person space and time to be alone. You might say, "I want to understand your position when you feel like talking about it." This gives him an opening to raise his concerns later. If you believe he uses this style in an indirect way to manipulate you, you might be more effective using the assertive style.

Describe: "I heard you sigh, but you haven't said a word in over an hour."

Express: "I have a feeling something is troubling you.

Specify: "I'd like to talk about it."

Consequence: "I cannot read your mind so I can't talk with you without knowing what is wrong."

SUMMARY

How do the assertive and aikido styles compare? What do these two styles have in common? How do they differ? When might it be best to use assertiveness? aikido? The following chart summarizes both styles of communication.

The differences between the assertive and aikido styles of communication are general ones. You may feel you are more comfortable with one style of communication. In many instances, you can use either style.

ASSERTIVE VS. AIKIDO STYLE

Assertive	Aikido
"Standing tall"	"Standing with"
Positive style	Positive style
Direct, clear, straightforward	Less direct; more gentle and supportive
Especially useful in:	*Useful to:*
◆ setting limits	◆ defuse emotionally charged situations
◆ asking for help	
◆ advocating for another	◆ help others feel they are understood
◆ making difficult decisions	◆ reduce anger
◆ dealing with difficult styles of communication	◆ balance emotions to allow dealing with issues

Overview

Chapter Four

Communicating to Take Care of You
Communicating Your Limits
Asking for Help
Expressing Criticism
Expressing Anger

Expressing Yourself Under Special Circumstances
Talking on the Telephone
Communicating Effectively with the Doctor
When Getting Needed Information is a Problem
Communicating with Older Adults
If the Care Receiver Mistreats You

Challenging Communication Styles

Setting your Goals and Making Action Plans

Summary

Communicating Effectively in Challenging Situations

Many caregivers say one of their biggest challenges involves uttering the word no. The feeling is that saying no is somehow not permissible. If you feel this way, ask yourself, "Is there courage and nobility in saying nothing and burning out? Or does true courage and nobility lie in taking care of yourself so you can be a caring helper longer?"

> A "no" uttered from the deepest conviction is better and greater than a "yes" merely uttered to please or, what is worse, to avoid trouble.
>
> Mahatma Gandhi

Keep those questions in mind as we discuss in this chapter tools for dealing with these caregiving challenges:

◆ setting limits

◆ asking for help

◆ expressing and responding to criticism

◆ expressing anger

We will also discuss how to communicate more effectively under special circumstances and with people who use the following communication styles:

◆ Passive/peacekeeping

◆ Aggressive/pitbull

◆ Factual/computer

COMMUNICATING TO TAKE CARE OF YOU

Caregivers frequently report they have difficulty setting limits and asking for help. Yet, these are critical tools for avoiding burnout, maintaining your well-being, and getting the support you need. It's equally important to express your feelings and give criticism in constructive ways. You want others to hear what you have to say, *not* to focus on how you said something.

Setting Limits

If you have never set limits, it can take time to feel good about doing so and to communicate your limits in positive ways. At first people may not take you seriously and you might back down a few times. But with time and practice, you can do it. You might be surprised at your family's reaction. Many caregivers discovered that their relatives were pleased and relieved when they began setting limits. It seems family members worried less knowing that caregivers were taking care of themselves.

Because only you know what your limits are, setting your limits is up to you. Setting limits is a form of self-respect and honesty. It's realizing that you can't do everything and that's okay. It also shows consideration for family and friends. It helps take the guesswork out of planning and problem solving when you tell others what you are able and unable to do.

Remember, your limits are not engraved in stone. You can be flexible and change them when your priorities change and when time, place, people, and circumstances demand it.

What happens if you don't set limits

As a caregiver, do you think setting limits is selfish? Do you believe people who set limits are uncaring? If so, think about what can happen if you don't set limits. Not setting limits can lead to:

◆ feelings of resentment on your part.

◆ caregiver burnout, and possibly, the inability to provide the help needed.

◆ concern by family about your health and even your survival.

◆ health problems related to stress and fatigue, or even death.

Limits carry risks

Relationships suffer when they are based on someone doing whatever another person wants or needs. If you lose closeness with a person because you set limits, ask yourself, "Am I better off without a relationship completely defined by what the other person wants?" Then weigh the risks, to yourself and the care receiver, of not setting limits. Think about the serious effects on you and the care receiver if your health fails.

Consider the consequences of setting limits

Before saying or doing anything about setting limits, review possible consequences of what you want to do. Ask yourself:

◆ What would be the worst outcome? How would I handle it?

◆ What are the chances the worst outcome will happen? Could I live with it?

◆ What are the consequences if I do nothing? Can I live with those?

◆ What is the best thing that could happen?

Some limits are not negotiable

Look carefully at limits you cannot exceed. These are your non-negotiable limits. What is the most you can give to others? This has to be clear, "I am able to help two days a week. That is all I can do."

Look at how you set limits now

Evaluate your current style of setting limits, particularly with the care receiver and other family members. Check the boxes that most closely describe how you set limits.

YesNo

❐ ❐ Do I set limits so seldom that people don't pay attention when I do?

❐ ❐ Am I so meek about setting limits that people don't take me seriously?

❐ ❐ Do I usually wait too long—until I can't continue   before I set limits?

❐ ❐ Do I hint or expect people to read my mind about what I can and can't do?

❐ ❐ Do I complain instead of setting clear caregiving limits with those who need to know my limits?

❐ ❐ Do I set limits and flip-flop by not sticking to them?

❐ ❐ Do I try setting limits once and then quit if people ignore them?

Did you check "yes" in answering any questions? If so, the following suggestions will help you set and communicate your limits.

Start small. If you have trouble setting limits, start with people outside your family and start with small matters, like telling a caller you can visit for only five minutes.

Start with the easy people. This means practicing saying a polite, firm "no" to someone either unrelated to you or that you don't even know, such as telephone sales solicitors, fund-raisers for questionable charities, or pollsters in the local mall. A simple "Thank you for your call, but I cannot donate to your cause" (or whatever the request is) is all you need to say. If the person persists, just keep repeating your statement and soon he will give up.

Start with easy situations. It's a good idea to warm up on situations or tasks that are impersonal or that you don't like. For example, if you enjoy volunteering but you don't care for the schedule or the assignment, try saying, "I enjoy volunteering but I must cut back. I'd be glad to help one Thursday a month at this time with…" Then work up to family situations, such as who will host the holiday dinners.

Communicating your limits

The following tools will help you communicate what you can and cannot do.

Be clear about your limits

Use "I" statements and be as specific about your limits as possible. "I am happy to stop by after work tonight but I have to leave by 6:30." (The formula is: "Up to this point I can do _____ . Beyond this point I will do_____," or "_____ happens.")

Offer choices within your limits

This is a way to replace what you can't do with a choice of what you can and are willing to do. "I can't take you shopping today, but I can do it either on Thursday afternoon or Saturday morning. Which is best for you?" (The formula is: "I am unable to do _____, but I can do _____ or _____. Which do you prefer?"). Sharon said to her son:

> I've enjoyed having the grandchildren stay at the house over the holidays every year. Because Grandpa needs more help these days, I can't ask them to stay with us this year. I would like to have them over to sing carols and decorate Christmas cookies with Grandpa. Let's talk during Thanksgiving.

Make no excuses

Giving factual reasons for setting limits aids understanding and is different from making excuses. Offering excuses sounds apologetic. Notice that the following statements contain no excuses or self-criticism:

- "I'd like to do that, but for now I can only handle these three things." (You are being factual and specific, and suggesting the limits are not permanent ones.)

- "I appreciate your suggestions. Right now I can't fit them into my day." (This is a good response to unsolicited advice.)

- "I need some time to think about it. I'll let you know tomorrow." (This gives you time if you feel like making excuses or if flattery or "guilt trips" undermine your resolve.)

If you want to make it easier, you can prepare people over the phone or in writing that you have to rethink how much you can do. You also can mention that your doctor advises you to cut down.

Some people may respond negatively to your limits. This doesn't mean you are wrong. It usually means things are changing that other people wish would stay the same.

Asking for Help

Some caregivers feel that by asking for help they are somehow falling short. But asking for help may be the only way they can continue to provide care at home. They are not falling short; they are adapting to changing care needs that cannot be met without help. It is a caregiver's responsibility to ask for help. If you feel uncomfortable asking for it, consider the following questions about asking for salt.

YesNo

☐ ☐ Do you expect people to pass the salt before you ask for it?

☐ ☐ Do you blame people for not knowing you want salt?

☐ ☐ Would you plead, hint, or whine to get the salt?

You probably answered "no" to the salt questions. Just as we expect to ask for salt in order to receive it, we also need to ask for the help we need in caregiving. As you ask for help, remember to use the tone of voice you use when asking for salt. It's probably pleasant and matter-of-fact, without blaming and hinting.

Prepare yourself to ask for help

Before you ask for help, consider the following suggestions.

Consider the person's special abilities and interests. Before approaching someone with a request, consider their likes, dislikes, areas of interest, experience, abilities, and knowledge. For instance, if someone enjoys cooking but dislikes driving, your chances improve if you ask for help with cooking.

Your chances for success also improve if you ask the person to help you with tasks he feels comfortable with and knows how to do. Tasks unrelated to caregiving are easier for some people.

Note: When one family member has a medical or nursing background, it is natural to expect that he is the best one to help with caregiving. Take care that other relatives are not automatically excused from responsibility because there is a health professional in the family.

Resist asking the same person repeatedly. Ask yourself if you are requesting help from a certain person because he or she has difficulty saying no. It is important to capitalize on your stronger speaking skills rather than on someone else's inability to set limits.

Consider the person's special needs. Personal, private time is hard to come by. As a caregiver, no one knows this better than you. Other obligations in people's lives may limit the time and energy they have to give. Consider these matters before asking for help and talk them over. "I need more help with the _____. I know you are very busy and I'm concerned about asking too much of you. Would helping me a few hours during the week be more than you can do comfortably?" Out of concern for everyone's needs, you may decide it's time to inquire about hiring in-home help.

Decide the best time to make a request. Timing is important. A person who is tired, hungry, stressed, or busy is not a good candidate for a request.

Prepare a list of things that need doing. If you are unsure what people prefer to do, and relatives say they don't know how to help, make a list of tasks you need help with (cooking, errands, yard work, someone to visit with the care receiver) and let them choose.

Some caregivers turn providing help into gifts given. The idea is that when people give their time and energy to help, they are giving the caregiver a valuable gift. They may call their list "Gifts of Help" or "Gifts You Can Share/Give."

Be prepared for hesitance or refusal. Your request might be answered with a simple no or silence. The person may be unable or unwilling to help and is setting personal limits. Sometimes refusals upset caregivers. Realizing the refusal has hurt the caregiver's feelings, the person may change his mind and decide to help, but the relationship will suffer. If the person hesitates, ask, "Would you like time to think about it?"

Suggestions for asking for help

The following communication tools may help if you feel uncomfortable putting your request into words.

Use your please-pass-the-salt style to make requests. This is the tone you want to use when you ask someone for help. Practice making a request: "I would like to go to church on Sunday. Would you mind staying with Grandma?" in the same tone you would use to ask for the salt.

Use "I" statements to make clear, specific requests. A statement like "I need more help" is vague. A specific request sounds like, "I would like to go to church this Sunday. Would you stay with Grandma from 9:00 a.m. to noon?"

Avoid weakening your request. If you say "Could you think about staying with Grandma?" you weaken your request. Saying, "It's only a thought, but I'd like to go to church," sounds like your request isn't very important to you. Notice the strength of the statement, "Would you stay with Grandma from 9:00 a.m. to noon?"

Use an "I" statement to express appreciation for any help even if it is given reluctantly. "I want to thank you for staying with Grandma so I could go to church today."

If your request is turned down

If your request is turned down, try not to take it personally and give yourself credit for asking. Most likely the person is turning down the task, not you. Or he may worry about doing the task the way you want it done. Consider asking, "Do you have any concerns about what I have asked?" Then express appreciation for the person's willingness to hear your request. "Thank you for taking the time to listen."

Try not to let a refusal prevent you from asking for help again. The person who refused today may be glad to help another time.

Expressing Criticism

If setting limits and asking for help seems risky to caregiving relationships, expressing criticism may seem even more risky. But sometimes you must speak up whether you want to or not. This is especially true when health or safety are involved. Because the person may not like

> *I never give them hell.*
> *I just tell the truth and*
> *they think it is hell.*
>
> Harry S. Truman

what he hears doesn't mean you shouldn't speak up. Usually, how criticism is given affects people more than the criticism itself. Consider Grace's approach:

> Don't load the dishwasher that way. Always put the glasses on the upper rack and the cups in rows behind the saucers. You're wasting detergent. I never use that much.

How would you feel about loading Grace's dishwasher? Was the way you were doing it wrong or simply different? Grace could use some advice on more effective ways to correct people.

Before offering criticism

Constructive criticism helps people learn. It focuses on problems, not personalities. It shows you care enough to level with the person. A courteous, respectful tone makes your words, not your behavior, worth remembering.

Before you say anything, reflect on why you are criticizing. Use the following checklist to be certain you are criticizing for the right reasons.

YesNo

❑ ❑ Are you in a bad mood?

❑ ❑ Do you want to appear wiser, more knowledgeable or more experienced?

❑ ❑ Do you want to punish someone?

❑ ❑ Are you criticizing because something is done differently (not wrong or worse) than you do it?

Re-evaluate your "yes" responses because all are invalid reasons for criticizing. Valid reasons include unsafe activities and behavior that violates the rights and feelings of others. Once you decide your motives are valid, think about the timing and possible pitfalls before you offer criticism.

Address problems promptly. Timing is important. If you ignore a problem or delay addressing it, you give someone the message that he is doing fine. Then when you do speak up, the person wonders why you didn't say something earlier. Delays in addressing the problem may also allow it to grow worse and your feelings about it to build. This often leads to blaming "you" statements like, "Why don't you ever…?" "You always…," or "You never…"

Avoid the pitfalls. Before you say anything, mentally review pitfalls you want to avoid. It's important to:

◆ resist offering an opinion about the person's motives for doing what he did.

◆ avoid mind-reading and judging the other person's motives for doing what he did.

◆ avoid making comparisons with other people.

◆ avoid raising questions about the person's loyalty or commitment.

Ways to deliver constructive criticism

Bringing up a problem can be the hardest part of communicating effectively. If the person has seen you (or others in the family) do what you will be discussing, mention that you are also working on this problem. This makes you partners against the problem.

Grace has done this in the following scenario. Compare this with her statements earlier about loading the dishwasher. Do you feel differently about the way the criticism was given?

I'd like to talk about the way the bathroom is left after Grandpa has his shower. I know he throws his damp towels on the floor; I would like them put in the laundry. I step in puddles of water when I go in the bathroom and I worry about slipping and falling. You can use the mop in the kitchen closet or the damp towels to soak up the puddles. I would appreciate it if you would make sure the floor is dry. Thanks.

Grace's criticism was constructive because she applied the following suggestions. She used an "I" statement when she said, "I step in puddles." She focused on the problem, not the person, by saying, "I'd like to talk about the way the bathroom is left." She was specific when she said, "You can use the damp towel to soak up the puddles." She focused on the issue of concern—the bathroom. She didn't mention the dishwasher.

The following are additional tools for giving constructive criticism:

Phrase questions carefully. Your questions and comments can help or hurt. Asking why the person did something sounds accusatory. Frequently people don't know why they did something. Questions beginning with "how," "what," and "when" sound like you are gathering information, not blaming.

◆ "How do you usually do this?"

◆ "What do you think went wrong?"

◆ "When does the problem arise?"

Offer face-saving comments. Your intent is to protect the person's pride and feelings by offering valid, impersonal reasons for what has happened. Ask yourself the aikido question when a criticism must be given, "What does this person need from me to feel better or to save face? Protection from embarrassment? A chance to improve without having to apologize?" Some examples of face-savers are:

◆ "I can see how a mistake could be made. The directions are confusing."

◆ "This is easy to forget, especially when it's a busy time."

◆ "I hope we can continue to talk things over at a later time."

End on a positive note. You can end on an upbeat note by mentioning positive, helpful contributions the person has made and expressing your belief that things will work out. For example, Gerald said to an in-home worker:

> I notice how patient you are when talking to Dad, especially when he keeps asking who you are. One thing I've become more sensitive to when talking to Dad is to say 'you' instead of 'we.' It sounds more respectful to say 'How are you today?' instead of 'How are we today?' With a little forethought, this can be an easy change to make. And it's a change I will appreciate very much.

Remember the tools for how to best express yourself:

1. Use "I" messages.
2. Respect the rights and feelings of other people with what you say and do.
3. Be clear and specific.
4. Speak directly to the person(s) involved.
5. Be a good listener.

Responding to criticism

Although you may do your best to offer criticism in a constructive manner, you may not always be treated in the same way. This can be infuriating even when you sense a criticism has merit. Being open to criticism isn't easy, but it's important. As a caregiver you may be offended by criticism you feel is neither deserved nor wanted. How does one deal with criticism? The Boy Scouts say it best: "Be prepared." Here are some other tools that will help:

Think about the merits of the criticism, not just how it makes you feel. Does the criticism have merit? Did the person truly criticize or was he expressing a concern that you viewed as a criticism? For example, if you were told you needed help to provide care, would you see it as a criticism of your ability? Are there times when you could be wrong? If so, it shows true grit to admit a mistake and apologize. Just be sure your apology doesn't have the word "if" in it. Saying "I'm sorry *if* I was wrong" suggests you don't really believe you were wrong. A genuine apology has no "ifs" and says, "I was wrong and I'm sorry."

Use your aikido skills if the criticism is valid. Step into the other person's shoes and try to see things from his point of view. Ask what needs to change for him to feel better: "I need to understand what you want done differently." Perhaps you can't make the changes he wants, but you can listen with respect and concern. That might be all he wanted. (See Chapter 3 for information about aikido.)

Don't take unjust criticism to heart. Another part of readiness is the ability to disregard unfair criticism. You can ignore the criticism by simply saying, "I find your remarks interesting" and dropping the subject. If ignoring the criticism isn't the answer, you can calmly assert yourself by returning the problem to the critic with a statement like, "It would help me if you would share how you would have done _____." Or, to deflect criticism, try a remark like, "That is another way of looking at this…" If you need time to collect your thoughts, tell the person, "I will think about what you've said."

Responding to criticism from the care receiver

Taking criticism from the person receiving your help can be particularly difficult. This is especially true if you are the brunt of all the criticism and you are doing the most.

If the criticism is undeserved or invalid, try using aikido to respond and try not to take the criticism personally. Aikido is a very useful tool to use in these situations. It tends to disarm the person because he has no opponent and is not given "fuel" for an argument.

Some caregivers have also found it helps to calmly interrupt when the care receiver takes a breath and suggest talking later. Other caregivers quietly state that they can't listen any longer: "I need to excuse myself for a while," and leave the room. Offering a snack or something to drink gives you a reason to leave the room and may reduce the stress of the moment.

Another option is to suggest the person put his criticisms in writing because you can't remember everything. (The idea here is that people who criticize for the sake of criticizing often will not take the time to put

their criticisms in writing.) This also may help to focus you and the care receiver on legitimate issues that need to be addressed.

Remember, you do not have to listen to a barrage of unfair and hurtful criticism. Regardless of the criticism or its source, how you react to it affects how you will feel about yourself later. It's gratifying to look back on a challenging situation and say to yourself, "I handled that very well."

Expressing Anger

Like most of us, you can probably relate to this quote. Being able to express anger in ways that are positive and not hurtful is critical. This can be especially true when you find yourself facing emotionally charged problems and decisions. This happened to Betty when she least expected it.

> *Speak when you are angry and you will make the best speech you will ever regret.*
>
> Ambrose Bierce

Betty is 50 years old. She is the youngest of three children in the family and the only one who lives near their parents, who are both in their nineties. Her sister, Catherine, lives on the East Coast and her brother, Allen, lives in France. Betty thought the family should get together at least once while both the parents were alive. After much planning, a family reunion was held.

Betty still gets a knot in her stomach when she thinks about what happened that weekend. Catherine had said she felt the folks should move in with Betty because they "shouldn't live at home alone at their age." Allen agreed with Catherine. Betty became upset and angry.

Betty: "You're both fine ones to give me advice. You do none of the work. You never offer to send a dime to help me with the folks' expenses. I end up doing all the work and paying for everything. Now, you have the nerve to suggest that they move in with me so I can sacrifice what little free time I have left to take care of them!"

Catherine: "I didn't realize you would be so touchy about my idea."

Allen: "You never asked for any help or money. How was I to know you needed it?"

Betty: "Just forget I said anything. You're obviously too busy with your own lives to care about your own parents and me."

Silence descended on the group. The rest of the time was spent avoiding each other while trying to be polite in front of their parents. The family reunion ended with polite good-byes. Nothing had changed, except Betty wishes she had handled her anger in a better way.

The goal of expressing anger effectively is to share your feelings in a positive way so that people hear what you say versus hearing only your anger. Reaching this goal requires taking the time to regain perspective and to prepare.

Begin preparing by taking a look at what triggers your anger. Is it advice from people who don't help? Is it repetitive questions or behavior? Is it a request for help just when you have a moment to yourself? Once you identify the triggers, think of ways to cool off before you say anything. Deep-breathing and stress reduction activities might help you regroup. Counting to ten remains an effective way to calm down and think about what to say. Once you feel composed it helps to apply the following communication tools:

Use "I" messages in a non-threatening manner. Be aware of your body language. For example, don't tower over people when you talk to them. Place yourself at or below eye level when you say, "I get upset when I get advice instead of help taking care of Mother."

Avoid "you" messages. Blaming, accusing, and mind-reading are huge pitfalls. They usually lead to strong feelings of remorse later.

Speak in a normal tone of voice. Talking fast with a raised voice implies anger, regardless of what you actually say. Maintaining a moderate tone, volume, and rate of speaking suggests you are in control of your anger.

Getting angry is only human and saying so is not a bad thing as long as you follow the tools for how to best express yourself.

Responding to anger

When we respond to anger, our goal is to defuse the anger and calm the situation. Applying the aikido style of communication is an effective way to do this. If Catherine and Allen would have responded this way, the family reunion might have turned out differently.

Catherine: "If I believed that my brother and sister didn't care about me or the folks, I'd feel the same way you do."

Allen: "I don't know exactly what you need from us. Give us an example of what we can do from such long distances."

Betty: "I figure I spend about $200 a month on the folks. I would really like some help in covering my out-of-pocket expenses."

Catherine: "I can see we have a problem. What would you like me to do to help? I don't have much money."

Betty: "If you could come out once a year and keep an eye on the folks so I could take a vacation, it would be a big help."

In this example, Catherine and Allen aligned with Betty. They empathized with her feelings and asked for more information. This told Betty they cared. Meanwhile, they received information from Betty to redirect the conversation and move toward resolving the problem.

Other possible tools for responding to anger

Be careful with the following tools because they can backfire and make people angrier. Your knowledge and experience with the person will help you decide if these responses are appropriate in your situation.

Excuse yourself and leave the person alone. Sometimes anger builds as it is being expressed. You may decide to say, "I have to excuse myself. Let's talk when we both feel less emotional," and calmly leave the room. This is an option if your presence is making the person angry, if your safety is at risk, or anger is building and the person usually calms down when alone. Be careful about using this response. There are times when even politely leaving the room will increase someone's anger.

Use humor to ease tensions. Humor, used wisely, can recast unfairness into nonsense. It can help people rethink a problem. The difficulty is that not taking someone seriously is a powerful act of defiance. Using humor can come across as insulting or arrogant when it isn't meant that way.

Either way, there is a risk of increasing anger if the person feels you are making fun of him or light of an issue.

Refer to yourself, *not* the other person, in using humor. "So, I guess I'm not 'person of the week'" or "Here we are, madder than hatters at each other, and Dad is the one with the driving problem."

Change the subject. This is risky, too, because the person may think you don't understand or don't care. He needs to feel you have heard him before you change the subject. A remark like "You have a good reason to be upset. I have news I hope will help you feel better…" may work to lighten the atmosphere.

Expressing anger with blaming and accusations or responding to anger with anger doesn't promote family unity or help to solve problems. The assertiveness and aikido communication tools will help you accomplish more.

EXPRESSING YOURSELF UNDER SPECIAL CIRCUMSTANCES

Talking On The Telephone

Bob lived several hundred miles from his father. He called his father weekly, but was increasingly concerned about his father's well-being after the calls. He said:

> My dad is 85 years old and very frail. He is hard of hearing and has poor vision. Lately he seems more forgetful. I learned from a neighbor that my dad had a blood test at the hospital the previous day. Dad didn't remember anything about it. Every time I call, he tells me "Everything is just fine." But his voice sounds weaker when he says it. I have a feeling something just isn't right, so I'm going down for a visit.

Although telephone conversations can reveal clues about potential problems, they also can lead you astray. Miscommunication can occur because you don't have "the messages" that body language and facial expression provide. If you want to understand what the person means or feels, you might have to check with the person to make certain you both understand each other. For instance:

◆ "From the sound of your voice, I have the feeling you are worried. Is there something that is worrying you?"

◆ "I'm having trouble understanding what you mean. Can you explain a little more?"

◆ "It sounds like you mean (want, need, feel) _____. Am I right?"

Some people feel safer talking on the telephone than they do face to face. It's possible to capture honest thoughts, concerns, and feelings that would not be disclosed in person. If you discover this, try to schedule your calls when you won't be interrupted and you have time to talk. You don't want to cut off someone who finally trusts you and opens up to you. If your time is short when the person calls, mention in advance how long you can visit.

Telephone skills

A skilled, considerate telephone listener will:

◆ listen for clues in the tone of voice or manner of speaking that are different from earlier conversations.

◆ ask open-ended questions to get more information about those clues, like "How did you feel?", "What do you mean?", or "What do you think about…?"

◆ confirm what was meant: "Are you saying Dad won't agree to stop driving?"

◆ stop other activities such as housework or driving while on the phone.

◆ take notes. Details of telephone conversations are easy to forget, perhaps because there is no visual information to support what has been said. Taking notes helps you remember key concerns and to refer to them during future calls.

◆ summarize the conversation at the end to clarify what you both said.

Communicating With The Doctor

As you provide care over the years, you wear various hats. You are an expert in the care of your relative, a consumer of health care services, and the person who works with the doctors. You may also be a patient occasionally. In any case, you want to build a partnership with the physician and other

health care providers. You, as well as the physician and his or her staff, have a role in forming and maintaining this relationship.

What to consider before going to the doctor

Think about the main reasons for your visit and what you expect from the doctor as you prepare for your visit. Consider the following tools.

Prepare your questions. Make a list in advance of your most important concerns and questions. This increases the likelihood your office visits will meet your needs.

Consider other reliable sources of information. Before you decide what questions you want to ask the doctor, consider other reliable sources of information. Your pharmacist can answer questions about medications and the office nurse may have answers to your caregiving questions. Most caregiving issues relate more closely to nursing than to medicine. Also, the nurse usually has extensive knowledge about the doctor's patients, their illnesses, and the treatments prescribed.

Don't worry about asking the nurse questions the doctor should or prefers to answer. The nurse will refer you to the doctor for those questions. Depending on her background and the doctor's wishes, you can usually ask a nurse questions regarding:

◆ what you can learn from various tests and examinations.

◆ scheduling tests and what you have to do to prepare for tests or surgical procedures.

◆ providing personal care and measures to prevent problems such as pressure sores.

◆ managing medications at home.

You also can obtain information from support groups, specialty clinics, your local health department, and organizations dealing with certain health problems such as Parkinson's and Alzheimer's diseases, and stroke. These organizations offer free or inexpensive educational materials or can tell you where to get them. Sharing this information with non-caregiving relatives gives them an objective overview of the illness and related caregiving issues.

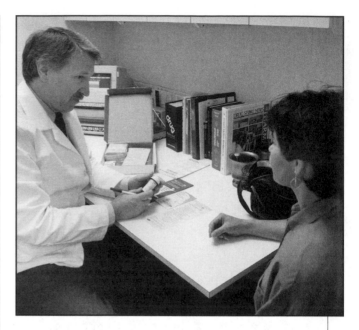

Make sure appointments meet your needs. When you call for an appointment, be clear about the reasons for the visit so the receptionist schedules enough time for you or the care receiver. Experience has shown that the first appointment in the morning or after lunch, and the last appointment of the day, are the best scheduling times.

Call ahead. Office staff suggest calling before you leave for the appointment to see if the doctor is seeing patients on time. If the appointment is for a memory-impaired relative, mention problems the person might have if kept waiting. Remind the receptionist of these special needs when you check in at the desk.

Take someone with you. Take a friend or relative along if you feel uncomfortable asking questions. They can ask questions you don't want to ask and help you remember what the doctor said.

Build a relationship with the office staff. Introduce yourself to the doctor's office staff. After you get acquainted, consider sending a card during the holidays or dropping a note to a staff member who provided exceptional service. Getting to know the staff often means better service.

Talking with the doctor

The following tools can help you get the most out of your time with the doctor.

Discuss your main concerns first. This is important because if you wait until the end of your appointment there may not be time to properly deal with the main reasons for your visit. You can say something like:

◆ "I have something important I want to talk about."

◆ "There are three things I need to understand better."

◆ "I have three important questions to ask."

Be concise. Clearly, briefly, and frankly discuss your concerns. The doctor will ask questions to get the necessary details. Lengthy, detailed descriptions of past experiences and old health problems are usually a waste of your time.

Refer to a second party. If you want a second opinion but you hesitate to ask for it, tell your doctor. "My _____ and I have discussed the importance of getting a second opinion." (Remember, there is a better chance of getting a second opinion if you ask for it than if you don't ask.)

Get your questions answered. Ask about tests and treatments and the reasons for them.

◆ What do you expect to learn from the test?

◆ When can I expect to hear the results of the test?

◆ How will I (or my relative) feel afterward?

◆ Are there other options to having this test?

Ask about treatment plans. Ask about medications and treatments that don't seem to work. Ask about alternatives for any treatment you find burdensome, such as a medication that must be taken in the middle of the night. Ask for clarification about the diagnosis and treatment plan and the reasons the doctor recommends it, what the treatment will accomplish, and restrictions on activities, food, or driving and the reasons for the restrictions. Find out about recovery and how long it will take to get back to normal, not just to feel better.

Telephone calls to the doctor

Most of us have called the doctor and waited for a call back. Because a doctor may not be able to return a call right away, caregivers and health care providers recommend that you briefly describe the reason for your call and ask when you can expect the doctor to return your call. Be prepared to answer some questions. If you're calling about a new symptom, the doctor will probably want to know what the symptom is, when it appeared, what you think causes it, and if it is getting worse. Be prepared to answer such questions.

When Getting Needed Information Is a Problem

Some caregivers find they can't get the information they need about their family member's condition and functioning because their relative won't tell them. It is important to understand the reasons a person may not want to disclose health matters. Some people fear losing privacy or control.

This lack of trust on the part of the care receiver can hurt and frustrate caregivers. If you have this problem, you face some difficult choices.

◆ Do you ask the care receiver if you can talk to the doctor?

◆ Do you politely tell him you will be talking to his physician?

◆ Do you contact the doctor even though you were told not to?

◆ Do you just talk to the doctor without telling the care receiver at all?

Everyone's situation is unique, but it's better to ask your relative about talking to the doctor. Would you agree or disagree with Judy's response in the following conversation?

Judy: "Dad, I need a better understanding of how you are doing. I realize you don't want to talk to me about it so I'd like to talk to your doctor."

Dad: "No, I don't want you to. No."

Judy: "What is it about my talking to your doctor that bothers you?"

Dad: "Frankly, I don't think my health is anybody's business but mine."

Judy: "I agree that your health is a private matter. Privacy is important to me too. I will keep what the doctor says in strict confidence. But I can't help you if I don't know what to do. I have questions that need answering."

Judy called the doctor. She briefly explained the caregiving situation and told the doctor she did not have her dad's permission to call, but he knew she was calling. She asked for the information she needed and the doctor gave it to her. Leona's story is a little different.

Today, Leona's doctor told her she had Parkinson's disease. Leona told her doctor that under no circumstances did she want her daughter Elaine to know her diagnosis. Leona fears the diagnosis will be the last straw because Elaine already helps Leona manage her diabetes, take care of the house, and run errands. She strongly believes Elaine would pressure her into moving to an assisted living facility.

Leona's demand places the doctor in an awkward position. While he respects her right to confidentiality, he also needs assurances his prescribed treatment can be carried out. Leona clearly needs Elaine's help to do this. Faced with dilemmas like this one, some doctors may decline to provide further care. The prospect of losing the doctor usually changes the patient's mind.

If you suspect that, medically, more is going on than your relative will tell you, talk to the doctor about it. If possible, mention specific problems your relative is having that worry you: "I'm helping my mother get along at home and manage her diabetes. I've noticed she has a tremor and seems unsteady when she walks. I need to know if she has other health problems besides her diabetes because I am responsible for her care."

The following tools may also help to deal with this difficult situation.

Tell your family member you cannot help without certain information from his doctor. Mention that health care professionals require similar information to provide the best care possible. If your relative still refuses to share information, you could say:

◆ "I'd like your permission to talk to your doctor about…"

◆ "I can't help you without talking to your doctor."

◆ "I will have to tell your doctor I can't help carry out his treatment orders without knowing what's wrong."

Get the doctor involved. Talk with the doctor. Ask for information on a "need to know" basis. Tell the doctor about the care receiver's objections. Be clear that you are requesting only information you need to help your relative. If the doctor reassures your relative that only information about his current illness will be shared, your relative may agree.

Talk to a trusted friend, relative, or religious advisor. Without betraying confidences, explain that you cannot provide the best possible care without knowing your relative's medical problems. If they agree to get involved, it is best to tell the care receiver up front that you talked to them because you were concerned.

Respect your relative's need for confidentiality. Build trust by sharing only caregiving problems that do not undermine the person's dignity and privacy. Ask, "If I had this problem would I want it discussed with others?" If you still aren't sure, ask permission from your relative before you discuss a concern with someone else.

Communicating with Older Adults

The communication tools discussed so far also apply when communicating with chronically ill, frail, older people. However, it's important to consider how health-related problems may affect communication. Age-related changes in vision and hearing affect 50 percent of people over age 75. Approximately 10 percent of people over age 65 experience memory loss as a result of Alzheimer's disease or a related disorder. You will be able to communicate more effectively if you try some of the following tools.

The hearing-impaired

To communicate more effectively with the person who is hearing-impaired, try these tools:

◆ Approach the person so he can see you to avoid startling him.

◆ Stand or sit between three and six feet away from him.

◆ Get the person's attention before speaking.

◆ Place yourself so the light is on your face for better visibility of lip movements, facial expressions, and gestures.

◆ Speak at a normal rate using normal lip movements.

◆ Do not shout. Yelling distorts sound, making it even more difficult for the person to hear.

◆ Use one-sentence explanations.

◆ Use gestures (nod, point, beckon) and demonstrate what you mean.

◆ Avoid eating, chewing gum, smoking, and turning away from the person while you are speaking.

◆ Do not speak directly into his ear. He will hear you more loudly but not more clearly.

◆ Reduce background noise and activity.

◆ Remember that hearing aids make all sounds louder, not just your voice.

◆ Be aware of false impressions. Head nodding doesn't necessarily mean "I understand."

◆ Give time for the person to respond.

◆ Explore adaptive and assistive listening devices. These include pocket size amplifiers and speakers.

The visually-impaired

Use these tools with the person who has limited vision.

◆ Announce your presence. Speak as you enter the room to avoid startling.

◆ Ask if the lighting in the room is adequate.

◆ Speak normally and directly. Remember, just because a person is sight-impaired doesn't mean he can't hear or talk.

◆ Use a gentle touch, if appropriate. It may help him focus on you.

◆ Tell him when you are leaving the room.

◆ Obtain low-vision aids. These devices help a person make the best possible use of remaining vision.

The memory-impaired

Figuring out how much a person with memory problems understands takes some detective work. It can get confusing because some people can read aloud without understanding a word they read. Others may respond with smiles and nods to your words without understanding a word you said. Still others understand what they see and hear but cannot find the words to respond.

Once you realize what aids the person in understanding, you can take measures to communicate in those ways. For example, if your relative cannot understand writing, pictures may be helpful. If he can't find the bathroom, a picture of a toilet on the bathroom door may solve the problem. If your spoken word is not understood, try using gestures and demonstrate what you mean. For example, pat the seat of the chair while saying, "Please sit down," or demonstrate a task one step at a time, allowing time for the person to imitate what you do. These tasks may range from getting dressed to making a sandwich or setting the table.

There are many special tools for communicating with people who have memory loss. Organizations dealing with such problems as stroke, Parkinson's disease, and Alzheimer's disease, have materials written specifically for families. Look in the telephone directory under the name of the disease or call the social services department of your local hospital. Chapter 17, "Caring for Memory-Impaired Elders," addresses this topic in greater detail.

Additional information about hearing and visual impairment is available through local hearing and speech specialists or specialty clinics.

Setting the stage
for effective communication

Choose a time to talk that is best for the person. Select a day when little else is going on. Select a time when the person feels rested and medication levels are at their most effective levels. Try to fit your visit in his routine so he doesn't have to delay or skip a daily activity or miss a favorite television or radio program. Make sure he has eaten and doesn't need to use the toilet. Adjust the room temperature and lighting to his liking.

Remove as many distractions as possible. As we grow older, we are more easily distracted by noise and activity in the surroundings. See the list of potential distractions discussed in Chapter 3.

Speak directly and clearly. Older people respond better to clear messages. "I noticed some meat has spoiled in the refrigerator. May I throw it away?" or "Your doctor wants to see you this month. I'll be glad to take you." They may not take a subtle hint like "Hasn't it been a long time since you saw your doctor?"

If the Care Receiver Mistreats You

Bill, a 48-year-old son, said:

When my mother died, my wife and I decided to turn the daylight basement into an apartment for my dad, Joe. At 78, he was lonely and becoming more forgetful. He moved in six months ago. My wife, Marie, provides most of his care. It is just not working. Our teenage sons avoid him because he constantly criticizes them. Lately they've been spending a lot of time at their friends' homes. When he wants something, he yells at us. The stress of putting up with this is too great. Last night we decided Dad will have to move into an assisted living facility.

Charlotte, a retired nurse, said:

Robert's cold, angry look stopped me in my tracks and he wasn't even looking

at me. He was looking at his wife. Even though it was years ago, I still remember how he silenced his wife without saying a word. I was attending a stroke support group meeting. The man I'm talking about actively participated in the group discussion while his wife sat quietly behind his wheelchair. I wondered how long the woman could continue caring for someone who treated her so unkindly.

What do you do if the care receiver trespasses on your rights or hurts your feelings? Do you feel you must suspend your rights because of the person's age or health problems? If the person speaks or, like the men in the stories, communicates in such a way that you feel hurt or "put down," do you just "grin and bear it"?

If a care receiver mistreats you or uses helplessness to control you, you will likely become resentful. Your feelings of resentment will eventually affect your ability to provide care. Letting resentment build and saying nothing is a disservice both to you and to the care receiver. If he sees no consequences to mistreating you, the behavior will continue.

The reality is that a price is paid for mistreating the caregiver. The cost comes as the caregiver's physical and mental health suffers and talk of placement surfaces. Another consequence of mistreatment may come in the use of medications to control aggressive behavior. Often these medications are powerful and may have unwanted side effects.

Caregiver burnout, placement, and the use of potent medications are high prices to pay for not dealing with mistreatment. If you need a refresher, refer to assertiveness (in Chapter 3) and dealing with anger and criticism sections of this chapter. You may also find support groups and professional counseling helpful. Your effectiveness as a caregiver and your relative's ability to remain at home may lie in your ability to communicate limits and consequences in a clear, kind, but firm manner.

CHALLENGING COMMUNICATION STYLES

The challenges of providing care increase when communication breaks down. This can happen with certain communication styles. These styles frequently emerge when stress is at peak levels or when people must make difficult decisions. Also, sometimes people use these styles because they have always worked. This section will briefly discuss tools for communicating more effectively, with three such styles: passive/peacekeeping, aggressive/pitbull, and factual/computer.

Passive/Peacekeeping Style

"Peace at any price" is a motto for people who use the passive/peacekeeping style to communicate. However, when honest concerns and feelings are not raised, it can potentially undermine important relationships and decision making. Making sound decisions becomes difficult because the true nature of problems remains hidden and cannot be clearly identified and resolved.

Sharon: "Usually I say nothing when my father-in-law ridicules my family and me because I'm afraid of making him mad. Or I end up saying 'I don't mean to sound disrespectful' and apologizing to him, even though I've done nothing wrong."

Judy: "When our family gets together to decide how to help Grandma, my sister Christy won't tell us what she wants to do. She always wants the rest of us to choose what we want to do first. When we ask her to tell us what she wants, she says, 'Anything is fine with me.'

Yesterday, Ken told me Christy gets tired of doing what nobody else wants to do."

We have called the passive style Sharon and Christy used a peacekeeping style. This is the style where people hope and hint rather than speak directly. They use apologetic, self-defeating language such as "I don't mean to sound…" Their personal needs nearly always take second place to the needs of others. Christy did this when she said, "Anything is fine with me."

It's also easy to fall into this peacekeeping style when providing care because often caregivers don't feel they can speak openly to someone who is elderly or sick. Some people who receive care may feel the same way for a different reason. They might feel uncomfortable speaking up because they are dependent on the goodwill of the caregiver to meet their needs.

Sometimes people use a passive style because they fear speaking honestly to a person who comes across as judgmental or controlling. Perhaps Sharon felt that way when she said "I don't mean to sound…" Sometimes people are passive because they are afraid of rejection or they don't want to jeopardize an important relationship by being open. The peacekeeper's intent is to please, not to deceive. People seeking to please may also:

◆ seek approval and want to stay in another's good graces.

◆ avoid confrontation; they might even go so far as to agree with their own critics.

◆ feel they are accountable for everything that goes wrong.

- feel they are responsible for other people's happiness.

- be unable to ask for things and therefore use compliments or guilt to manipulate others.

Tools for communicating with peacekeepers

You want to be clear that it is safe to speak openly to you. You may have to say directly that you won't get upset or think less of the person. A gentle, assertive style may be effective. The aikido style may not be direct enough to ferret out hidden information. However, the aikido style may work to encourage the person to share his feelings with you (see Chapter 3 for a review of aikido). In either case, you encourage peacekeepers to speak openly if you apply the following tools:

Recognize how you come across. If a person uses the peacekeeping style to relate to you, ask yourself if you may be the reason. For example, are you coming across as judgmental or controlling? Being aware of your role allows you to act on it by reassuring the person he can say "No" or express his feelings without fear of criticism, retaliation, or judgment. For instance, you might say:

- "Please tell me more. I didn't realize…"

- "I won't get upset if you tell me how you feel about what happened."

- "I want to understand. I'm not here to criticize."

Use a direct, calm, unhurried speaking style. This relaxing manner encourages openness. You can see the aikido style in the following openers:

- "I can only imagine how hard this is for you."

- "I understand how (sad, annoying, worrisome) that would be."

- "I'm interested in what's important to you."

Give the person your undivided attention. This shows you respect him and what he has to say.

What happens if you use this style?

If you communicate in a passive manner you voluntarily give up your right to:

- have a role in making decisions.

- advise others of your limits and needs.

- get the information and help you want and need from professionals and family members.

Aggressive/Pitbull Style

Joe is a 78-year-old widower. Alone and becoming forgetful, he agreed to move into the basement apartment his son constructed for him. Joe's wife was the quiet type, so Joe is used to "wearing the pants in the family." Living with his son and two teenagers isn't easy. Marie, his daughter-in-law, is easygoing, but must cope with Joe's speaking style.

Joe shouted to his grandsons: "Turn down that terrible music! You never stop to think someone else might not want to hear that junk. And, look at you! You are wearing jeans with holes in them. Why don't you ever wear clothes that look decent? (Turning to Marie) Why don't you put your foot down, Marie?"

Marie: "Boys, turn down the music, it's upsetting your grandfather. I wish you three could get along."

The person who uses the aggressive/ pitbull style of communicating is focused on getting his way and ignores the feelings and the rights of others. Joe's "you" statements accuse his grandsons of being thoughtless and slovenly. Joe, and others like him, use this style to maintain power and to control other people. At times, people who need assistance use this style to regain some control over their lives. People using an aggressive style may:

◆ use anger and temper tantrums to intimidate.

◆ use criticism and ridicule to discourage the efforts of others.

◆ make jokes at other people's expense to undermine their self-esteem.

◆ list failings for the other person's "own good," injuring their self-confidence.

◆ blame others by using red flag phrases such as "even you," "don't you even (care)," "you should," "you always," "you never," and "why don't you ever?"

Tools for dealing with aggressiveness

The intent is to stop the aggression. If you reply in a pitbull mode, a shouting match develops. But if you wait without interrupting, the aggressor eventually runs out of things to say.

You can also reduce the need to be aggressive. If the person is angry, deal with his anger. (Re-read the dealing with anger section in this chapter.) If the person wants more control over his or her life, find ways he can regain it by offering choices whenever possible and encouraging independence.

Some tools for dealing with aggressiveness include:

Try the aikido-aligning style. Agreeing can have a disarming effect on people who are communicating in an aggressive manner. It is the last thing they expect and it surprises them. When a person's emotions get out of control, agreeing seems to initiate some calmness. Marie might have said, "Yes, the boys do wear jeans with holes in them. I know it's hard to believe, but it's the style these days."

Concentrate on areas of common concern or agreement. Asking the individual to elaborate on areas of common concern is pure diplomacy. For example, Marie could have said, "Sometimes I have trouble accepting how the boys dress, too. When I went to school, wearing clothes with holes in them was embarrassing. Was it that way for you?"

Ask about feelings. Sometimes agreement doesn't work. Asking about feelings is usually the next best step. Marie might say, "I need to know what has upset you."

Express appreciation. Sometimes people attack indirectly. They may offer criticism about the way you provide care "for your own good" or for the good of the ill person. It is difficult, but often effective, to respond to this type of aggression with, "Thank you for sharing that. I'm always open to new ideas."

Deal with indirect put-downs directly. Jokes made at another person's expense in the name of "good fun" are a form of aggression. The aggressor acts surprised when the person expresses indignation and may say, "Just kidding." Consider the following situation in which Bert put a stop to Betty's little jokes and he did it with class.

Bert: "Betty, I felt insulted at your remark that I couldn't balance a checkbook if my life depended on it."

Betty: "Can't you take a joke?"

Bert: "I know the joke wasn't meant to insult me but I don't think jokes made at my expense are funny."

Betty: "You are really getting thin-skinned."

Bert: "I don't want it to happen again. If it does, I will call you on it. It won't be funny when I say, 'I don't think jokes made at my expense are funny, Betty.'"

Bert did a lot of things right. He prepared himself ahead of time. He privately practiced what he would say and how he would say it. He gave Betty a face-saving excuse for her remarks: "I know the joke wasn't meant to insult me." He used "I" statements and he used the DESC method.

Describe: He described what Betty said by using quotes.

Express: He expressed his feelings: "I don't think jokes made at my expense are funny."

Specify: He told her he didn't want it to happen again. (He also ignored Betty's "thin-skinned" remark and kept his focus on the "joke.")

Consequence: He told her what would happen if she did it again: "I will call you on it."

What happens if you use this style?

Aggressive behavior creates a vicious cycle for those dealing with chronic conditions because the mere threat of an angry outburst can keep friends and family away. It distances people. This distancing reinforces the aggressor's belief that no one really cares. If the aggressor is the care receiver, the stress caused by aggressive behavior may hasten moving the person into a professional care setting.

There are times when all of us use the pit-bull style to get what we want or to express our frustration or anger. The hardest, shortest, and best way to get back on track is to acknowledge our misstep and, using an "I" statement, apologize for it.

Factual/Computer Style

Some people seek to prevent closeness by using a factual manner to relate to others. The belief is that people use this style of communication to avoid showing their true feelings. Not only do they wish to remain emotionally anonymous, they usually show little or no interest in how other people feel.

Ed is an example of the factual style. Ed and his sister, Nan, were meeting at a local cafe to discuss their mother's driving. Nan saw it as a problem and Ed didn't.

Ed: "Some older people drive until they are well into their 90s. One wouldn't think driving to the grocery store would be such a problem. Most elderly need the independence driving gives them."

Nan: "You're right, many older people do continue to drive. Many older people also voluntarily quit driving and remain independent by using local transportation services. Mom's driving worries me. Did she tell you about the parking meter she totaled last week? Did you know that she got a ticket for passing a school bus unloading children, and that Tuesday she got lost on her way to my house?"

Ed: "Actually, not driving would save on insurance and car maintenance. The money saved could go for cab fare. There are definitely advantages to consider."

Nan gave Ed the telephone numbers of the city bus service and the closest senior center to contact. They discussed contacting businesses that offer delivery services. She knew Ed would be comfortable doing the research and she would help her mother deal with her feelings and concerns.

"Calm, cool, and collected" describes the factual style of communicating. Unwilling or unable to share feelings, the person speaks in impersonal terms, such as "some," "most," "one," and "everyone" instead of "I" and "we." "Some" and "most" are also commonly used words. A factual-style sentence sounds like "Some older people drive well into their 90s," or "Most older people need the independence driving gives them."

Tools for relating to the factual style

The goal in responding to people who use the factual style to communicate is to adapt to it. The goal is not to make these people express their feelings. Using assertiveness or mirroring the factual style works well. The following suggestions may help you communicate more effectively.

Imitate the person's style. If you try to solicit the person's feelings with a question like "How do you feel about that?" the person may retreat further. Use the same impersonal language he uses. For example, change your question to "What do you think about that?" When responding, replace "feeling" words such as "concerned" or "happy" with the word "interesting" to describe what was said. Nan might have said "It's interesting that some older people drive until they are well into their ninetieth year."

Give the person credit for being right. We all like to be told we are right. Once you have agreed on the person's "rightness," he will generally become more receptive to different options and your ideas. Nan did this when she agreed that "many older people do continue to drive."

Give the person intellectual tasks. People who relate to others in this way often prefer dealing with caregiving problems that involve facts or research, rather than emotions. They might do well and enjoy helping in areas of researching resources and dealing with finances and taxes.

What happens if you use this style?

There is good news and bad news. The good news is, you can use this style. Because it is a neutral response, it is effective in emotional, guilt-laden, no-win situations. For instance:

Non-caregiving expert: "Your mother seems lonely. I'm sure she would love to live with you."

You (in factual style): "Many people think older people want to live with their children. Research shows they actually prefer living in their own homes even when they live alone."

The bad news is, if you are like most caregivers, you occasionally want praise or approval. If you want praise or approval from a factual/computer-style communicator, you have to ask for it.

∾

SETTING YOUR GOALS AND MAKING ACTION PLANS

Perhaps as you read the information on communication you found some areas to work on. Improving your effectiveness as a listener or a speaker is easier if you decide on specific goals. Setting goals provides focus and direction.

The next step is making an action plan. An action plan is like a short-term contract to meet a goal. An action plan should include with whom, what, and when you will apply a communication tool. The activity in the box on the next page can help you with your action plan.

Finally, write down how confident you are that you will do it (1 = not confident; 10 = fully confident).

Write one goal for listening:

_____
_____
_____
_____

Write one goal for expressing yourself:

_____
_____
_____
_____

Check the goal you want to work on first.

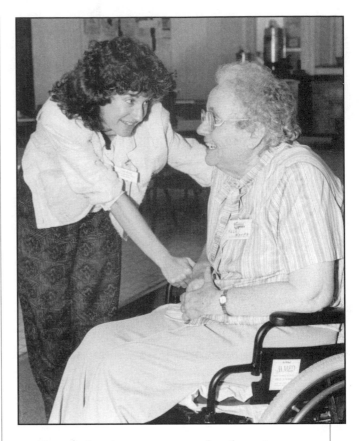

Caregiving is not easy, and enhancing your "box of communication tools" is extra work and does take practice. However, improved communication skills results in better relationships. And being able to communicate your limits and ask for help in positive ways will decrease feelings of frustration and resentment.

You deserve rewards for your efforts. Think of some way to congratulate yourself for applying the communication tools discussed in this chapter.

SUMMARY

Common themes reappear throughout the communication chapters. Here are some qualities and principles to strive for as caregivers:

◆ Listen carefully in an accepting and nonjudgmental way to show you care.

◆ Stand up for yourself without stepping on the rights and feelings of others.

◆ Create an environment in which people feel safe sharing with you.

◆ Respect your needs by setting limits and asking for help in a clear, direct, positive way.

◆ Find a mutual benefit in redefining common goals.

◆ Focus on issues as problems and not on people as problems.

◆ Avoid blaming others.

◆ Prepare ahead of time for contacts with health care professionals so you and the care receiver obtain the best care and advice possible.

◆ Continue to refine your communication tools to enhance your effectiveness in dealing with daily concerns.

IMPROVING MY COMMUNICATION SKILLS
Action Plan

This week I will_____ (what)

_____ (with whom)

_____ (when)

On a scale of 1 to 10, with 1 being "not confident" and 10 being "highly confident," how confident are you that you will reach your goal? _____

Check the day you reached goal.   **Comments**

Monday   _____   _____

Tuesday   _____   _____

Wednesday   _____   _____

Thursday   _____   _____

Friday   _____   _____

Saturday   _____   _____

CHAPTER FIVE

Learning From Our Emotions

As you and the person receiving your care adjust to the reality of living with chronic illness, you may be struggling to find the strength just to survive. You may find yourself "within a dark wood." But with time, as you gain knowledge and understanding, your goal may change from seeking survival to finding ways to rebuild your lives and recapture broken dreams.

Whether you are seeking to survive or to rebuild your life, at times you probably feel painful and complex emotions. You are not alone. Most caregivers experience difficult emotions at one time or another. However troublesome, your feelings are a natural response to whatever is happening in your life.

Your feelings, whether positive or negative, directly affect your situation, and your situation directly affects your feelings. One feeds the other. Negative feelings can affect your situation adversely, which, in turn, may generate feelings of helplessness and depression. But the cycle can be broken. You can learn to manage your emotions and make changes that affect your situation.

This chapter explores the difficult emotions connected with caregiving—to help you understand and learn from them—and offers tools to help you manage your feelings.

> *In the middle of the journey of our life I came to myself within a dark wood Where the straight way was lost.*
>
> - Dante
> *The Divine Comedy*

ABOUT EMOTIONS

Emotions serve a purpose. They are messages, telling us to stop, look, and listen, to pay attention to what is going on. They can indicate that change is needed. Listening to our feelings prompts questions like: "What is wrong?" "Why do I feel this way?" "What can I do about these feelings?" "What will help?" Asking these questions is the first step toward finding answers.

Remember these characteristics of feelings:

◆ Feelings exist.

◆ Feelings are real.

◆ Feelings are neither good nor bad.

It is how we respond to our feelings that makes the difference in how they affect us and our lives. What will your response be? To simply survive or to find a better way? Do you respond to difficult situations and suffering in a way that allows you to rebuild your life?

Anne Morrow-Lindbergh, a well-known writer and the wife of Charles Lindbergh, famous aviator, offers wisdom gleaned from the nightmare experience of having their 18-month-old son kidnapped from their home and later found dead. She writes:

> I do not believe that sheer suffering teaches. If suffering alone taught, all the world would be wise, since everyone suffers. To suffering must be added mourning, understanding, patience, love, openness, and the willingness to remain vulnerable.

Anne Morrow-Lindbergh's words are hopeful. They are a reminder that we can learn from hard times and difficult feelings. We can make a choice about how to respond to life's challenges. And we can grow in wisdom.

It's also important to consider the feelings of the person for whom you are providing care. His feelings are an undeniable part of the caregiving situation and affect you, just as yours affect him.

Mixed Feelings

Caregiving often involves a range of feelings. Some feel comfortable. Others feel uncomfortable. Feelings are referred to as positive and negative, not because they are good or bad, but based on how they often feel. For example, guilt and anger feel uncomfortable to most of us and are often referred to as "negative." Love feels good and is referred to as "positive."

Compassion, caring, and commitment are feelings for many caregivers. However, they seldom stand alone. Often positive feelings are accompanied by those we find less acceptable—like anger, resentment, and guilt. This mixture of contradictory feelings, more often referred to as ambivalence, is natural and human. Accepting ambivalence is crucial in coping with emotions involved in caregiving.

Identifying and accepting all emotions becomes the challenge.

◆ Do you have positive feelings as well as strong and difficult feelings?

◆ Is your caring and compassion mixed with anger, hostility, and frustration?

◆ Do you feel guilty about having "negative" emotions like anger or resentment?

Acceptance is the first step in moving forward. When we accept ambivalent feelings we come to recognize and accept loss.

Kinds of Losses

You and the care receiver may be experiencing many different losses. Losses may be large or small. They may include loss of companionship, financial stability, healthy partner or friend, sexual relationship, dreams for the future, independence, lifestyle as you've known it, weekly lunches with a friend, walks with your spouse, and more. Only you know your losses since your situation is unique and what you perceive as a loss is based on how you view your situation. Another person may perceive the same situation differently. It is important to understand and accept the losses you and the care receiver have experienced.

The care receiver may also be struggling with strong feelings, some of them like yours. He may be feeling sad, depressed, or angry due to the effects of the illness and loss of independence and control. He may experience fear and frustration about loss of his ability to function, or be fearful of the ultimate loss, death. If at all possible, it is helpful to share your feelings and thoughts, as a way to better understand each other's experience.

In certain situations people are unable to share their experiences. For example, those who suffer from dementia or the disabling effects of a stroke may be unable to put their thoughts and feelings into words. This reality limits your ability to communicate, and is perhaps your greatest loss. If the care receiver is unable to talk about his feelings and fears, then you must find other ways to communicate. Observing his behavior and emotions can give you insight into what he is feeling. It is possible to gain an increased awareness of, and an ability to "read" body language, tone of voice, and facial expressions. Many caregivers have found that much can be said with touch. And, touch can be meaningful to both of you.

Marlene, caregiver to her husband who has Alzheimer's disease, made a choice to communicate in a positive way.

As Paul gradually became increasingly helpless, Marlene became frustrated by their inability to talk to each other. She felt at her wits end much of the time. She had loved Paul for more than 40 years and wanted that love to be part of the way she communicated with him, not frustration and anger. A counselor suggested she try "self-talk," which is the repetition of positive statements to yourself as a way to counteract negative thoughts. She repeatedly said to herself "I choose love".

Gradually Marlene became adept at replacing negative, frustrated thinking with the positive phrase she chose. This gave her a sense of control over her thoughts. Marlene found it easier, even in the most frustrating and stressful times, to use gentleness, touch, humor, and loving actions to communicate with Paul instead of lashing out in anger. When she was able to change her response, Paul appeared more relaxed.

The exercise on page 92 can be helpful if you and the care receiver are able to communicate verbally. Do the exercise individually and then discuss it as a way to understand each other's perception of what is lost.

As you and the care receiver discuss the responses elicited by the exercise, it will help reduce the stress created by illness and loss. Sharing may also help you maintain and build your relationship, a concern of many caregivers and care receivers.

Chapters 3 and 4 offer important help with communication skills, including the use of "I" statements, active listening, and assertive and aikido styles of communication. These tools can be helpful in what could be a sensitive, difficult conversation.

IDENTIFYING LOSS

This activity is designed to help you identify your losses and what they mean to you. It is important to recognize both major and minor losses. Use extra paper if you need to. Be specific. Identify each loss individually, and follow it with a statement about what the loss means to you. The first one is an example.

1. *I have lost: personal freedom. This means: I can no longer choose how to spend my time without first considering another's needs.*

2.

3.

4.

5.

Recommendations for coping with loss are addressed later in this chapter.

THE ESSENCE OF GRIEF

In completing the "Identifying Loss" exercise you may have recognized multiple losses. When you lose precious parts of your life, grief is a natural response. Loss begets grief. If you dare to love and make commitments, grief will be part of your experience. It happens to all of us.

Your grief response is uniquely yours and is determined by what the loss means to you. Was it a large or small loss? How attached were you to what was lost? How will the loss affect your life? How have you coped with change and loss in the past? These are valid questions and the answers will determine, in part, how you respond to loss and how you grieve.

Grief brings with it many strong, complex emotions, which may include loneliness, frustration, anger, anxiety, confusion, fear, guilt, resentment, sadness, and depression. These are legitimate emotions and may be

part of your experience. As you give yourself permission to feel these emotions, your hurt will lessen. However, you must first allow yourself to feel the pain of your loss. Denying, avoiding, or minimizing feelings only complicates your grief response.

Grieving can be lonely. It is well recognized that grief follows a death. However, people may not recognize that caregivers and those with chronic illness go through a comparable grieving process, so they may not offer support. It is important to let others know how you feel and what you need. This can be difficult, but support is critical when you are dealing with a loss.

We can learn much from the way Ernie and Jean handled their situation.

Ernie, a physical therapist, had two serious illnesses, a moderate stroke at age 37 and a diagnosis of Alzheimer's disease at age 55. An insightful man, he clearly told those who knew him how important it was that he be allowed to grieve his losses. He sought out people who accepted his feelings and avoided those who were uncomfortable with them. He talked openly about past and present losses and those he anticipated in the future. He spoke with a sense of urgency, sensing his limited time for clear expression of feelings.

Jean, Ernie's wife bravely dealt with both of their losses. She, too, felt grief, as she dealt with their changing relationship and roles. She was a compassionate, committed caregiver. It disturbed her to have feelings of anger and guilt that seemed incompatible with her caring nature. When she realized that ambivalent feelings are a normal part of grief, she was able to be more supportive to Ernie.

Grieving Your Own Way

Grief is an experience that is unique to each of us. There are many different responses to loss. One is not better than another. There is no right or wrong way to grieve, only your own way. It is helpful to honor each person's grief response. That makes it easier to accept the differences rather than let them be a source of conflict. Lillian and Rob had different ways of dealing with their feelings.

Lillian was angry because her son, Rob, seemed distant and withdrawn. Rob and his dad had always been close, but now that his dad was "leaving" because of Alzheimer's disease, Rob stayed away more and more. When Lillian tried to talk to him about this he became angry and tearful. He was grieving and finding the "long goodbye" extremely sad and stressful. Rob had always found it difficult to talk about his feelings. Lillian, meanwhile, openly expressed her feelings of anxiety and sadness.

Lillian's and Rob's responses to the same situation were neither right or wrong, nor were they more or less caring; they were just different. Rob and Lillian talked about the situation, which helped them to respect each other's feelings and become more supportive of each other.

As you and others cope with losses, try to accept that each of you is experiencing grief in your own way. Respect and honor each other's uniqueness.

Anticipatory Grief

Anticipatory grief is a grief response that can be experienced before an actual death. It is a response to loss. We grieve present losses that are caused by the illness, and we grieve those losses anticipated in the future. It is difficult to adjust to these losses because you can't anticipate a happy ending, that is, a return to "the way things used to be."

Jack felt overwhelmed when his mother, Louise, suffered loss upon loss. Louise had Parkinson's disease for many years and her losses gradually rendered her unable to care for herself. The final "insult" occurred when Louise had eye surgery which was unsuccessful, leaving her blind. The loss of sight triggered intense feelings of loss and grief for Louise. She raged at the world and felt very sad and depressed. She expressed a wish to die and could find no reason to go on living. She talked of suicide.

Jack, as his mother's caregiver, felt sad and angry at the injustice of his mother's losses. He also felt the loss of a friend and loving parent. As Jack assumed increasing responsibility for his mother's care, he felt like the parent. He found this change very difficult. In a very real sense, Jack was feeling the loss of his mother while his mother was still alive. He felt lonely, bereaved, and resentful.

Jack is grieving present and anticipated future losses. As caregiving requirements increase, he feels the loss of her independence as well as the loss of a mother-son relationship. In addition, Jack is anticipating the ultimate loss, the death of his mother.

Jack's situation is just one example of an anticipatory grief experience. Caregivers of loved ones who have Alzheimer's disease have said, "It's like a funeral that never ends," "I lost my family member long before his body died," and "I've already watched the death of my husband, due to Alzheimer's disease; now I'm watching the death of the disease."

Caregivers of people with progressive dementia, as in Alzheimer's disease, understand uncertainty, stress, change, and loss all too well. Nancy's husband was a successful accountant and now he cannot add the simplest numbers. Ralph's wife of 35 years no longer recognizes him. These situations are filled with grief.

Caregivers could be consumed by grieving ongoing change and loss. It is helpful to accept the disease and changes yet to come. Acceptance does not eliminate the hope that some new drug, surgery, or treatment will be discovered to change the medical reality of "what is."

Tasks of Grieving

In his book *Grief Counseling and Grief Therapy,* J. William Worden describes four tasks people must complete to reconcile loss and begin healing after a death. These tasks also apply to people who experience loss as a result of chronic illness. The tasks are:

1. Accept the reality of the loss. Identify and acknowledge each loss. Do not deny or minimize them. This is an emotional and intellectual process and takes time.

2. Work through the pain of the loss. Feel your feelings, however painful. If you don't work through your feelings you can compromise your physical and emotional well-being, which may result in depression, health problems, and other symptoms. Doing grief "work" is a difficult task. It is made more so when others are uncomfortable with your feelings and give you the subtle message that you "shouldn't feel that way," or that you should "pull yourself together."

3. Adjust to your losses. Adapting to ongoing loss and change requires that you recognize and accept what you can't change. At the same time, efforts to change what you can will help you focus on pleasures that remain. This can give you a much-needed sense of mastery over your environment. If you strive to hold on to what is lost, you lose the precious opportunities that remain, and your frustration and grief will get worse.

4. Reinvest in life. Reinvesting in life empowers you to move forward. Rebuild your life, incorporating change and loss. There is still a life to be lived in which you can find renewed hope and meaning.

These tasks are an ongoing, sometimes slow process. They do not move in orderly stages, but rather in a fluid process that is interwoven with the rest of your life.

A Different Kind of Loss

We have assumed that many caregivers feel compassion and caring, and therefore feel loss and grief. If you are the caregiver for a person with whom you have had a difficult relationship, and are caregiving out of a sense of duty, you may still feel loss. This is not an uncommon occurrence. Your losses no doubt have more to do with what has never been and can never be, as in Gerald's situation.

Gerald's father had never told him he loved him. Gerald became the caregiver for his father, in part because he hoped that he would hear the words "I love you" or receive some expression of love from him. His father did not respond in that way and Gerald grieves his loss.

Gerald's feelings included a mixture of regret, resentment, anger, loneliness, and sadness. As in most difficult relationships, his feelings were ambivalent, complex, and difficult to sort out. He found it helpful to talk to a mental health professional.

Grieving your losses

The following tools may help you grieve your losses:

◆ **Express your feelings in constructive ways.** These may include physical activity, writing, or other stress reduction activities. Do what is helpful to you.

◆ **Talk about your feelings with understanding people.** There is comfort in being heard and supported by those you trust. Professional bereavement counseling can help people cope with feelings of loss.

◆ **Give yourself permission to cry.** Crying is a valid way to release feelings and tension.

◆ **Get support.** Contact with caring friends, support groups, family or others is important. Well-intentioned people may surround you; you may or may not perceive them to be helpful. A disappointment for many caregivers is when friends they thought would be supportive are not. Support groups offer safe gatherings of people with similar problems and concerns. They are helpful to many.

FEELINGS AND CAREGIVING

The feelings you experience as a caregiver are a normal and natural response to your situation. Most of us experience strong, complex feelings when confronted with loss and difficult situations. It's important to realize you are not "going crazy" because you feel intense emotions.

The Caregiver's Feelings

Your feelings are affected by situational factors. Examples include:

◆ Your relationship with the care receiver. Has it been positive for the most part? Or has it been difficult and full of conflict?

◆ The caregiving situation. Are you a 24-hour-a-day caregiver? Do you manage a full-time job and full-time caregiving? Do you find time for yourself?

◆ Your support system. Do other family members share caregiving responsibilities with you? Do friends help out? Or are you "doing it all?"

◆ Your strengths and coping skills when dealing with loss and change. Do you find healthy ways to release stress and feelings? Can you say no when that is best?

◆ Your reasons for entering the caregiving role. Did you feel you had no choice? Did you do so out of love and caring for the person?

◆ The care receiver's personality. What impact has the disease had on him—emotionally, behaviorally, or physically?

What is your situation? How does it affect your feelings?

Feelings can be helpful. They can be a signal to **stop** and:

◆ assess what is going on for you.

◆ determine how you feel about the situation.

◆ make necessary changes.

David's situation with his father illustrates this point.

David found it increasingly difficult to visit his dad in the nursing home. He often felt irritable and lashed out at his dad, after which he felt guilt and sadness. His dad responded with increasing sadness and despair which the staff noted. The nurse talked with David and helped him recognize that anger was his way of handling feelings of grief over his dad's deteriorating health. The way David was expressing those feelings was affecting both of them.

David responded to the nurse's suggestion that he find a safe outlet for his anger. He began to play racquetball three times a week, an activity that provided physical activity and time with friends. David also began writing in a journal. This provided a safe outlet in which to express and sort out thoughts and feelings. Visits to his dad soon began to improve dramatically.

David's feelings and behavior clearly affected his dad and the situation overall, which made him feel worse. To his credit, David took responsibility for his feelings and accepted support from the nurse. She helped him identify healthier ways to let go of his anger.

Like many people, David wasn't comfortable expressing feelings. He didn't realize that underlying his anger were feelings of loss, grief, and hurt. What he expressed outwardly was different from what he felt inwardly. As David found constructive ways to cope with his feelings, the situation with his dad improved. Consequently, when his dad died, David took comfort in how their relationship had healed.

There can be another ingredient in this mix of loss and grief.

Jean, the wife of Ernie, mentioned earlier in the chapter, was surprised to find that she had overwhelming feelings of sadness and loss over the death of her mother. She spoke of this to the social worker who asked Jean when her mother had died. Jean related that her mother had died when she was 16 years old. She was now 54. Jean was surprised because she thought she had finished mourning her mother's death. In reality, she had not. No one talked about her mother's death after it happened. As a result, she had not dealt with her grief but rather had suppressed feelings all these years. Now, the feelings surfaced and Jean was grieving the loss of her mother.

Jean's experience is common. Current loss often resurrects past losses and feelings. Unresolved feelings of grief surface later in different ways, as evidenced in Jean's case. The feelings don't go away, no matter how good we are at denying or avoiding them. Jean now had to deal with the death of her mother as well as current losses.

Getting in touch with your feelings, which is often difficult, is a very important step to effective caregiving. No matter what the source of your feelings, it is important to identify and express them. This isn't easy when we live in a society that doesn't always accept the expression of feelings. If you have difficulty sorting out your feelings and grieving your losses, a counselor can help. Jean found the support of a grief counselor immensely helpful. Ways to find help are discussed later in this chapter.

Remember, feelings are:

- a normal response to your situation.
- fluid and changeable.
- an aid in self-understanding.

It's important to identify your feelings, accept them, and learn from them.

The Care Receiver's Feelings

A difficult aspect of caring for people with a chronic illness can be dealing with their emotional responses. Anger is a common response to chronic illness and it is often displaced onto others. It may be that the care receiver directs anger and bitterness toward you and you bear the brunt of his hostility. This no doubt seems unfair since you may be doing the most for him. But you may simply be the one who is there; or perhaps you are the one who is most closely associated with the loss. Maybe you are the safest person for the care receiver to express anger toward. Whatever the reason, a person usually shows displaced anger when he isn't aware that he is angry.

Sometimes emotions are caused by the disease, as in the case of Alzheimer's disease or a stroke. In this situation, it's important

to understand all you can about the disease to better cope with the care receiver's feelings and not take emotional outbursts and expressions personally. This can be hard to do.

When anger, resentment, and other negative emotions are directed at you, remember these are complicated emotions and the care receiver's anger contains hurt and pain. The care receiver is responding to being chronically ill and dependent. Part of his adjustment, as well as part of yours, is learning to cope with difficult feelings. The better you both are at identifying and managing feelings brought about by the illness, the more your situation will improve. See Chapters 3 and 4 for communication tools that are helpful in handling difficult feelings.

COMMON EMOTIONS OF CAREGIVING

The emotions most often experienced by caregivers (and care receivers as well) are denial, fear, anxiety, anger, resentment, guilt, depression, and hope. Although we discuss them separately, these feelings are often experienced together.

Denial

Denial is the way people protect themselves from reality. There are times when reality is too painful to absorb all at once and denial serves its purpose. For example, when a person is first diagnosed with a chronic illness, it often takes time for everyone to believe it and accept it. Remember, to accept "what is" is often difficult and brings with it painful feelings.

Denial lessens as you tell the story of your situation to someone you trust. The situation becomes real with the telling of the story. Sometimes this requires telling it again and again. This breaks down denial naturally and helps you accept "what is."

Fear and anxiety

Caregivers and care receivers frequently live with fear and anxiety. The ongoing uncertainty and stress of living with chronic illness is a breeding ground for these feelings. It is sometimes difficult to tell them apart.

Fear is directed toward a specific threat that you can identify. For example, a person

who is chronically ill may have a fear of becoming dependent or a fear of pain. You, as a caregiver, can have similar fears, such as:

◆ fear of loss of control over your life.

◆ fear of abandonment by others and the loneliness that entails.

◆ fear of expressing strong emotions.

◆ fear of death. Facing chronic illness, debilitation, and loss may raise your awareness of death and the feelings you have about it.

Anxiety is defined as feelings of apprehension in the absence of a specific danger. It occurs when you are trying to control an unpredictable situation. With caregiving, anxiety has many sources, including:

◆ concern about something happening to you—then who would be the caregiver?

◆ anxiety about an uncertain future—will you be able to maintain your mental and physical health?

◆ living with continuous change—emotional, financial, and social.

◆ changing roles and responsibilities.

Often with fear and anxiety, a sense of dread and a vague sense of impending loss accompany a variety of physical symptoms and increased feelings of helplessness. Physical symptoms may include a feeling of uneasiness or agitation, cold hands and feet, and uncontrollable shaking or trembling. Muscles may be tense, especially in the neck and shoulders.

Circumstances alone do not cause fear and anxiety; it is what we think about them that affects our response. The following is a situation in which fear and anxiety are interwoven.

Eve felt anxious when Al first came home from the hospital after suffering a stroke. She was concerned about his ability to resume his place in the family as father and husband. Would she have enough strength to care for him? Now that they were home, would they have enough support? How would anyone know how lonely she felt? Would she ever feel comfortable leaving the house again for fear he would have another stroke and die? Eve was also afraid that her feelings and thoughts meant she was crazy and "cracking under pressure."

Eve felt relief when she was told that what she was experiencing, in the face of major uncertainty and loss, was normal. She gained strength in remembering that she had coped with difficulties successfully in the past, and that she could cope, and feel anxious at the same time. Eve's continual anxiety was making life with Al more tense and troublesome. She recognized this and sought professional help. In fact, Eve continued monthly meetings with the counselor for the remaining six years that Al survived. Just knowing she had an understanding, helpful person to talk to on a regular basis helped to reduce her anxiety.

Eve found the following steps helpful as a way to manage her feelings of fear and anxiety. She took a bold look at the worst thing that could happen. She:

1. Asked herself what was the worst thing that could happen.

2. Prepared herself to accept the worst.

3. Focused on enjoying what she and Al could do, since the worst hadn't happened.

For Eve, the worst thing that could happen would be for Al to die. As a way to prepare for the worst, Eve and Al talked about their wishes for the end of life and did planning which included drawing up a will and making funeral arrangements. This was difficult to do but it was also a relief. Both Al and Eve had been fearful of "the worst." Having accepted the worst thing that could happen, they were able to look forward to opportunities still available to them.

Whatever your anxieties and fears, identifying the worst thing that can happen, accepting the worst, planning for it, and finding the energy to live, even with your fears, is a substantial help. As the Chinese philosopher Lin Yutang said, "True peace of mind comes from accepting the worst. When we have accepted the worst, we have nothing more to lose and everything to gain."

If you are anxious or fearful about a situation, the following tools may help:

- **Confront the worst that can happen.**

- **Educate yourself.** Learn about the disease of the care receiver, his treatment, and what you can expect. Knowledge and understanding can lessen anxiety.

- **Break fear and anxiety down into specific components.** It is easier to cope with specific, identified concerns than with vague general feelings.

- **Problem-solve.** Get the facts, analyze the facts, make a decision, and then act.

MANAGING ANXIETY AND FEAR

The following activity in problem solving is designed to help you focus and redirect your thoughts in a way that will help you feel less fearful, anxious, and indecisive. See Chapter 1 on solution-seeking for further information.

Answer the following questions. Be specific. Identify each one of your concerns. Make a specific plan. (You will feel an increased sense of mastery as you make decisions about your anxieties and fears.)

1. What am I anxious (fearful) about?

2. What can I do about it?

3. I will take the following action:

4. I will start doing this on (date and time):

Anger

Anger is a normal response to the loss of something or someone valued. We protest when this happens, sometimes loudly and strongly. At times life hurts and that hurt generates anger. In our society, feelings of anger are often not understood or accepted. Consequently, we often have trouble accepting and expressing anger. It may seem easier to deny these uncomfortable feelings.

Anger is complex. It would be an oversimplification to speak of anger alone; hurt, pain, frustration, and fear often underlie feelings of anger. As a caregiver, it is necessary to recognize anger for what it is.

> Jan was angry at her friend Marge for not visiting or calling. They had been close friends for years. Now that Jan was caregiver for her husband and needed support, it appeared that Marge had withdrawn her friendship.

In the situation above, Jan felt angry at Marge for not being there when she needed her. A large part of her anger consisted of deep hurt and disappointment. Jan also felt the loss of a cherished friendship.

Anger can stem from many facets of caregiving. The constant changes and losses in your life serve as a wellspring of anger. Perhaps your physical and emotional burdens are increasing as a loved one with Alzheimer's disease worsens. As his personality changes, you may become the recipient of his hostility. When a person has a stroke, uncontrollable emotional outbursts can occur. It may be hard to remember that this is the disease "speaking" and not the care receiver. Perhaps your family has not met your expectations and you feel abandoned and alone. What's more, your efforts have not stopped, or even slowed the progress of the disease. The possible sources of anger go on and on.

If you are an older caregiver, you may experience losses unrelated to caregiving— loss of physical ability and health, reduced income, and the deaths of your friends and loved ones. Perhaps you feel overburdened and are called upon to be a caregiver just when you are least able to do so. This can seem unjust and can cause angry feelings.

You might direct your anger at the care receiver, yourself, or others. And, the care receiver may direct anger at you. Undeserved anger, when directed at you, hurts.

> Roger was losing his physical abilities because of Parkinson's disease. He was often angry and lashed out at Ginny. Ginny asked Roger, "How can you treat me like this?" He replied, "If I can't be angry with you, who can I be angry with?"

This is the case more often than not. You may be the one person with whom it feels safe to be angry. Not that it's any easier to be the recipient of anger, but it helps to understand.

When you feel you are the recipient of unjust anger, the following tools may help you handle the situation:

◆ **Set realistic limits.** For example, when listening, look the person in the eye and allow him to vent his feelings. If this feels too uncomfortable, excuse yourself and leave the room with the comment, "I would like to discuss this at another time. Can we talk about this later today?"

◆ **Count to 20.** During this interval, ask yourself: Is this anger really directed at me? Try to reframe the provoking statement. For example, you might view the situation as:
  – He must be having a rough day.
  – This is not a personal attack.
  – I don't have to get angry just because he is.
  – I don't have to feel like a victim.
  – Easy does it, this could be a tough situation.

◆ **Use humor.** Sometimes humor can lighten a situation but it must be appropriate.

◆ **Develop an awareness of your own feelings.** This makes it easier to respond without anger. Here are some self-statements:
  – I feel tense—take deep breaths.
  – I'm clenching my teeth—time to relax.
  – I have a knot in my stomach—let it go, this is not my anger.

◆ **Develop defusing statements.** For example, you might say to the care receiver:
  – "This must be a rough day for you."
  – "I love you," if appropriate.

◆ **Use the aikido style of communication.** Be an "aikido friend." Remember, emotional situations are opportunities to use this style of communication.

Your own anger may appear as frustration, impatience, resentment, and perhaps withdrawal. Caregivers often find it difficult to deal directly with anger. How can you admit anger about a spouse having a stroke and totally disrupting your lives? After all, "he's the one who's sick, how can I be angry at him?" Sometimes anger is displaced onto others like the doctor or nurse. People in the medical profession are frequent targets.

Anger is not a "bad" feeling. It just is. However, it is often an uncomfortable feeling, particularly if you believe nice people don't get angry. Anger doesn't mean people do not love each other. Rather, it probably means they care deeply.

It is very important to find healthy ways to manage anger. "Swallowing" your anger may have physical effects on your body. Symptoms such as backaches, headaches, increased blood pressure, ulcers, and colitis can be evidence of holding anger in. Turning anger inward can contribute to feelings of low self-esteem and depression. On the other hand, it is generally self-defeating to release anger in uninhibited outbursts. It usually serves to make matters worse. Striking out in anger at others can destroy relationships.

Use the following tools to manage anger in constructive ways.

♦ **Recognize and accept your anger.** You are less apt to displace your anger onto others.

♦ **Use "I" messages.** Avoid using "you" messages and blaming others (see Chapter 3).

♦ **Structure situations so it feels safe and comfortable to express feelings.** For example:
  – Use a private room or place to talk.
  – Agree that you will allow each other to express honest feelings without blaming the other. Use "I" messages.
  – Set a time limit of 5 to 10 minutes for each of you to speak.
  – Take turns talking. One talks, the other listens. Do not interrupt.

♦ **Select the best time to express anger.** It is not always necessary to express angry feelings immediately. In fact, there is often good reason for the old adage, "When angry, count to ten."

♦ **Set realistic limits.** For example, when you are the recipient of unjust anger, say, "I will not stay in this room and listen to anger I don't deserve."

Most important, use the energy and fire of anger to make positive changes. Use anger constructively; make it work for you. Martin Luther understood the benefit of anger:

> When I am angry I can write, pray, and preach well, for then my whole temperament is quickened, my understanding sharpened, and all mundane vexations and temptations gone.

Resentment

When you are taking care of someone else, it is important to balance what you give with what you receive in nurturing and support. When you lean too far in the direction of giving and it becomes burdensome, resentment naturally follows. Self-sacrifice and giving "until it hurts" are not helpful to anyone, least of all to the person receiving your help. No one wants to be a burden to others.

An ideal goal is to be able to enjoy the care receiver and still give needed care. This requires that you balance your own needs with those of the person you are helping.

You can't be a good caregiver unless you take care of yourself. Realistically determine your limits and decide just how much you can do. It helps to realize that no matter how much you do or how often you visit, you can't take away the loneliness or change the diagnosis of the care receiver. You can't live their life for them or make it all better.

The following are tools to help you avoid feeling resentful.

- **Give yourself permission to take care of yourself.** Find ways to maintain activities you enjoy. Make a pledge to find time for yourself. Self-neglect can lead to a decline in your health, which can include serious illness.

- **Get adequate rest.** This is extremely important, and in fact, critical to caring for another person. An exhausted caregiver is of no help to anyone.

- **Set limits.** Learn to say no and communicate this honestly: "I'm sorry, Cal, but I'm very busy at work this week and won't be getting home until 7 P.M. tonight. I've left food you can easily prepare for your dinner. We can have coffee together when I get home." In this situation, the caregiver is making a change that will make her feel less burdened. She is setting the expectation that the care receiver fix his own dinner, which she is sure he can do.

- **Find small but important ways to help yourself.** This is something only you can do. Saying no is sometimes the only way to assure that the care receiver does not become overly dependent but continues to do the things he can. This is important for promoting his self-esteem and reducing your feelings of resentment.

- **Take time for pleasure.** Plan and do activities or projects together that are pleasant for both of you. Don't let the tasks of caregiving dominate your relationship. Set aside a few minutes each day to share some pleasant time. Whether this is having a cup of coffee together at the end of the day, reading aloud, or reminiscing about good times, your choice will be a conscious one and it will be meaningful to both of you.

Guilt

Guilt is natural in the caregiving situation. It is also a difficult and painful emotion. "What ifs" and "if onlys" may be frequent thoughts. "What if I had taken him to the doctor earlier?" "If only I had paid attention when he told me he was feeling dizzy," "If only we hadn't had that argument the morning he had the stroke," "What if we had kept mother at home instead of placing her in the nursing home—perhaps she wouldn't be so depressed and angry."

> *An appropriate sense of guilt makes people try to be better. But an excessive sense of guilt, a tendency to blame ourselves for things which are clearly not our fault, robs us of our self-esteem and perhaps of our capacity to grow and act.*
>
> Rabbi Harold S. Kushner

There are endless reasons for feeling guilt when living with chronic illness. Some guilt feelings are legitimate and realistic but many are not. Guilt is an emotion that can become inflated and take on unrealistic proportions. Whether realistic or not, guilt feels bad.

Caregivers often feel guilty about the complex, difficult emotions they feel. The anxiety, anger, irritability, and frustration that are part of the caregiving experience lead to feelings of guilt. Also, mixed feelings about the care receiver, the role of caregiver, or the increase in responsibility for decisions may create feelings of resentment and guilt.

A less mentioned situation exists when the caregiver suddenly feels the loss of an unlived life. She is forced into focusing on another person whose life is changing, perhaps drastically. As she assumes the burden of caring for another and ignores her own needs and wishes, the possibilities for her own life may seem diminished. She may be filled with a fierce need to live. Imagine the potential for feeling guilt in this situation.

If you plan enjoyable activities in order to have a life somewhat independent of the care receiver, you may feel guilty about the fact that you are able to do that while he cannot. Experiencing pleasure when a loved one is ill can feel like a betrayal of your relationship. It is not. Sharing your experiences can enhance your relationship, giving it a new dimension. For example:

> Carol went to a concert with a friend. As a way to share the event with Gil, she brought him a program and tape of the concert.

Carol and Gil shared the concert, in their own way. Balancing their lives in this way takes cooperation and planning. However, they both gain, as Carol feels less resentful and "tied down" and Gil's world is broadened. Also, they continue to do those activities they can still enjoy together.

Moving on with your life while your loved one's life slows down is difficult. However, it is wise for a caregiver to continue on with life, as much as possible, from the onset of the disease. A pattern is then established with the care receiver and he does not expect otherwise.

Perhaps guilt has always been a frequent companion of yours. If so, you are not alone. Early in childhood many people learn to feel responsible for anything bad that happens. This willingness to accept blame seems to be a human tendency.

Do you have unrealistic expectations and take on too much responsibility for things over which you have no control and are really not responsible? If so, guilt may be the result. When things go wrong, it is not unusual to start the "what if" and "if only" dialogue with yourself. Assuming that if you had acted differently things would be better is usually just not so. This kind of thinking leads to unrealistic, excessive guilt. It is more helpful to realize that you did the best you could, under the circumstances. If guilt causes you trouble, talk with a professional counselor.

What about those times when you have caused hurt or pain to another? When you really have been responsible? It is impossible to care about others without hurting them in some way at one time or another. This is the human condition. At those times, it is important to assume responsibility and to make amends.

In the case of Mary and her mother, Bea, it became necessary for Mary to place Bea in a nursing home.

> Bea's condition had declined and she needed almost total care. Mary was unable to meet all of her mother's needs and maintain energy for herself and the rest of her family. Her spouse and two daughters were increasingly irritable with each other. They all loved Grandmother but her needs were greater than they could manage.

> The family agreed that a nursing home seemed the only alternative. They found one nearby that met their criteria for care. They felt sad about placing Grandmother

in a nursing home, but also a sense of relief at not having responsibility for her total care. Mary, especially, felt guilty about placing her mother in a nursing home. She had promised Bea she would always keep her at home. Now she had not kept her word and had broken her promise. Of course, it was a mistake to make the promise in the first place even though Mary's intentions were good.

As Bea became increasingly angry, hostile, and depressed, Mary felt responsible and began to feel depressed. Fortunately, Mary talked about the situation with an understanding social worker at the nursing home. Mary came to realize she had done her best for her mother and had no other option.

Friends and family tried to relieve Mary's guilt feelings by telling her that she had done all she could for her mother. But it was not until Mary forgave herself that she could release her guilt. This happened after she told Bea that she deeply regretted placing her in the nursing home after promising not to. Mary explained that her intent had been honest but none of them could have predicted how difficult it would be to care for Bea at home. Mary assured Bea that she would not abandon her and would always see to her needs as much as possible. Mary realized that caregiving for her mother was really continuing, in a different way, as she visited Bea often and played an active role in supporting her. The time they now spent together was more loving and less focused on providing "hands on" care.

Mary and Bea's story is a reminder that guilt is personal. Others can try to reassure you and relieve your guilt but only you are able to release it, in your own time.

Mary caused hurt by making a promise she couldn't keep. For this she felt guilty. She made amends by apologizing to her mother and maintaining her commitment to certain aspects of caregiving even though Bea was in the nursing home. Promising to "be there" for her mother reduced Bea's fears of abandonment. Mary was then able to forgive herself and let go of guilt.

We all make mistakes and feel guilty. When that happens, the following tools might be helpful:

1. Admit your mistake and apologize. Saying "I'm sorry" can be healing.
2. Correct the situation in whatever way possible.
3. Forgive yourself.
4. Ask forgiveness from the injured person(s).
5. Try to learn from the experience.

If you feel guilty without clear cause, ask yourself:

◆ Did I actually do something wrong, or do I just wish I had done something differently?
◆ Am I feeling guilt or regret?

Regret is a sister to guilt and a feeling that is often present in situations involving loss. For example:

Mark had been meaning to call his mother for several days. When she died suddenly, he regretted that he hadn't called.

Certainly, all of us can recall times when we have felt regret. We are sorry that we did something or did not do something. This is a natural reaction in times of stress. **Regret, however, does not qualify as guilt.** Regret is "a feeling of disappointment or distress about something that one wishes could be different." Guilt is "a remorseful awareness of having done something wrong" or "self-reproach for supposed inadequacy or wrong-doing." Healthy regret is easier to live with than guilt.

Mary felt guilty when she placed Bea in the nursing home because she felt she had done wrong in breaking her promise to her mother. When she was able to make amends and forgive herself, she was able to relinquish feelings of guilt. However, regret was often with her as she wished the situation was different.

Guilt is often a complex, familiar, and frequently undeserved feeling. If you are having difficulty with guilt, try these tools:

- **Talk with a supportive, understanding person about your feelings.** This can help you clarify and come to terms with your feelings.

- **Stop blaming yourself.** Ask yourself, "Is this my fault? Or do I just wish things were different? Am I feeling guilt or regret?"

- **Ask yourself, "What did I do that was good and right?"** Identifying the positive things you have done is a counterbalance to feelings of guilt and blame.

- **Understand the limits of your responsibility.** Identify unrealistic expectations.

- **Accept the fact that no one is perfect.** Remember, "to err is human." Mistakes happen. It's what we do with them that makes the difference.

- **Seek professional help.** This is especially important to do if guilt persists.

Depression

Abraham Lincoln suffered from depression most of his adult life. His suffering is embodied in this quote. He knew the full range of emotions associated with depression— overwhelming sadness, despair, hopelessness, and thoughts of death as a release from the pain of depression. Lincoln suffered many losses in his life both personally and publicly. He struggled with difficult feelings. But he achieved great things and

> *I am now the most miserable man living. If what I feel were equally distributed to the whole human family, there would be not one cheerful face on earth. Whether I shall ever be better, I cannot tell. I awfully forebode I shall not. To remain as I am is impossible. I must die or be better, it appears to me.*
>
> Abraham Lincoln

grew in wisdom. His life is a clear message of hope and meaning in the midst of suffering.

When you experience loss, it is natural to feel sad and to grieve. With a chronic illness, distressing changes take place for both you and the care receiver. Hopes and dreams are thwarted. You both may feel depressed. For those with a chronic illness, depression can be a response to chronic pain, loss of function, low self-esteem, increasing dependence, and fear of death. You, as a caregiver, may also feel a deep sense of loss as each of these changes happens.

Studies show caregivers have a higher incidence of depression than the general population. Depression is even higher among caregivers of brain-impaired adults. When a care receiver has Alzheimer's disease, a caregiver may experience a long, unfinished goodbye as the person gradually "leaves," and may feel "suspended in grief."

We will discuss two types of depression—grief-related depression and clinical depression. These are most relevant to the feelings experienced in chronic illness and caregiving. There is much more to be said about depression. You can find more information at your local library, hospital medical library and from your personal physician. You can find much information on the Internet. The National Institutes of Health have information on depression on their Web site at http://health.nih.gov.

Symptoms of depression

Grief-related depression (the normal depression of grief) and clinical depression (depression that requires treatment) can look very much alike. For example, both grieving and depressed people can experience sadness, tearfulness, sleep problems, and appetite and weight changes. However, there are differences. If you understand these differences, then you can better recognize depression in yourself (and others) and seek professional help. Grief-related depression, while a natural response to loss, can develop into clinical depression.

Compared to grief-related depression, clinical depression tends to be characterized by:

◆ An inability to experience *any* pleasure.

◆ A sense of hopelessness and pessimism about the future.

◆ Low self-esteem, low self-image, and feelings of worthlessness.

◆ Suicidal thoughts or attempts.

Symptoms of clinical depression are more severe, last for an unusual length of time (present most of the day nearly every day for two weeks or longer), and gradually affect a person's ability to function. Clinical depression is diagnosed by a cluster of at least five symptoms, not by any one symptom. Symptoms may include:

◆ Persistent sad or "empty" mood.

◆ Loss of interest or pleasure in previously enjoyed activities, including sex.

◆ Increased fatigue, being "slowed down."

◆ Marked change in sleeping habits (insomnia, early-morning waking, oversleeping).

◆ Marked change in appetite; significant weight gain or loss.

◆ Feelings of guilt or worthlessness.

◆ Difficulty concentrating, remembering, and making decisions.

◆ Thoughts of suicide or death.

Thoughts of suicide must be taken seriously. If you, or someone you know, has thoughts of killing himself, get professional help from your doctor, clergy, or mental health professional. With help, these feelings will pass and you will feel better.

Managing depression

Depression itself is not a tragedy. Rather, the tragedy is when depression is ignored, undiagnosed, or untreated.

Depression is treatable, with good results. According to the National Institutes of Health, "With available treatment, 80 percent of the people with serious depression—even those with the most severe forms—can improve significantly." Modern treatment for depression is a combination of short-term talk therapy and antidepressant medications.

Short-term therapy. Two short term therapies, cognitive therapy and interpersonal therapy, are highly effective in the treatment of depression.

Depression distorts our perceptions. When depressed, we tend to see the glass as half-empty rather than half-full and to view situations negatively. Cognitive therapy helps a person identify distorted, negative thinking and learn how to "reframe" those perceptions in a more accurate way. Cognitive therapy does not attempt to change "what is," but rather to help you perceive your world accurately, both the good and the bad. For more information on cognitive therapy, refer to the book *Feeling Good* by David D. Burns.

Depression affects relationships. It affects how we think, act and feel toward others. Difficult relationships also can be a factor in causing a person to become depressed. Interpersonal therapy is designed to help people in their difficult relationships with others. It emphasizes communication and relationship skills.

Cognitive therapy and interpersonal therapy have many concepts that overlap. They work so well together that many therapists combine both in their work. Both therapies deal with current thoughts, feelings, and behaviors. They emphasize the present, not what happened in childhood. The focus is on current difficulties and patterns that contribute to depression. Therapy lessens depression by helping you learn new skills and ways of looking at and doing things.

Antidepressant medications. There are many antidepressants from which to choose. None are addictive or habit-forming, and are generally safe when taken as prescribed. The overall effect of any antidepressant is the same. They affect the chemical process in the brain by restoring balance to the neurotransmitters, thereby restoring balance to brain function.

Antidepressant medications can take a few weeks to provide full benefits, although some people feel an improvement within a few days. If you are given an antidepressant, it is important to stay with treatment and report any side effects to your doctor. If symptoms are troublesome, call your doctor instead of waiting for an appointment.

Antidepressant medications must be monitored carefully, and it may be that your doctor will prescribe a different one. Or, he may tell you to continue with the present medication as the side effects can be expected to disappear in two or three weeks. You may feel the results are worth the temporary discomfort. At any rate, do not discontinue or change your medication without first consulting your doctor.

Alcohol, drugs, and depression.

Depression is not helped by alcohol or drugs. They do not offer an escape from the pain of your feelings. They only mask them temporarily. Alcohol and tranquilizers are central nervous system depressants and will make depression worse.

If you find yourself having a couple of drinks to calm your nerves or to help you sleep, stop, before it becomes a habit. Stress situations precipitate heavier drinking which can lead to depression and addiction in certain people. This is a complication you do not need.

For more information on depression, see Chapter 20, "Your Mental Health," pages 217–224.

℘

CARING FOR YOURSELF

You are your most valuable resource. Treat yourself as you would anyone you cherish. Be gentle and compassionate with yourself, not demanding or judgmental. Accept your human frailties, but at the same time, see your strengths. Who you are as a person is the single most important thing you bring to your role as a caregiver.

Taking care of yourself includes managing the difficult emotions of caregiving. This, in turn, can give you an increasing sense of control over your situation. The following tools may be helpful.

- **Participate in activities you enjoy.** This may include hobbies or activities of special interest. Rediscover those accomplishments that build your self-esteem.

- **Treat your body well.** Eat properly. Adequate nutrition is important for overall well-being. Set a regular time each day to exercise, whether it is yoga, running, walking, aerobics class, or other activities. This is also a constructive way to release tension.

- **Use relaxation techniques.** Learn to relax as a cat does. Develop an awareness of tension in your body by doing frequent body scans. To do this, mentally scan your body for tension, noting areas that are tense. Then "go limp" all over your body, with special attention to the tense areas. This can be done anytime, anyplace.

- **Make use of books and tapes.** They can give you information and tools for working with depression, stress, emotions, and relaxation.

- **Get a good night's sleep.** Insomnia is very common in people who are under stress. This is often temporary. Try not to worry about it. Worry causes more stress than sleeplessness. The following can help to manage insomnia:
  - Give up caffeine.
  - Avoid sleeping pills. They may disrupt your normal sleep patterns. Use sleeping pills only as a temporary measure, if at all.
  - Try meditating if you are unable to sleep (see Chapter 2). Or, try repeating prayers.
  - Get physically tired. Clean the house, garden, exercise; do any activity that will tire you.
  - Get up and read or work until you are tired.

- **Get social support.** Have at least one friend you can tell your troubles to. Sustain and nurture old friends. Avoid isolating yourself from others.

- **Attend a support group.** Again, this can be a safe, supportive environment in which to meet others who share similar experiences. Other benefits are:
  - You will find others who are experiencing similar feelings.
  - There is opportunity to give and receive support.
  - You learn from each other and realize you are not alone.
  - You can find encouragement, support, hope, and friendship.

- **Write your feelings down on paper.** Writing in a private journal is a way to keep in touch with and examine your feelings, as well as a constructive way to release them. Writing is a private way to talk to yourself about how you feel. It gives you uninterrupted time to express anything you want, without fear of judgment from others.

◆ **Change negative self-talk to positive self-talk.** Your emotions are derived from your thoughts.

Do the following activity frequently, as feelings are ever-changing. Remember, your feelings affect your situation. Take responsibility for them and learn from them. The changes you make help create a situation in which you can rebuild your life and find hope, even in the midst of loss and change.

IDENTIFYING FEELINGS

In earlier activities you identified your losses and anxieties. The following activity is designed to help you to get in touch with the feelings that are most difficult for you, and to plan actions that will help you manage them. Do the following steps:

1. Identify your feelings, one at a time.

   (*Example*) *I feel: afraid.*

2. Identify what would help you deal with the feeling. What do you need?

   (*Example*) *I need: to get more information about the disease John has.*

3. Plan to do at least one thing that would help.

   (*Example*) *I will: call his nurse and ask her to send me information about his condition, or refer me to where I can find it.*

4. Decide when you will carry out the plan.

   (*Example*) *I will do it: today while John is napping.*

HOPE

Hope is the beacon of light by which we travel. Without it, we become lost. Hope is as necessary as breathing. Without it life has little meaning or purpose.

Difficult feelings, including depression and suicide, can be the result of hopelessness and despair. An attitude of optimism and hope contributes to your well-being and even creates the potential for slowing the progress of an illness.

As a caregiver, you may hope to just make it through one more day, or hope to find respite, to get a break. Whatever your hope, it is crucial. Also, it is important to remember that even if you feel your situation is hopeless, it does not necessarily follow that the care receiver is without hope.

A sense of hope is "Knowing that your present moment has meaning."

Robert Randall

Hope is necessary and will change in nature throughout an illness, for both of you. Early in the disease process there may be hope for a cure. When you live with a chronic illness, you may hope for remission and relief from pain and symptoms. If your condition worsens you may hope for a better quality of life.

It's important not to take hope away from another nor to instill false hope. Statements like, "You're going to get better," when that isn't the case, will ultimately lead to a sense of resentment and betrayal. In fact, those who are ill are often the first to know when they are not going to get better. Sometimes the only real hope you can give another is to affirm your wish to care for him to the best of your ability.

Hope is entwined with meaning. As we find our way, we make choices that help us find hope and meaning, perhaps even wisdom, in suffering.

As you walk through your "dark wood," hope can help you find your way. There are lights to guide you and people who can help.

We need not walk alone...

We reach out to each other with love and understanding and with hope. We come together from all walks of life, from many different circumstances...

We need not walk alone!

The Credo of the Compassionate Friends

Overview

Chapter Six

Mastering Caregiving Transitions

As a caregiver, you face changes no matter what level of care you provide—whether you are a full-time caregiver providing hands-on care, a part-time caregiver helping an older relative remain in his home, a long-distance caregiver, or you oversee a relative's care in a care facility. Dealing with caregiving changes is seldom easy.

> *Everything changes, nothing remains without change.*
> The Buddha

In *Managing Transitions*, William Bridges states that it isn't change that does you in—it's the transition. Change is the external situation—the increased needs of the care receiver, the decreased ability of a caregiver to meet the care receiver's needs, or moving the care receiver to a care facility. Transition is the internal emotional process we go through to come to terms with what has changed. It's these feelings that can be particularly difficult.

The ability to cope with change and transition is an important caregiving tool that can affect your health, the quality of care you provide, and how long you can provide care. This chapter will help you to:

◆ gain confidence in your ability to master change and transition.

◆ examine how your attitude affects how you deal with change.

◆ identify ways to reduce pessimism, that is, negative thinking.

CHANGING FAMILY ROLES

Both you and your family member who needs care may face the difficult task of letting go of old roles and accepting new ones. New roles can challenge everyone involved. They often distress caregiving spouses who must take over what was the other person's role before the illness. The person receiving care may resist and express resentment toward the caregiver. Marge, a 67-year-old caregiver, said:

> Norm had his stroke a year ago today. It left him with weakness on his right side and some speech problems. As I read the notes from my journal, I realize how much Norm and I have changed and how far we have come. Before his stroke Norm managed our finances, took care of the yard, and did the driving. Now I do nearly everything Norm did. I also help Norm bathe and dress, and I still do all the work I have always done. It feels uncomfortable taking Norm's place and I sense he resents it too. The stroke hasn't ruined our lives; we still travel and fish, we just do it a little differently than we did before.

If you are an adult child, you may be providing support, caregiving, or making decisions for a parent for the first time. This is particularly difficult if your parent has always made his or her own decisions, if you have tried to maintain distance between you and your parent because of a poor relationship, if you looked to your parent for assistance, or if you viewed him as a "pillar of strength." Pat said:

> It's not the actual caregiving that is difficult for me. It's seeing the disease rob my mother of who she was and all she could do. She was a very bright woman. I miss the mother-daughter relationship we had. Now I feel more like a parent, rather than a daughter, to my Mom. My Mom helped me make decisions in life. I never had helped her make a decision, and now I am forced to make decisions about Mom's life. It's not easy.

Dealing with changes in your family member may be even more difficult because of competing demands from family and work. The situation of Stephen, a 45-year-old son and caregiver is not unusual.

My mother, Pearl, is 85. She has Parkinson's disease. She needs more help than I can provide but she has refused to let anyone but me help her. Increasing pressure from work and lack of time for my wife and children made me realize that something had to change.

Reluctantly, I discussed my problems with my mother. Mother resisted any change. Finally I said, "I worry about you being alone, and yet we can't live together. I'm afraid I'll lose you if you fall and hurt yourself. I have to find help for you when I can't be here." She said, "Go ahead, I probably can't stop you anyway."

After considerable searching I found and hired a student nurse who needed money and a place to stay and wanted the experience. Mother seems to be adjusting to an outsider helping her, but I'm having trouble getting over the feeling that I let her down. Even though I made the best decision I could under the circumstances, I still feel guilty.

Stephen's experience is not unusual. Even when a change needs to occur or "the best decision" has been made, you may experience emotional turmoil. Particularly difficult is when you must make a decision you had hoped you wouldn't have to make.

A LOOK AT CHANGE

A change involves not just a beginning of something, but also an ending of what was. In dealing with chronic illness, this ending of what was (and generally will not be again) is the reason that even when something is done because it is "the best," you (or the care receiver) may not feel good.

For example, some caregivers experience mixed feelings when they decide to hire paid help because it means their role as the sole provider of care has ended. Caregivers who cannot let go of their old role may have trouble keeping paid helpers or working with care facility staff. They may consider workers deficient if everything is not done exactly the way they do it. Caregivers who accept the ending of their old role are more likely to be flexible in the way quality care is provided.

You and the care receiver face many uncontrollable changes in health and lifestyle. However, whatever a change, you can choose:

◆ whether or not you deal with making a change.

◆ how you deal with a change.

◆ your attitude about the situation.

◆ whether you look ahead and plan for potential changes or ignore them and wait for a crisis.

How other people respond to caregiving changes is beyond your control. You can *influence* peoples' attitudes and actions but you can't control them. Relatives may deny a change in your family member's functioning that worries you. For example, you may be concerned about your father's memory but your brother insists there is no problem, saying, "Dad has always been forgetful." In such a situation, a relative may not support your decisions. In this case, you might ask your brother to spend a couple of days with Dad in hopes of helping him to see your perspective. However, you can only control how you deal with the situation.

What happens if you do not deal with change? Caregivers who deny change, who try to restore the past or maintain the status quo, may unintentionally:

◆ waste time and energy trying to keep things the same.

◆ lose opportunities for a memory-impaired person to take part in planning for his future (because he may not be able to participate later because of the illness).

◆ develop unrealistic expectations because they are more likely to believe that the impaired person can function as he did in the past if he would just try harder.

◆ "burn out" because they can't accept that care needs have grown too great for them to handle.

It is only natural to want to return to earlier and better days; however, if you try to recreate the past, both you and the care receiver will likely experience frustration. Focusing on "the way things were" will make it even more difficult to deal with current circumstances. Trying to resurrect the past also prevents appropriate decision making and moving forward. However, do not confuse "resurrecting the past" with "reminiscing about the past." Reminiscing can be useful and beneficial.

❧

UNDERSTANDING TRANSITIONS

Caregiving changes and decisions are difficult, in part, because they usually lead to some type of loss for the care receiver. And, sometimes for you, the caregiver. They also frequently create powerful feelings of self-doubt and guilt.

A change involves emotions and adjustments for both you and the care receiver. Too often people are told, or even feel them-selves, "This is for the best." Then they wonder, "If it's for the best, why do I feel so bad… so sad?" Or "If the change is for the best, why doesn't the care receiver realize this instead of being so upset with me?" Such feelings are a natural reaction to change and to being in transition.

In *Transitions*, William Bridges says that whenever a change occurs, a transition follows. A transition is the internal emotional process we go through in dealing with a change in our lives. Understanding the transition process can help you master caregiving changes and deal better with your feelings. Each transition includes three phases.

Phase one: the ending. Endings are the starting points of transitions. To make a

transition you have to let go of what has ended. Even a positive caregiving change generally involves a loss, that is an ending, of something. It's important to be able to identify and let go of what has ended.

Phase two: the wilderness period (neutral zone or down time). This is the core of the transition. It is the "no man's land" between the old and the new—the old is gone and the new may not feel right yet. Feelings of confusion, emptiness, grief, and anxiety are common.

Phase three: the new beginning. A beginning is only achieved after an ending has been experienced and time has been spent in the wilderness. This can be frightening because it confirms the ending was real and the old ways won't work anymore.

Phase One: The Ending

Bridges reminds us that change is the external situation in which something new has begun. For example, "Grandma cannot remember to throw spoiled food away. So, now I'll have to do it."

Emotionally, the change in Grandma means more than our concern about her eating spoiled food. It is a sign of Grandma's declining abilities and it saddens us. We remember that Grandma was always there for us when we needed her. Now we have to let go of our old image of Grandma and be there for her. It's this internal process of letting go of "what was" that really bothers us, not the spoiled food.

When we speak of an ending we speak of a loss. However, not all endings are serious or sad; some may be positive. For instance, if the care receiver recovers and no longer needs help, there is a loss of dependency and this is a positive change. A caregiver who accepts this positive change is likely to find ways for the care receiver to be independent. A caregiver who is unable to accept such a change may continue to provide unnecessary care and therefore encourage dependency.

> *What we call the beginning is often the end, And to make an end is to make a beginning.*
>
> *The end is where we start from.*
>
> T.S. Eliot
> *Little Gidding*

Signs of an ending

For some caregivers, incontinence may be a sign that their ability to provide care without help is ending. If they accept this ending they are more likely to seek or accept help. The caregiver who can't accept that he has reached his caregiving limits may burn out and the quality of his care may suffer. This affects everyone involved, especially the care receiver.

Some endings never end

Chronic, progressive illness that causes a gradual decline in abilities or a steady worsening of symptoms may force both you and the care receiver to cope with ongoing endings. Caregivers of people with Alzheimer's disease have described their experience as "the funeral that never ends" and "a long goodbye." They deal with a succession of changes and losses due to the progressive nature of the disease. For many families, these losses multiply without the benefit of a "wilderness time" to grieve and come to terms with them.

Many memory-impaired people face endings but cannot understand what has changed and why. For instance, Dad doesn't remember his near misses while driving. He hears news like "Dad, driving isn't safe for you anymore" as if it is the first time. He may react with shock, anger, and disbelief every time he hears the news. His loss of recent memory robs him of the ability to make sense of what changed and why decisions were made about his not driving. Meanwhile, his remaining long-term memory contradicts what others say. He may argue, "I am a safe driver. I've never had an accident, except once when someone else ran a stop light and hit me." It is unrealistic to expect a person who has no memory of recent events to accept not driving, no matter how many times he hears it, because he does not think that his ability to drive has changed.

Dealing with endings

In any ending there must be a letting go. You may have to argue with an inner voice that tells you not to change, to keep on being the "old you," and to do whatever it takes to keep things the same. To silence such an inner voice, tell yourself, "Something has changed (ended) and I must find ways to deal with it."

Accepting a change or ending does not mean you approve of it or that you have given up. It means you are doing what you must in order to move on to whatever is next in your life. Often this involves a period of grieving as you let go of the way things were or something you once had. This is the purpose of the "wilderness period."

Phase Two: The Wilderness Period or Neutral Zone

The second phase of a transition, the wilderness period, is a time to help you come to terms with change and loss. Some people call it their "down time" because they feel "down." You may experience feelings of grief, confusion, emptiness, depression, uncertainty and anxiety as you search for the meaning in a change. This is a difficult phase. It is important to be patient and self-forgiving during this time. This is also the time to ask questions like these:

The lowest ebb is the turn of the tide.

Henry Wadsworth Longfellow

◆ What has changed? The person? The situation? Me?

◆ What has ended? For my relative? For me? In our lives? In the caregiving situation?

◆ How do I feel about this change? Sad? Angry? Guilty? Relieved?

◆ What do I do now? Try to change things back? Accept change as a challenge? Learn new ways to deal effectively with the change?

In the following story, Stephen spent time in his wilderness period questioning himself and his decision.

Even though I knew I had made the best decision possible, I still felt terrible about employing an outsider to help mother. I questioned my loyalty. Was I such a good son after all, letting a stranger take care of my mother? I wondered about my character. Was I being selfish and lazy by hiring help instead of helping Mom myself? My conscience bothered me too. My mother raised and cared for me. Was this how I repaid her?

After considerable soul-searching I felt better about my decision. I also realized it did not mean I abandoned my mother; it meant my role as caregiver had changed. Now I manage her care. I am her advocate and spokesman.

During the wilderness period, Stephen dealt with his feelings and realized he was still a caring, loyal, unselfish son.

Getting through the wilderness period

Stephen's story reveals how the wilderness period provides an opportunity to think about what has changed and to decide what must be learned and done for the next step. This is why the wilderness period should not be rushed. This is the time to decide if the direction you are headed is the right one. This "down time" is the crux of every transition. The following tools may help you through the wilderness period.

Maintain structure and order to your life. Plan your day's activities and set small goals you can easily achieve. This gives a sense of control and predictability during this unsettling phase. Give yourself credit for seemingly minor victories and accomplishments.

Take care of yourself. Don't add to your losses by giving up more than you need to. It's important to stay in touch with supportive people and continue enjoyable activities. These provide stability and continuity during transitions.

Identify the reasons you feel troubled. Feelings of confusion, anxiety, and tension commonly surface during transitions. Feeling distressed doesn't necessarily mean something is wrong; it usually means things are changing. Talk to a nonjudgmental listener to help you understand what is happening. Simply being able to identify feelings and describing problems can give you deeper insight and a clearer sense of direction.

Look for the positive in the change. If something forced change upon you, such as a spouse's stroke, look for something positive that came from it. Give some thought to "Things I learned about myself from this" or "Things I had no idea I could do." Consider making a list with one of these titles and adding to it. It may reinforce the positive for you during those tough times.

Avoid doing something just for the sake of taking action. Unless you have to take action, avoid making unnecessary changes during this time. If you make decisions and take action just to fill the void, you may regret these changes later.

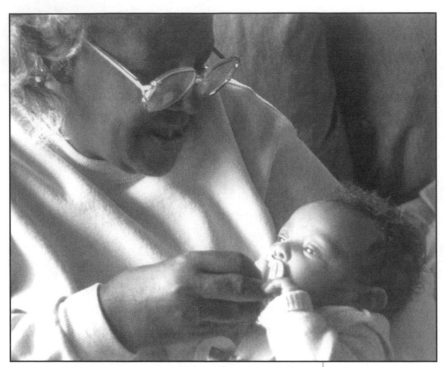

Phase Three:
The New Beginning

Bridges says you come to the new beginning only at the end—that is, only after you have completed the ending and the wilderness phases of a transition. He claims beginnings are vague and "unimpressive."

How do you know you are ready to begin? It would be helpful if you could identify a clear sign. The reality is that you may have only a subtle feeling that you are ready for "a new beginning." You may feel more refreshed and ready to move forward than you have for a while. New ideas and opportunities may surface and you begin looking into these new possibilities. A neighbor mentions she provides companionship services and you hear yourself saying, "I want to learn more about your work." You picture yourself doing things.

Sometimes comments made by other people may repeatedly return to your mind as though prompting you to pay attention. A support group member told Marge: "Your sense of humor about your caregiving mistakes brightened my day and helped me realize I'm not the only one who makes mistakes." For two months Marge kept remembering those words. Finally, one Sunday she talked to the editor of her church newsletter about writing a caregiver's idea and advice column. The editor of the local newspaper asked to print her second column, "Planning to Enjoy the Holidays." This shows the indirect, almost subconscious nature of beginnings. When you start looking for ways to enhance your new and still-changing life, you have begun.

> *When we are ready to make a beginning, we will shortly find an opportunity.*
> William Bridges

LEARNING FROM PAST TRANSITIONS

Sometimes it helps to look back at earlier transitions (endings, wilderness periods, and beginnings) to see what you learned from them. In the following example, Marge read her journal to reflect on the changes and transitions she experienced after Norm's stroke. She asked questions about how she handled each phase of the transition: What did I learn? How did my attitude help or hinder me? How do I feel about the choices I made? If I had to do it over, what would I do differently?

Using Marge's example, think back to a caregiving event/change that led you through a period of transition, such as accepting your role as caregiver or deciding to relinquish day-to-day care.

◆ What comes to mind as your ending?
  – Accepting a diagnosis?
  – Accepting that changes in your loved one are caused by the illness?
  – Accepting and adjusting to your role as caregiver?

CHANGE AND TRANSITION

Event/Phase	What helped me deal with the event	Things that made it difficult for me
Norm's stroke, right afterward	My friends' support. Confidence in the doctors and nurses. My religion. My relaxation exercises.	Didn't understand the nature of the stroke. Worried about losing Norm, future, money.
2 weeks later	Norm's improvement. Felt encouraged. All would be OK.	Stayed at hospital until exhausted.
2+ months later (still dealing with ending)	Got information about stroke. Learned how to help Norm with his rehabilitation exercises. Realize I did OK at a crisis time and that Norm is getting better but will not be the same as before.	Let Norm's moodiness rub off on me. His progress slowed no matter what I did. Saw friends less. Felt not right to have fun.
6 months later (wilderness)	Went to support group. Learned OK to feel bad. Realize have limits, can only control me. Try to take one day at a time.	Wouldn't accept help from family and friends.
1 year later (new life style)	Try to stay in touch with positive people. Involve Norm in activities with friends and family.	Still worry about future and money.

◆ What helped you through the void?
 – Family?
 – Friends?
 – Support group?
 – Religious beliefs?

◆ How did you know when you were ready to begin dealing with what had changed? With caregiving? With your own needs?
 – Did you take a closer look at the care receiver's remaining skills?
 – Did you begin thinking about favorite activities and considering how you and the care receiver could still enjoy them?
 – Was it getting harder to summon the energy to do things in the old ways?
 – Did you find yourself skimming the classified ads and reading the employment, home help section?

◆ What would you do differently in each phase?
 – Learn more about the illness earlier to help yourself accept it?
 – Ask for more help?
 – Attend a support group?

◆ What did you learn and do that you can apply to future:
 – Endings?
 – Wilderness periods?
 – Beginnings?

◆ What did you learn about yourself?
 – That you are more patient than you ever imagined?
 – That you are able to deal with the challenges of change?
 – That you are more willing to accept help from other people?

Reflecting on how you dealt with past changes and transitions can help you to identify and build on your effective responses to change, and to discard the ineffective ones. As you identify what worked and didn't work for you during past transitions, copy the following form on a separate piece of paper for your notes. Writing down what you learned from your experiences can be a useful tool to help you with future transitions.

CHANGE AND TRANSITION

Event/Phase	What helped me deal with the event	Things that made it difficult for me
Event/Phase	What I plan to use next time	What I plan to do to adjust and begin anew

THE POWER OF A POSITIVE ATTITUDE

Your attitude toward the challenges of caregiving will make it easier or more difficult for you to deal with them. If you have an optimistic attitude, you are more likely to expect that a positive outcome is possible and to focus on what you can do when faced with a change or decision. With a pessimistic attitude, focus is on the negative. Being optimistic doesn't mean you suppress your feelings when dealing with a difficult situation or decision. It's perfectly normal to feel discouraged, angry, fearful, anxious, sad and uncertain. However, people who are optimistic get beyond these feelings to make the most of a situation.

An optimistic attitude helps you avoid depression, helps you focus, and motivates you to move forward. Studies also show that an optimistic attitude may help you avoid getting sick during stressful times. On the other hand, a pessimistic attitude— for example, thinking nothing can be done—will probably keep you from looking for ways to deal with the changes you face and will increase feelings of helplessness. And, it might even put your health at risk.

Optimism creates possibilities and hope; pessimism destroys them. How you view events can either enhance or undermine your ability to master a transition. As Delores said, "It's difficult to remain optimistic when things aren't going well, but a pessimistic attitude makes the job of caregiving even harder."

Learning to Be Optimistic

It has been said that an optimist sees a glass as half full while a pessimist sees the same glass as half empty. The optimist usually sees a favorable outcome and tends to focus on the most hopeful aspects of a situation, whereas the pessimist tends to take the gloomiest possible view of a situation. In his book *Learned Optimism,* Martin Seligman says that if you learned to be pessimistic as a child you can learn to become more optimistic. A pessimistic attitude is not set in stone.

To determine if you tend to be optimistic or pessimistic, complete the following. Check "yes" if you agree with the statement; check "no" if you don't agree.

Yes	No	
❐	❐	Caregiving problems are never-ending.
❐	❐	Good things that happen are only brief moments in time.
❐	❐	Chronic illness casts a dark cloud over every area of my life.
❐	❐	I am responsible for making the care receiver happy.
❐	❐	Nothing can be done to make my situation better.

If you checked "yes" to any of the previous statements, your attitude tends toward pessimism and may be inhibiting your ability to deal with change and to make sound decisions.

Seligman claims your attitude depends on how you explain to yourself things that happen in your life, especially life's negative events and setbacks. You can become more optimistic by applying these tools:

◆ View setbacks as temporary.

◆ View bad things as specific, not universal.

◆ Seek solutions to problems.

◆ Give yourself credit for what you do.

◆ Recognize beliefs are not facts.

◆ Practice positive self-talk.

View setbacks as temporary

An optimist sees good things as permanent or lasting and problems as temporary. For instance, Diane said that she will always feel Alzheimer's disease brought her closer to her mother. Although the effects of this disease are permanent, she found something positive in it. Diane's optimism was evident in her ability to see an increased closeness toward her mother even though her mother's illness was a downhill slide.

A pessimist tends to see good things as temporary or fleeting and problems as permanent. Pessimists frequently use words like "always" and "never." If Diane's opinion had been that her closer relationship with her mother probably wouldn't last, her attitude would have been pessimistic.

View bad things as specific, not universal

An optimist tends to see good things as universal or widespread and bad things as specific. For example, Marge saw the stroke (a bad thing) as affecting only part of her and Norm's daily life, not their whole relationship. They still enjoyed each other

and went fishing and on guided tours.

A pessimist tends to see good things as specific and bad things as universal. He may view that unpleasant events will last forever, perhaps even a lifetime. If Marge believed fishing was the only good thing left in their lives and that the stroke ruined their future, it would be a pessimistic attitude.

Seek solutions to problems

Optimistic people generally will look toward hopefulness and at prospects of "what can I do." In other words, when problems develop, they focus on finding solutions. Pessimists tend to feel helpless to change anything.

Give yourself credit for what you do

An optimist is more willing to take credit for the good things that happen and not feel responsible for the bad things over which he has no control. For example, Stephen credited himself with finding and hiring in-home help for his mother.

Pessimists tend to take things personally and blame themselves for the bad things that happen over which they have no control. They credit the good things that happen to outside causes. A pessimistic person might say, "I just make matters worse. If it wasn't for the doctors, my relative wouldn't be getting better."

Recognize beliefs are not facts

Seligman says that many people make the mistake of assuming that the negative things they think about themselves must be true. He suggests we need to challenge self-recriminations in the same way we would challenge someone who accused us of something we believed was not true.

Practice positive self-talk

People who are optimistic practice positive self-talk. Positive self-talk builds confidence and self-esteem; negative self-talk increases pessimism and vice versa.

How do you explain unfortunate events that happen to you? Do you give yourself the credit you deserve for the good things that happen? Are you hopeful about your capacity to deal with changes? As you read the comparisons in the box below, which outlook most closely fits yours?

Optimistic Outlook	Pessimistic Outlook
"Things usually work out eventually." (*Sees bad events as temporary that will pass. Shows hopefulness.*)	"Things never seem to work out." (*Sees bad things as permanent and unchangeable. Sees good as fleeting. Believes nothing can be done so does nothing.*)
"Despite the stroke we still enjoy each other and our fishing trips." (*Sees life as generally good with a negative event affecting only a part of life.*)	"The stroke has ruined our retirement years." (*Sees a negative event affecting entire life. Causes feelings of grief and loss for a future now viewed as gone.*)
"Strokes happen. I'm looking at what we can do to prevent another stroke." (*Does not blame self for situations or behavior cannot control. Willing to take credit for good things.*)	"If I had insisted Norm quit smoking and fixed healthier meals, he probably would not have had a stroke." (*Blames self for negative situations over which has no control.*)

When Being Realistic Looks Like Pessimism

Sometimes your outlook may seem pessimistic because you are looking at a situation from a realistic point of view. This doesn't mean you're a pessimist; it means you're a realist. Seligman calls this "flexible optimism" or "optimism with your eyes wide open." You might view the increased care needs of your family member as beyond your capacity. In this instance, your perspective may guide you toward making a decision to seek help. An optimistic but unrealistic expectation of your ability to carry on might lead to "caregiver burnout."

When something does go wrong, an optimist focuses on why it happened, learns from the situation, and considers "what can I do to make it better." An optimist doesn't gloss over a difficult situation, nor does he fall into despair (which is typical of a pessimist).

Realism is healthy and useful. It aids in successful future planning and in learning from misfortune. However, sometimes when under stress, realism can unintentionally slip into pessimism. With pessimism comes an avalanche of negative self-talk. When one is used to frank, realistic self-talk, it can be difficult to recognize, catch and reword the negative self-talk (for example, switching from "hardly anyone helps…" to "I'm fortunate to have the help of…").

How Negative Thinking Undermines Optimism

Negative thinking magnifies problems. Emotions build and problems tend to grow and get worse, fueled by pessimism. Then you usually get what you expect. A situation created solely in your mind can create needless stress and feelings of anger or sadness even though nothing actually happened to change the situation.

> Marge was fixing dinner but she was still thinking about breakfast. Since his stroke, Norm had begun pointing instead of trying to ask for things. Over and over, Marge has to guess what Norm wants. When she guesses wrong, Norm gets mad. Marge became furious when Norm did this at breakfast today. All day she thought about what would happen if they were destined to treat each other this way. It would spoil the rest of their years together and ruin what was a wonderful marriage.

A cycle of negative thinking can begin with a minor problem that builds in the mind to a major one. Marge began a cycle of negative thinking in which Norm's pointing lead to thoughts about a breakdown in communication and ultimately, destruction of their marriage. Nothing had changed since breakfast. This depressing outcome was born totally in Marge's mind.

Negative thoughts can become like habits and come to mind automatically. "I can't do anything right" or "Nothing seems to work out" might surface each time you make a mistake or something goes wrong. These automatic negative thoughts undermine optimism, increase stress, and contribute to depression. According to Seligman, "a recipe for severe depression is an existing pessimism encountering failure." Pessimism does not cause depression, but it provides fertile soil in which depression grows.

Negative thinking can be controlled, but it takes conscious effort. Seligman claims that once you are aware of your pessimistic thoughts you can deal with them with two tools. The first is to distract yourself—to shift your attention to something positive. The second is to challenge or dispute negative thoughts. Challenging is the most effective, long-lasting technique.

Distraction

Distraction works because the brain can only think of one subject at a time. Deliberately shifting your attention to something else forces the mind to abandon its original thought. Tasks that require concentration like writing a letter or doing a crossword puzzle work well.

Interrupting habitual thought patterns is another simple distracting technique. Some people put a rubber band around their wrist and snap it every time a negative thought surfaces. Others carry a 3×5 card with the word STOP written on it in large red letters. Clapping hands and yelling *Stop!* is another technique. Yelling "Stop" is not the same as saying to yourself, "I'm not going to think about (Norm's pointing) anymore." Telling yourself not to think a negative thought actually focuses your attention on that thought. Saying the word "Stop" simply interrupts the thought process for a short time.

You can strengthen the interrupting technique by combining it with a positive statement. For example, when you think,

"Nothing I do helps," use an interrupting technique, then restate the thought, "This situation is demanding. What I do helps tremendously." Once the positive statement is made, shift your attention elsewhere. It often helps to write down positive statements and place them where you will see them. Mirrors, refrigerator doors, and car visors are ideal places.

When you combine interrupting and shifting attention you will get longer-lasting results. For instance, after you snap the rubber band, direct your attention elsewhere or select a task that requires concentration such as reading or working on a hobby.

You can also stop the cycle of negative thinking by rescheduling it. When a thought nags at you, you can tell yourself, "Stop, I'll think about this after dinner."

Challenging negative thinking

In most cases, negative thoughts are distortions. Therefore, the best method for breaking the cycle of negative thinking is to challenge the truth of it. This works better and lasts longer than distraction and it usually stops the "gathering gloom of depressing thoughts." It also defends you against being victimized by your own self-criticism.

You can effectively challenge negative thinking by playing detective. Ask yourself, "What is the evidence to refute this belief? Is there an alternative way to look at this?" Recall facts and actual situations that contradict negative thoughts.

It was 2:00 a.m. and Stephen was wide awake. He was thinking about how hard he tried to be a productive employee, a good dad, a faithful husband, and a loyal son. His thoughts led him to the conclusion that people only cared about what he could do for them; they really didn't care about him. He began feeling depressed. Then he asked himself: Was his thinking true? Was he being fair? After all, didn't he just get a raise at work? Didn't his boys save their allowance to surprise him with tickets to a Chicago Bulls basketball game? Isn't his wife the one who just spent all day cooking for his Super Bowl party? And weren't there tears in his mother's eyes when she said, "Your dad would have been so proud of you, Stephen."

Stephen challenged the truth of his thoughts. Once he discredited his thoughts with facts he could reject them as false and meaningless. To challenge negative thinking and silence your inner critic, try these steps:

1. **Identify your negative thoughts so they can be evaluated and challenged.**

2. **Make a mental or written note of your negative thoughts. Then ask yourself:**
   - Do I think in terms of "always" and "never"? For example, "No matter what I do it never makes a difference." "Something always goes wrong."
   - Do my thoughts make sweeping claims like, "Nobody ever helps me"?
   - Do my thoughts make me feel guilty? Do I blame myself by using terms like, "I should have…" and "If only I had…"?

3. **Challenge your negative thoughts with facts. Confront your inner critic with evidence that makes your self-talk untrue.**
   - Is it true that I have never made anyone feel better, comfortable, safe, and loved?
   - Is it a fact that no one ever helps? No one ever does anything?
   - Is it really true that I am responsible for things over which I have no control?

   It's a good idea to challenge negative thoughts before expressing them to others. Someone else may be accidentally hurt or offended and may challenge them less kindly. The caregiver who says, "Nobody ever helps me," may be challenged with, "What do you mean? I have helped you."

4. **Identify specific ways to change what you can.** If your attitude about a problem tends to be pessimistic, identify something about the problem you can modify. This encourages a positive outlook because it disproves your view of the problem as permanent or unchangeable. If your thoughts say "No one ever helps," asking for help could change these thoughts.

Using the example below, jot down anything negative you say to yourself. Then challenge your claim with a factual statement that makes your negative thoughts or self-criticism untrue.

CHALLENGING NEGATIVE THOUGHTS

Negative Statement	Challenge
I feel like I never do anything right.	*I found and hired a student nurse to help my mother.*
I can't keep anything straight anymore.	*I manage the finances.*

SUMMARY

The goal is to achieve a positive attitude based on present reality. Because you have control over your attitude, reaching this goal is up to you. If your current attitude is based on wishful thinking about the past, you can change it by how you deal with change and transition.

If you view a setback as "ruining your entire life forever," you can change your perspective by identifying parts of your life untouched by the setback. If you view mistakes as opportunities to learn instead of signs of personal failure, you can avoid repeating them. If negative thinking and unfair self-criticism undermine your self-confidence, and paralyze your creativity, you can challenge the negativity with facts that make the criticism untrue.

CHAPTER SEVEN

Making Tough Caregiving Decisions

Increased needs of the care receiver, a decrease in your ability to provide care, or other changing circumstances may require making a difficult decision. This may include hiring in-home help, determining if the care receiver is still safe driving, moving the care receiver into a professional care setting, or legal and financial questions.

Making caregiving decisions creates stress and anxiety for many caregivers because such decisions mean a change in the care receiver's life, and there are no guarantees a decision will work. It's a tremendous responsibility to make decisions on behalf of someone who cannot take an active part; you can do your best but still wonder if you are making the right decision.

You may feel guilty if a decision also serves your need for relief from stress. However, it's just as important to consider *your* needs as well as those of the care receiver. Decisions based on reality, rather than emotions and past promises, have a better chance of working. This chapter provides you with tools for:

◆ making the best possible caregiving decisions.

◆ conducting a family conference.

◆ planning ahead.

Chapters in the "Caregiver Issues" section (page 151) focus on specific major decisions.

BEFORE MAKING A DECISION

Even seemingly minor decisions can be difficult and have significant impact. Consider the decision Diane, a 55-year-old daughter and caregiver, made.

I am a full-time caregiver for my mom, who has Alzheimer's disease. Two weeks ago I decided that both of us should resign from our church choir. Mom loves to sing but during the last few months she has been singing the wrong hymns and getting lost in the music. Her confusion caused problems for the entire choir.

I felt embarrassed for her and for me. Resigning from the choir was one of the most painful decisions I've ever made. Mom still asks me, "When are we going to choir practice?"

Diane decided her mother's memory problems made it impossible for her to continue singing in the church choir. Diane's attitude was that her mother's problems were lasting. She assumed her mother's confusion was so widespread that she couldn't participate at all. In reality, there were certain hymns, especially Christmas carols, her mother knew by heart and could still sing.

Diane would have been better prepared to make this decision if she had explored the basis for it. What was driving the decision—was it embarrassment or the true facts of the situation? Did she investigate ways her mother could participate in the choir in a limited way? Or did she decide her mother simply had to quit? After asking these questions, Diane might have reached the same decision. However, if she had

explored possible options and found them unworkable, her doubts and sad feelings about making the decision would be somewhat relieved by knowing that she tried.

Before making a decision it is important to:

◆ understand your motives, attitudes, and feelings.

◆ learn from past experiences and those of others.

◆ understand the care receiver's needs and feelings.

◆ involve the care receiver in decisions.

◆ investigate potential options.

◆ recognize the care receiver's right to take risks.

Understand Your Motives, Attitudes, and Feelings

Your attitudes, feelings, and motives will influence your ability to be objective and thus, your effectiveness as a decision maker. Ask yourself:

◆ What are my motives? What do I want? Do I want to open the door for discussing concerns or do I want my relative to do what I believe should be done?

◆ How would I describe my attitude about the situation? Can I be objective?

◆ How do my feelings fit into the decision? Would this decision make me feel better, less worried, or less embarrassed? Are my feelings distorting or exaggerating the problem?

Talk to someone you trust if you are uncertain about your feelings or if you suspect you are exaggerating the problem. Another person may give you the needed objectivity.

Learn from Past Experiences and Those of Others

Reflect on past caregiving decisions and consult other caregivers in your circle of family, friends, or support group members who have made similar decisions. Learning from past experience is a valuable way to prevent repeating mistakes and to guide future decisions. Ask yourself:

◆ What about the timing of past caregiving decisions? Were decisions made too hastily? Were they made too soon or too late? Or was the timing about right?

◆ What would I do differently to reach a decision?

◆ What helped me to make a sound decision that can be applied to the current decision?

Ask other caregivers:

◆ How did you decide it was time to make a decision about a similar problem?

◆ What would you do differently next time?

◆ What professional help (social services, private agencies) did you find useful or would you recommend for evaluating the situation or to provide caregiving services?

◆ What would the care receiver do in a similar situation?

Understand The Care Receiver's Needs and Feelings

An important step is to evaluate the care receiver's needs and to strive to understand his thoughts and feelings. This can be especially difficult if you are a long-distance caregiver. To get a complete picture, you may need to obtain information from a wide range of people, including the care receiver, health care providers, family members, neighbors, and local business and delivery people.

Identify areas where help is needed

Before deciding what must be done, you need to know how well the care receiver functions in daily activities and in performing specific tasks such as driving and managing finances. The more you understand his or her needs, the better prepared you will be to make a decision.

Some of the areas in which people often need help are:

◆ diet and meal preparation.

◆ home safety and maintenance.

◆ housekeeping.

◆ health care.

◆ personal care.

◆ medication management.

◆ mobility and transportation.

◆ legal and financial issues.

◆ socialization, companionship.

◆ activities and recreation.

Identify the care receiver's skills

In addition to understanding the ways the care receiver relies on others for help, consider what he still does independently. Based on your assessment of what activities he performs easily or with some difficulty, you can try to anticipate what help may be needed in the near future. Answering the following questions will help you clarify the care receiver's needs and remaining skills.

◆ What specific change(s) is the care receiver experiencing? What problems or needs are these changes creating?

◆ Are his needs temporary or permanent?

◆ Does he need occasional or continuous help?

◆ Does the care receiver see these changes as problems?

◆ In what ways does he compensate for these changes?

◆ Which, if any, of these changes are harmful to him or others?

If you need or want a professional evaluation, contact a care manager, nurse, or social worker who specializes in evaluating the needs and functioning of ill or frail individuals living at home. The care receiver's physician, the local senior center, the area agency on aging, or disease-related support groups may be able to refer you to reputable individuals or agencies that provide this service. In addition to providing an objective assessment, a professional evaluation may give you more confidence as you face making a decision.

Be sensitive to the care receiver's perspective

Try to understand the care receiver's thoughts and feelings in regard to accepting help, giving up driving, having someone else manage finances, or moving. Sometimes people welcome a change because they have been worrying about how they will manage. Frequently, however, a change is traumatic and stress-producing.

Involve the Care Receiver in Decisions

Charlie, age 85, is a widower and a retired commercial fisherman. Once a robust man, he has become frail and hard of hearing. Last week he tripped over his pant leg, fell, and bruised his arms and knees. When his daughter Jennifer asked him about the bruises, he said he couldn't remember what happened. Upon hearing this, Jennifer insisted Charlie let someone stay with him during the day. Charlie resisted. He had other ideas. But Jennifer persisted. She advertised for and hired a home care worker. It seemed perfect, except Charlie decided he didn't like the worker and fired her a week later.

Jennifer's plan didn't have a chance to succeed because she made plans *for* Charlie instead of *with* him. She needed to put herself in her father's shoes. Would she want other people making decisions for her without asking what she wanted? Would she be upset if her dad told her what she should do?

Let's consider how the situation might have been different if Jennifer had actively involved her dad in the decision.

Jennifer asked her dad, if someone helped him around the house, what would he want that person to do? She also asked him if he would prefer the person who did the chores to be a man or a woman. Charlie said, "I'd like a man but men don't do housework." She asked him if he'd consider hiring a woman if a man couldn't be found. He said, "Maybe."

A week later she told her dad she had talked to several qualified men over the telephone who were interested in working for him. She asked if he would like to meet them. She said, "After you meet them you may decide if you want one of them to work for you."

Although there is no guarantee, Jennifer stands a better chance that her dad will accept help this time. The goal is to help the care receiver meet his needs so he can live the life of his choosing instead of yours. No adult wants decisions made for him no matter how wise those decisions may be. Talk with the care receiver about his desires and priorities. When he sees his ideas or wishes incorporated into the decision, he has a vested interest in making the decision work. Involving him increases the likelihood he will consider a suggestion and accept a change, even if he prefers a different one.

Including the care receiver in decision making does not mean decisions are left totally up to him. The tasks within the decision-making process must be within the skill level of the care receiver. When a person has memory loss or reduced mental capacity, others must take an active role in making and carrying out decisions. Be careful not to leave necessary decisions completely unaddressed because you inappropriately gave the power of the final "yes" or "no" to the care receiver.

Decisions should not burden others unnecessarily. You can set limits on what you and other family members can do. Then within those limits the care receiver can make the decision. For example, if your mother can no longer drive, you can make a list of times you would be able to drive her and she could make a list of times she

---

QUESTIONS TO ASK

The following are important questions to answer when faced with a decision:

YesNo

❐ ❐ Do I know the care receiver's current and long-term needs?

❐ ❐ Do I understand his capabilities as well as his limitations?

❐ ❐ Have I gathered information on all available options to meet the care receiver's needs?

❐ ❐ Am I aware of how the care receiver feels and thinks about his situation and needs?

❐ ❐ Do I know and understand his preferences?

❐ ❐ Do I respect his preferences, even if they conflict with mine?

❐ ❐ Am I willing to allow him to take some risks which may have negative consequences for him alone?

❐ ❐ Do I know how other family members will be affected by the care receiver's risk-taking?

❐ ❐ Am I fully informed about the care receiver's financial situation?

❐ ❐ Will he be involved (as much as possible) in making decisions?

❐ ❐ Do I know how other family members (e.g., brothers and sisters) feel about the situation?

❐ ❐ Do I know how others are willing to help?

The more "yes" answers you have, the better prepared you are to make a decision.

usually runs her errands. Compare the lists to see if any of the times match. If no times match, you can seek a compromise that reflects your needs and her needs.

Investigate Potential Options

Try not to have preconceived ideas about what is "the best." It's important to identify all potential options and the benefits and limitations of each—from both your perspective and that of the care receiver. If possible, the care receiver should have at least two options from which to choose. Having some choice often helps to give a sense of control and reduce resistance.

Recognize the Care Receiver's Right to Take Risks

Sally's Aunt Mamie spent the last 60 of her 86 years living on her own in an old three-story house that badly needed repairs. The only bathroom was upstairs and Mamie had trouble climbing stairs. Increasingly concerned about her aunt's safety, Sally tried to talk her into moving to an assisted living facility near Sally's own home. It seemed like a good idea to Sally.

"Nothing doing," said Aunt Mamie firmly. "I've lived here more than 50 years and I'm not moving now!"

Many families worry about a mentally competent elderly relative whose safety is at risk. They may try to work out other alternatives with their relative without success. If an accident occurs, they frequently blame themselves for not stepping in. It's

important to remember that mentally competent adults have the right to make choices regardless of age, as long as they are not putting others at risk. You cannot force change or overrule the decisions of a person who is not mentally incapacitated. However, the person who has the ability and the right to make a decision is also responsible for accepting the consequences of his choices.

If you find yourself in a dilemma like Sally's, communicate your fears and talk about the potential consequences of an injury. The care receiver may think that you will provide needed care should an accident occur, or that an accident wouldn't affect his living situation. Unspoken expectations need airing. Saying, "I worry about who will take care of you if you fall and are seriously injured," might open the door to a frank discussion of "what ifs." Faced with reality, the person might reconsider your suggestions about safety. If not, and your fear of an injury comes true, remember the decision was the care receiver's, not yours—you had no control over it.

A MODEL FOR MAKING DECISIONS

Strong emotions can arise in making decisions. Family members (including the relative you are concerned about) may have different views of a situation, the options, and the decision. They may have different priorities: one may feel the person's safety is most important while another may believe the person remaining at home is more important than safety issues. A decision can become bogged down over emotions and philosophical differences.

Many caregivers find it helpful to have a plan to follow as they make decisions. The figure illustrates a seven-step model for systematically approaching a decision. It can help you to make the most thoughtful and best decision.

1. Identify the Problem

You need to agree on what the problem is before exploring options or trying to reach a decision. Family members may disagree about what the problem is or they may agree on the problem but have different views of it. Present specific facts and situations if one person doesn't see a problem at all. It may help to answer the following questions:

◆ How does the problem present itself? What has been observed?

◆ Why is there a problem?

◆ What makes it a problem?

◆ Who is affected?

◆ What is the current situation? How widespread is the problem?

◆ What are the consequences if a decision is not reached about the problem?

The goal is to pinpoint a problem as specifically as possible. It's important to move from generalizations such as "Dad is a poor driver," to describing specifically what has been observed. For example, "At least twice last week Dad did not stop at stop signs," "A month ago he was cited for running a red light," "He straddles the center line when he drives," and three neighbors have expressed concern about the safety of their young children when Dad is driving in the neighborhood." Without identifying the specific problem(s), a problem can seem too large or vague to tackle. This can lead to feeling overwhelmed and not making a decision or taking action.

2. Gather Information

Your goal is to make an informed decision. Often families are so concerned about solving a difficult situation that pertinent questions, which provide a stronger base for decision making, go unasked and unanswered. It's important to have objective information about the person's health and level of functioning, and to gather information from all relevant sources. This

3. Generate Options

Once the problem has been clearly identified, it's time to brainstorm options. This is thinking of as many ideas as you can to address the problem. The likelihood of selecting the best option is increased if all available alternatives are considered in decision making. Keep this step separate from evaluating the options. It's important not to evaluate or censor ideas as they are presented. The purpose of brainstorming is the free exchange of ideas without fear of criticism or rejection. Critical thinking comes later. Health care and social service professionals can help identify options.

may include information about community and family resources and family finances.

4. Evaluate Options

With most decisions there is no one "right" or "perfect" course of action. You are trying to find the best choice among the available alternatives. Remember, any decision you make is likely to have both positive and negative consequences.

The next step in decision making is to figure out which option will have the best outcome for your family. After all options have been identified, think about the positive and negative consequences or benefits and limitations of each one. The following questions may be helpful:

◆ What are the potential benefits of this option for my family member? For myself?

◆ How likely is it that these benefits will occur?

EVALUATING OPTIONS

Options	Benefits	Limitations

◆ What are the limitations or disadvantages of each option for the care receiver? For myself?

As you evaluate each option, consider both short-term and long-term consequences for you and the care receiver. Choosing the least restrictive option for the care receiver is an important goal. This is the option that allows the most freedom of movement and choice. However, an option should not unfairly burden anyone. Therefore, it's critical that everyone involved speak openly and honestly about what they can and cannot do.

Agreeing on standards for evaluating the options—criteria such as financial limits and personal preferences—also can help you select the best option(s). You might also find that combining two or more individual options results in the best decision. It may be helpful to prioritize the options and develop a possible back-up plan. It is possible your first choice may not work.

A good guideline to follow is "Be easy on people; be tough on issues." Good communication is an essential ingredient in making decisions as a family.

Writing identified options on a chart like the one on page 142 helps organize ideas. Recording points made can also help to reduce confusion and misunderstandings. And, it gives a visual model of how you reached the decision.

Another reason for evaluating options may be to streamline them. We often feel "the more choices, the better"; however, for some memory-impaired people too many choices can be overwhelming. Reducing the options to the best two or three may reduce confusion, and yet give the person a sense of control over the decision.

5. Create a Plan

This can be the most difficult part of decision making, especially if there doesn't seem to be a single best choice. At times, you may feel that you must select the "least worst" of the options. But, if your choice meets the care receiver's needs, if you tried to preserve the greatest control and freedom for him, consider that you made the best decision for now.

Developing a step-by-step strategy for implementing the plan, putting the plan in writing, and indicating who has agreed to do which tasks can reduce disagreements among family members. A written plan can also be useful later when you evaluate it.

6. Act on the Plan

Carry out the plan. Try to establish a trial period, using the perspective of "This seems like the best decision for now. Let's give it a try for _____ weeks/months, then look at our plan again."

7. Reassess the Plan

A plan should not be considered as "final and forever." Because situations change, flexibility is key to quality decision making. Reassessing a plan can be hard to do, especially if you want closure to a difficult situation. You might want to skip this step because it takes you back over old issues you want behind you. However, asking "How well is the plan working?" and making necessary adjustments is decision making at its best. Be prepared to try a different option or go back through the decision-making process.

This decision-making model is a guide. No plan is foolproof, but by following a decision-making process, you increase your chances of making a decision that works.

Decisions are influenced by many factors, including the personalities of family members, the quality of relationships, and communication patterns. Other factors include whether the older person is mentally intact and able to participate, whether a decision is being made in advance or at a time of crisis, and whether family members are living nearby or at a distance. In spite of these differences, quality decision making can occur by following a decision-making process and focusing on issues and options (not personalities or old grievances).

HOLDING A FAMILY MEETING

A family meeting is one tool for deciding how to share caregiving responsibilities and for making caregiving decisions. It gives everyone an opportunity to discuss concerns, identify current or potential problems and solutions, and negotiate the sharing of caregiving tasks. It can also reduce misunderstandings and clarify each person's expectations. The following guidelines can help insure the effectiveness of a family meeting.

Include Everyone

Involve everyone who is concerned and affected by caregiving decisions. This includes siblings, spouses, other relatives, housemates, the person for whom plans are being made, and perhaps close friends or neighbors. If illness prevents the care receiver from being involved directly, get his input and keep him informed.

A family member should not be excluded because of distance, personality, or limited resources. It's just as important to include a family member who is difficult, argumentative, or never visits, as those who are supportive. Telephoning distant relatives to get their input and keeping them informed will help them feel a part of decision making. Involvement of all family members in developing caregiving plans and making decisions ensures greater support, and helps prevent undermining of decisions.

Consider a Two-Step Meeting

Sometimes families find it helpful to hold a two-step meeting. The first meeting is held without the care receiver to air ideas and feelings, identify concerns, look at gaps in information, and discuss responsibilities. The purpose should not be to make the decision or to "gang up" on the care receiver. A second meeting is then held with the care receiver, who is actively involved in looking at the options and making decisions.

Plan for Success

A family meeting is most successful when you do the following:

- Before the conference, ask family members to list their concerns and the tasks they are willing to do.

- Hold the meeting in a neutral setting.

- Create a feeling of trust, support, and confidentiality.

- Keep the meeting focused on the current concern rather than on other issues or past conflicts.

- Be certain everyone has an opportunity to express feelings, voice preferences, and offer suggestions without being put down.

- Focus on the positive. Identify what each person can do, but encourage everyone to be honest about their limitations.

- Prepare a written plan, listing what each person will do and when they will do it. But, keep it flexible. A written plan can prevent later disagreements about who agreed to do what, and can assure that needed tasks will be completed.

Use a Facilitator

A family meeting is not always easy. Decision making is most difficult if family members have never discussed feelings or family issues, or if family conflicts already exist. When family members come together after years of separation, old conflicts can re-emerge with regard to relationships, family roles, expectations, and even inheritance.

If family conflicts or hidden resentments are likely to prevent rational discussion and decision making, seek professional guidance. A counselor, health or social service professional, private care manager, or a member of the clergy trained in family counseling may be able to help you deal with family conflicts. He or she also may be able to facilitate the family conference and provide objectivity.

MAKING DECISIONS UNDER TOUGH CIRCUMSTANCES

Special circumstances or difficult relationships may hamper decision making. Sometimes people hide problems, send mixed messages about what they want or will do, or cannot participate in decision making. This can place you in a quandary: Do I force a decision or let things ride? Letting things ride ultimately puts you in the position of waiting for a crisis before making a decision or addressing a problem.

When the Care Receiver Covers Up Needs

Some people cover up problems because they fear they will be forced to move or to accept in-home help. If involving them in the decision and reassuring them of your intentions doesn't help you to get needed information, try these steps.

◆ **Talk to others in the family.** Ask what they have observed. The information and opinions expressed might give you additional insight and alert you to potential areas of disagreement among family members.

◆ **Ask friends and neighbors** if they have concerns. You may be surprised by what friends and neighbors know and how much they do to help the care receiver. This is also an opportunity to strengthen the care receiver's support system and acknowledge their help by showing your appreciation.

◆ **Talk to local business people (grocers, druggists, fast food employees).** Individuals who provide services such as mail delivery and garbage pickup—also may have seen or suspected problems. This is also an opportunity to let them know you value their watchfulness and who to call if they suspect a problem.

◆ **Write down your findings.** Take notes. Use quotes. With permission, include names and telephone numbers of your business and neighborhood contacts. This information provides a broader base for making sound decisions.

◆ **Seek professional advice.** Ask the care receiver's health care provider for information about professionals who can evaluate the care receiver's functioning and needs. Public and private agencies offer care management services that include an assessment of a person's needs.

When You Receive Mixed Messages

How do you make a decision if you receive different messages on different occasions? What do you do if the care receiver agrees to hiring help, then the next day resists the idea? How do you decide about a move that the person wants to make in the morning and then opposes in the evening?

Often mixed messages indicate that the care receiver is thinking about the impact of a decision. Try sharing your observation of the mixed messages and talking with him about what they represent. Listen carefully. This allows him to express feelings and may reassure him that you are sensitive to his position, uncertainty and feelings.

When the Care Receiver is Memory Impaired

If a decision must be made and declining memory is an issue, consider the preferences the person has expressed over time and incorporate these into the decision. Advise relatives of the person's wishes and your predicament.

Consult the care receiver's physician. An assessment and "straight talk" may encourage the care receiver to agree that a particular decision needs to be made. However, if the care receiver suffers from memory loss, he or she may agree, then later forget. Even when this happens, you can feel more confident in moving forward with a decision because of the base of information you have. You may also use the doctor's opinion to persuade the care receiver: "The doctor says (this change) is necessary because…"

If memory problems affect the care receiver's judgment, if he poses a danger to himself or others and cannot make rational decisions, you are justified in making decisions and in taking preventive action on his behalf. However, you don't have to do this alone. The physician and other professionals involved can provide guidance.

PLAN AHEAD IF YOU CAN

One important decision-making tool is to plan ahead. Although we can't always predict change, we can discuss potential future changes and decisions with the care receiver, unless he is memory impaired or cannot communicate. Advance planning can focus on issues such as declining health and long-term care, living arrangements, financial and legal issues, end-of-life decisions, and death and funeral arrangements.

The advantages of talking about and making plans in advance of need is that it helps to reduce heartache, increases understanding about a person's wishes, makes decisions easier in difficult times, and reduces uncertainty and disagreements. Advance planning also enables care receivers to maintain maximum control over their lives, especially if a time comes when they cannot actively participate in decision making.

One approach is to talk with the care receiver about "what ifs." For example, ask "What if the doctor said I could no longer provide the care you need? What would you like to have happen?" Talking about future "what ifs" is not always easy, particularly if frank discussions of emotional issues have been avoided in the past. Also, planning ahead requires anticipating situations we consider negative. This can make everyone feel uneasy.

Look for natural opportunities to talk. For example, when the care receiver says, "When I die…" or "When I can no longer live here…," be receptive to a discussion. Too often others discourage discussion by saying things such as "Don't be so morbid," or "We've got plenty of time to talk about this. Let's not talk about it now," or "You'll probably outlive all of us." Other natural times for talking may be when a family member or friend experiences a health crisis, has a car accident, makes a change in living arrangement, or develops Alzheimer's disease, or you are preparing your own will or powers of attorney for finances or health care.

When making advance plans, it is important to explore options and to have more than one plan. Circumstances later on may require flexibility.

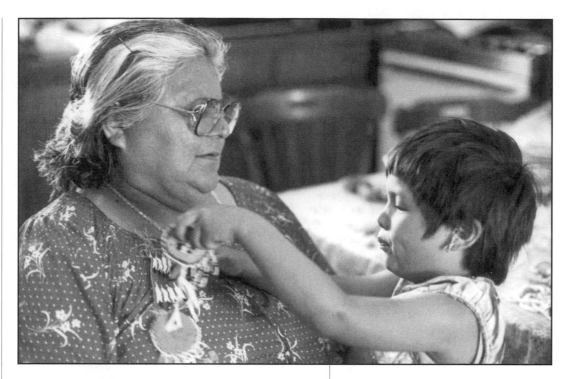

SUMMARY

Making sound, compassionate decisions is a skill that requires preparation, cooperation, and practice. It also involves the risk that you might make mistakes. But, there is a positive side to mistakes. They provide important information to guide future decisions. A realistic attitude about present and foreseeable caregiving needs is also important to effective decision making.

There are no perfect or easy answers. There are no ready-made solutions. Every caregiving situation is unique. Although it may seem that decision making is risky, remember that not deciding is still a making a decision.

Caregiver Issues

CHAPTER EIGHT

Spouses and Partners as Family Caregivers

Often the primary family caregiver is the spouse or partner of the person needing care. When the spouse/partner caregiver is healthier than the care-receiver, and is able to participate independently in many more activities of daily life, he/she is referred to as the "well-spouse/partner." The well-spouse/partner may be an older person, or a young adult, or a middle-aged person whose partner has developed a chronic condition at a relatively young age.

When one partner is significantly healthier than the other, the couple may face unique challenges.

CHALLENGES FOR WELL-SPOUSE OR WELL-PARTNER CAREGIVERS

◆ Experiencing the sudden shift in the relationship and the intense grief that accompanies the awareness that the couple's relationship as they have known it is gone forever

◆ Unsettledness due to the emotional roller-coaster of difficult feelings such as anger, guilt, resentment, and loneliness

◆ Dealing with feelings of intense sadness at the loss of shared hopes, dreams and activities

◆ Living through the "long goodbye," which may go on for months or years.

The person with the chronic condition may become less and less "the person I fell in love with" as the disease or chronic condition affects physical appearance, physical abilities, memory or thought processes, personality, and emotional responses

◆ The changes in roles and routines that were in place for many years

◆ Fear that care needs may become too great for the spouse/partner and that the couple may not be able to live together if out-of-home care becomes necessary

◆ Anxiety—Who is going to meet my needs now? Can I do this for as long as will be necessary? Do I want to stay in the relationship? Do I have a choice? Will this person I love still love me as a spouse or partner, or will we become more like parent and child? What about our children's lives?

◆ Financial concerns—Who will be the breadwinner? Will I have to give up my job or change career paths because of caregiving responsibilities? What if this goes on so long we run out of money? What if the medical assistance laws change and we can't get help if we can't do this ourselves anymore? Should I be doing something legal to protect our assets? Who do I turn to for questions about finances?

◆ Increased risk of caregiver depression, illness, or early death if the caregiver does not keep a commitment to care for himself or herself as well as for the care receiver

◆ Loss of any or all of the intimacies that have been a part of the couple's special relationship: verbal intimacy, physical intimacy, sexual intimacy, emotional intimacy, and social intimacy

There are particular challenges for families when both the caregiver and the care receiver are relatively young. There may be children or teenagers at home who are affected by the care decisions. The well-spouse/partner may have parenting and employment responsibilities, or may be a caregiver for one or both parents.

The younger the care receiver and the shorter the period of time the couple has been in a relationship, the more likely it is that questions will arise about the long term prospects for the couple's relationship. Many times, spouse or partner caregivers find it useful to connect with a well spouse group, or to seek individual or couples counseling, for help in dealing with the many complex and difficult challenges of caregiving.

If you are a well-spouse/partner, it is important to ask yourself:

◆ Am I taking care of my own health needs—taking my medicine, keeping medical appointments?

◆ Am I smoking or drinking more than before?

◆ Am I feeling isolated from friends?

◆ Have I given up activities I used to enjoy?

◆ Do I feel like I am "losing myself"?

◆ Do I need to ask for more or different kinds of help?

◆ Do I feel guilty for wanting to acknowledge my own needs and emotions?

◆ Am I increasingly irritable or angry?

◆ Am I having problems eating or sleeping?

◆ Am I experiencing increased anxiety or depression?

◆ Does my stress level feel overwhelming?

Many times, spouse/partner caregivers find it useful to connect with a well-spouse caregiver group or seek individual or couples counseling to help deal with these issues.

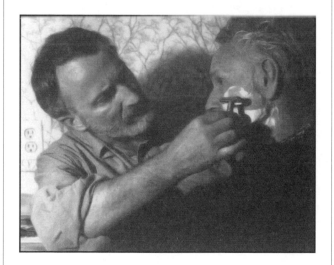

RESOURCES

Bridges, William. *Transitions: Making Sense of Life's Changes.* Perseus Books Publishing, 1980.

Lustbader, Wendy. *Counting on Kindness: The Dilemmas of Dependency.* McMillan Press.

Williams, Redford, and Virginia Williams. *Life Skills: Eight Ways to Build Stronger Relationships, Communicate More Clearly, and Improve Your Health.* Times Books/ Random House, 1997.

The Well Spouse Foundation, www.wellspouse.org

American Society on Aging, 800-839-0879

Lesbian and Gay Aging Issues Network (LGAIN), 800-537-9728

CHAPTER NINE

Family Caregivers in the Workplace

Family caregivers often describe their caregiving as a full-time unpaid job. In addition to their caregiving work, many family caregivers are also employed in either part-time or full-time work outside the home. They have been described as "invisible" in the workplace, as they often are without support from their employer or co-workers. They shoulder the responsibilities of caregiving while also trying to be a responsible employee. As the number of family caregivers has escalated, family caregiving has gradually become recognized as a social issue with significant impact on both employers and employees.

Research into the issues of caregiving and employment has found that:

◆ An estimated 10 percent of caregivers quit their jobs. This results in costly increased turnover for the employer, and lost income and benefits for the employee.

◆ In today's workforce, an estimated one in four workers cares for an aging parent.

◆ Twenty percent of caregivers leave their jobs at least temporarily to handle caregiving demands.

◆ Eighty percent of long-distance caregivers are employed full- or part-time and need to do many of their long-distance caregiving tasks during their work day.

These tasks can include phone calls to find resources, paperwork, talking with healthcare providers, and contacting other family members to coordinate care issues.

◆ Absenteeism among family caregiver employees is less of a problem for employers than "presenteeism"— employees who are on the job but distracted, working under the physical and emotional strain caused by their caregiving responsibilities. Studies have shown that "presenteeism" costs employers billions of dollars a year in lost productivity and safety claims.

◆ Some employers offer benefits such as flexible work schedules, funeral or bereavement leave, or health fairs that include information on aging services or services for people with chronic illness. Few employers offer classes, employee assistance counseling, or written information for their employees who are caregivers. Fewer still offer referral services for family caregivers about taking care of themselves.

◆ Employees generally underestimate the amount of time caregiving will take and the impact it will have on their work life. Caregivers report caregiving for periods from as short as a few weeks to months or years.

◆ Caregiving affects male and female employees in similar ways. Male caregivers often do not let co-workers know of their caregiving responsibilities and stress. When asked, both male and female family caregivers say they would use employee services addressing issues of caregiving if they were available.

◆ Retirement decisions are sometimes influenced by caregiving responsibilities. Wives caregiving for husbands often retire earlier than planned. Husband caregivers often work longer than planned because of financial concerns.

◆ Two of the major stressors for employed family caregivers are fear of unemployment and fear of loss of the health insurance benefit offered through the employer.

◆ Employees frequently use their weekends, sick days or vacation leave to attend to caregiving. This results in employees suffering from symptoms of exhaustion and burnout, since they have no chance to relax or find respite for themselves.

◆ Many employers express an interest in learning about caregiving support that could be made available to their employees.

RESOURCES

American Association for Caregiver Education – www.caregivered.org. Search using the terms *Caregiving: Workplace Issues* or *Employed Caregiver Issues*.

American Association of Retired People, www.aarp.org. Search using the terms *Caregiving: Workplace Issues*.

Family Caregiver Alliance National Center on Aging, www.caregiver.org, Search using the terms *Work and Eldercare*.

CHAPTER TEN

Long-Distance Caregivers

aregiving in any situation is not an easy job. When the caregiver and the care receiver do not live close to one another, it can be especially challenging.

Are you a long-distance caregiver?

◆ Does your care receiver live farther away than down the street or across town?

◆ Does it take a significant amount of money or time to make the trip to your care receiver?

◆ Do you use vacation time and money to see your care receiver or meet with the caregiving team?

◆ Do you have to depend on the "eyes and ears" of people closer to your care receiver to know what is really going on?

Whether you live several hours away, across the country, or halfway around the world from your care receiver, if you answered "yes" to most of these questions you are a long-distance caregiver. Many long-distance caregivers fall into the role suddenly and unexpectedly—someone they care about experiences a medical crisis or decline in functioning, and the amount or type of care needed changes drastically. It is not uncommon to hear stories from family caregivers about "the call that made me a long-distance caregiver."

Worldwide, there are more long-distance caregivers than ever before. It is estimated that in the U.S. alone there are over five million caregivers managing care from a distance. In all parts of the world it has become common for family members to live far away from each other. Children often live far away from their parents because of school, employment, relationships, or geographic preference. It is not always the adult children who move away. In the U.S. particularly, parents may move to a warmer climate or closer to medical facilities. There are some families where the younger generation has emigrated to a new country and the older generation has stayed behind.

CONCERNS OF LONG-DISTANCE CAREGIVERS

There are certain issues that come up frequently in long-distance caregiving. Some of the most common are those referred to in these quotes from long-distance caregivers:

"How can I know how my folks are really doing when I am unable to be there to see for myself? When I call, my parents always say things are fine!"

"How will I ever find resources in a place I have never lived? Who is going to supervise the people I find to help with my daughter's care?"

"I am worried all the time and feel guilty that I cannot be there to help out."

"My sister thinks I am getting off easy because I am not close enough to help out with my grandmother's regular care. I think she is mad at me for not helping more."

"I worry that I'll get sick from stress, or it will ruin my marriage, or I'll lose my job if this goes on for months or years."

These quotes highlight some concerns common to long-distance caregivers:

◆ How to get an accurate assessment of functioning and medical conditions

◆ How to find resources

◆ How to supervise care

◆ How to determine future housing needs

◆ How to handle the effects of long-distance caregiving on the caregiver's employment, family finances and relationships.

In addition, long-distance caregivers often find themselves needing to make decisions about matters such as:

◆ Medical, legal or safety decisions

◆ Transportation

◆ Payment of bills

◆ Insurance

◆ Nutritional needs or meal delivery

There is much useful information available to help long-distance caregivers. Finding and using this information will increase the likelihood that your long-distance caregiving plan is the best plan possible under the circumstances. It is important to remember that "the best plan possible" is "the best plan *for the moment*." It may need to be revised many times after it is implemented.

TIPS FOR LONG-DISTANCE CAREGIVERS

Prepare ahead whenever possible. If you anticipate that someone is likely to need long-distance caregiving in the future, plan for that time before it happens. Work with your care receiver to get as much information as possible. Locate records, papers, and important contact numbers—you will need this information to communicate with physicians, insurance companies, benefits offices, Veteran's Administration, Social Security, Medicare, etc.

You will need signed release forms in order to do any business on behalf of the care receiver. If you gather this information sooner rather than later, you will have it when you need it.

It will also help reduce your stress level if you are able to gather information on some basic resources before you need it. Having the phone numbers of a few key contacts on hand can greatly reduce the time it takes you to make or revise a plan from afar. Consider getting contact information in advance for resources such as home health services, case managers, hospice, paid caregivers, transportation, and home-delivered meals or medications.

Educate yourself about your care receiver's condition and get regular updates about the situation. If a family member is not able to gather this information in person, you might need to ask neighbors, health care providers, friends, or social service workers to assess the situation and relay that information.

Hold a family meeting as soon as an emergency or change in the care receiver's

functioning necessitates a new or revised plan. At this meeting the family caregiving team can decide what needs to be done next and who will do it. You should continue to make and revise plans over the entire time you and others are doing family caregiving.

Gather resource information. It will be helpful to develop some sort of file, resource binder or book to keep the information organized. You may want to consider using the services of a case manager if you need help in finding resources, assessing and re-assessing your care receiver's needs, and keeping up to date on changes that might require a new plan. Case managers can be a great assistance to long-distance caregivers. Some case managers are in private practice and others work for healthcare, social service, and disease-specific organizations. Many public programs for seniors or people with disabilities have case managers assigned to work with the people in their programs.

Identify possible sources of financial assistance as early as possible. If your care receiver has health insurance, is a veteran, or participates in a health care or social service program, there may be some services that are covered or provided at a lower fee or free of charge. It is important to research this early in the process, as many caregiving services are the out-of-pocket responsibility of the care receiver or his or her family.

RESOURCES

Heath, Angela. *Long Distance Caregiving: A Survival Guide for Far Away Caregivers.* Impact Publishers. Out of print. Available through used book dealers.

Lebow, Grace, and Barbara Kane. *Coping with Your Difficult Older Parent: A Guide for Stressed Out Children.* Quill/Harper Collins Publishers, 2002.

McLeod, Beth Witrogen, ed. *And Thou Shalt Honor: The Caregiver's Companion.* Rodale Books, 2002.

Family Caregiver Alliance. "Handbook for Long-Distance Caregivers" www.caregiver.org

American Association of Retired Persons, www.aarp.org

Alzheimer's Association, www.alz.org

CHAPTER ELEVEN

Grandparents as Caregivers

Grandparents raising grandchildren is a situation that is happening more and more frequently in the United States. Caring for the grandchildren can be temporary, permanent, part-time, or full-time.

There are many reasons why this situation occurs, ranging from a parent's need for help to parental failure. Some of the specific causes are:

◆ Serious illness or death of a parent

◆ Parent(s) away in the military or due to other occupations

◆ Drug and alcohol abuse in the home

◆ Child neglect and abuse

◆ Parent is mentally ill

◆ Parent is incarcerated

◆ Single parenthood or divorce

◆ Homelessness

◆ Unemployment

◆ Teenage pregnancy

◆ Abandonment of the child by the parent

◆ Parents working long hours

◆ Poverty

Grandparents come to the rescue in these situations to keep the child from foster home placement or to save them from further harm and despair and to keep them in the family.

Grandparents raising grandchildren

— 2.5 million households
— 52 percent of the grandparents are younger than 55 years old
— 31 percent of the grandparents are between 55–64 years old
— 17 percent of the grandparents are 65+ years old

Grandchildren living with grandparents

— 51 percent of the children are younger than 6 years old
— 29 percent of the children are 6–11 years old
— 20 percent of the children are 12–17 years old

— Census 2000, U.S. Census Bureau

REWARDS AND CHALLENGES

Some grandparents face rearing their grandchildren with ambivalence or even resentment, while others take on their role with gratefulness and an opportunity to develop deeper relationships with their grandchildren. Personality types, values, financial security, housing, health, and available time all come into play as grandparents take on this responsibility. The degree of resentment or acceptance often is related to whether or not they had a choice in the matter.

Rewards

There can be much satisfaction for grandparents and grandchildren alike when they are working together toward maturity. Grandparents can give a sense of security after the pain of divorce or domestic violence, which eventually will help to foster self-respect, self-confidence, and self-identity in grandchildren. These accomplishments are often aided by the child's participation in religious activities, sports. school activities and academics.

Grandparents can preserve values that are important to their family and culture and relate family history to their grandchildren, giving a sense of belonging, worth, and stability. As grandchildren gain strength and grow, grandparents may experience a sense of renewal. As grandparents work with the children in school, faith community or other activities, social contacts expand. Grandparents may be exposed to new environments and experiences that enhance their own sense of fulfillment and positive development. Even though these events bring pleasure, it is natural for grandparents at times to resent the responsibilities and inconveniences involved in parenting again.

Challenges

Parents often think they are through with day-to-day parenting once their children are raised or nearly raised. They begin to make plans for the future without children at home. When these plans change, sometimes suddenly, great stress can occur for grandparents and grandchildren alike.

Children placed with grandparents need a warm and loving environment. They are often dealing with major losses, feelings of abandonment and fantasies about being reunited with their parents. They have much psychological work to do and may take out their anger on their grandparents (the custodial parent). Even though this is another stressor for grandparents and certainly something they did not seek, grandparents can use their wisdom and experiences to aid these children.

Grandparent caregivers face physical, emotional, financial, legal and educational challenges. Sometimes these stresses can be overwhelming and complicated. They can range from learning the new philosophies in infant care to dealing with a belligerent teenager or one with anorexia or drug addiction.

SPECIFIC PROBLEMS
Parenting Skills

Grandparents are confronted with things that are different from when they were parents the first time around. They may have to learn about:

◆ Disposable diapers—sizes, shapes, and costs

◆ Numerous safety devices for home and automobiles, some mandated by law

◆ Society's influence on discipline issues

◆ Varying philosophies regarding childhood immunizations

◆ Recommended choices and preparation of formula and food for children at various ages

◆ Crib and sleeping safety—proper positions for sleeping

◆ Registration at school and requirements for enrollment and attendance

◆ Toy safety and what is recommended for certain ages

◆ Appropriate television and entertainment for children

◆ Teaching children regarding dangers of strangers, abduction, terrorism, drugs, and school violence

◆ Computer skills and the Internet—advantages and dangers

Health Concerns

Some grandparents have health problems that exist before they take on parenting tasks. These health problems can be made worse by the added burdens and responsibilities of child rearing. Yet many grandparents who are in good health say their vitality increases with the stimulation of children in their home. Common health problems that can occur in both groups are:

◆ Insomnia

◆ Hypertension

◆ Back problems

◆ Digestive disturbances

◆ Depression

Psychological and Social Issues

Because much of the grandparents' time is taken up with giving the care and attention their grandchildren require, the grandparents may lose friends and former social ties. Their world becomes limited and narrow allowing isolation to creep in. They may be overwhelmed with failure, guilt, and embarrassment as they view their own child's inability to parent. These emotions turn to grief and mourning that takes time to work through in a healthy way. If the parents of the children have died, the grief can be enormous, and it is accompanied by huge responsibilities for which they were not prepared. Resentment, bitterness and exhaustion can increase as more responsibilities are thrust upon them. Many grandparents worry about what will happen to their grandchildren if they die or are no longer able to provide care. Children with emotional or behavioral difficulties take an additional toll on grandparents, often leading to fatigue, depression, and an inability to cope properly.

Financial Problems

Grandparents may have very limited funds for themselves, before having to take more people into their household. For those grandparents still in the work force, they may have to quit their jobs, decrease their hours or sacrifice in other ways. Studies have shown that many female caregivers have lower income jobs without retirement or other benefits. In addition, they often do not have savings to make up for lost wages if they quit or reduce their work hours. Obtaining health insurance for grandparents and their grandchildren can also be a very difficult task.

Legal Issues

The legal status of grandparents is very important especially if the grandparent has

the grandchildren all or most of the time. When children are being bounced back and forth between grandparent and parent, as might happen in the case of parental substance abuse/remission/abuse/remission, etc., the grandparent's legal status with those children is tenuous and needs to be firmly established. A legal ruling regarding custody, guardianship or adoption may also be required when there are warning signs or physical evidence of domestic violence between the child's parents. A legal ruling helps not only the grandparent but also the children. Obtaining legal status helps to maintain a balance of power between the grandparents, the child's parents and society. Each state has its own rules and laws regarding custody (temporary or permanent), adoption, and guardianship. It is important to investigate the laws and determine what is best for the situation at hand. Often a county or state children's social service worker, a social worker, or school counselor can guide grandparents to the proper sources and channels for these answers.

Depending on the specific legal status obtained by the grandparents, they may have rights to such benefits as:

◆ Social Security

◆ Subsidized health insurance

◆ Social services

◆ Housing

◆ School enrollment and ongoing requests for parental permission and consent

◆ Financial assistance

◆ Giving permission for medical care

TAKING CONTROL—CARE FOR THE GRANDPARENT

Suggestions for the Grandparents

◆ Explore and take advantage of the many support services and systems that exist through organizations like AARP and Generations United.

◆ Join a local grandparent support group to learn from each other and advocate with government agencies, schools, insurance companies, and social agencies.

◆ Learn about your state's custody laws, determine what best meets your situation and pursue legal status.

◆ Once you obtain legal status, find out what rights and services are available.

◆ For mental well-being, develop flexibility in your roles as mentor, role model, playmate, parent, grandparent and nurturer.

◆ Try to maintain at least some of your former social contacts and activities.

◆ Make sure to maintain regular visits to your health practitioner.

◆ Follow good health practices of diet, rest and exercise.

◆ Arrange times for respite and getting away.

◆ Realize that the relationship grandparents have when they see their grandchildren periodically is different from the full-time relationship. As Arthur Kornhaber says in his book, *The Grandparent Guide: The Definitive Guide to Coping with the Challenges of Modern Grandparenting*, "…some of the magical qualities are gone and the grandparent may need to take more of a role as an enforcer."

◆ Acknowledge and let yourself grieve the losses you are experiencing, such as freedom and lifestyle.

CONCLUSION

There are challenges and rewards for both the grandchildren and the grandparents who are raising them. Each experiences a roller coaster of emotions and feelings. However, both can gain power and strength through working with community agencies, social service organizations and faith communities that focus on the well-being of children and the needs of grandparents who are taking on parenting again. The needs of the children must be met, but there must also be care for the caregivers—the grandparents who have come to the rescue.

RESOURCES

Kornhaber, Arthur. *The Grandparent Guide: The Definitive Guide to Coping with the Challenges of Modern Grandparenting*. McGraw Hill 2002.

American Association of Retired Persons Grandparents Information Center www.aarp.org

www.grandparenting.org

www.raisingyourgrandchildren.com

CHAPTER TWELVE

Caregivers of Children with Special Needs

Many parents and primary caregivers of children with special needs are faced with unexpected challenges and emotions. However, they are not alone. Although their individual experiences may differ, many parents/primary caregivers have similar emotional dynamics.

Children with special needs include, but are not limited to, those with medical/health issues, Autism Spectrum disorders, developmental delays, speech/feeding issues, blind/visually impaired, deaf/hearing impaired, physical disabilities, chronic diseases, behavioral or mental health issues, premature birth, sensory issues, and learning disabilities.

Many parents/primary caregivers can learn to cope with the demands of parenting a child with special needs once they learn about the emotions they are dealing with and how to address them.

WHAT EMOTIONS MIGHT PARENTS/PRIMARY CAREGIVERS EXPERIENCE?

Not all parents/primary caregivers may experience the following emotions. However, it is helpful for them to be aware of the various emotions involved and to realize that their experiences and feelings are normal.

◆ **Grief:** Loss of the "perfect baby/child" that was anticipated prior to the birth or diagnosis; Hopes and plans for child's future; Lifestyle prior to child's birth or diagnosis.

◆ **Anger:** Toward themselves, partner, child, medical system, educational system, treatment team, and/or religious belief system.

◆ **Guilt:** Unable to protect child; Child's suffering; Less attention toward other children; Relationship with partner; Less focus on self.

◆ **Feelings of Isolation:** Depression; Unable to leave home; Not wanting to interact with others; Avoid having to explain child's conditions and answer questions; Resentment toward others with "typical children"; "No one else understands" what they are going through; Can sense that other people are uncomfortable around child; Financially unable to do activities; Have difficulty meeting child's needs outside of home; Lack of accommodations.

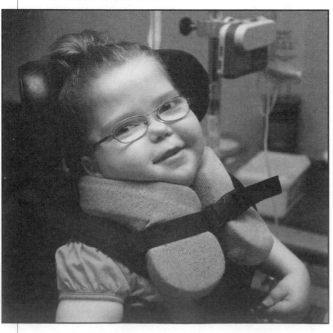

◆ **Low Self Esteem:** Interactions with many professionals who assign various labels and diagnoses of child; The "right parenting decisions" under normal circumstances may not work for child due to special needs; Society does not appear to value child equally to other children.

◆ **Fears:** Child's future; Ability to meet educational needs; Child's ability to live independently or "live a normal life" when older; Child's safety; Possible death of child; Maintaining a stable relationship with partner; Own personal mental health; Next "crisis".

◆ **Feeling Overwhelmed:** Lack of prior medical or advocacy experiences; Learning details of child's special needs and about related treatment; Managing appointments for various specialists; Dealing with insurance coverage and financial concerns; Advocating for accommodations; Managing time. Some individuals may become forgetful, miss appointments, and experience symptoms of stress.

◆ **Feeling Detached:** Over-involvement in work or other activities; Feelings of despair and hopelessness; Detachment in other areas of life due to focus on child's needs.

◆ **Other Stressors:** Balancing career and family; Lack of accommodations for child; Child's Individualized Education Plan; Attempting to meet needs of other family members; Making choices regarding child's treatment; Dealing with other people's reactions and opinions; Decrease in support system; Sleep deprivation; Poor eating habits; Lack of exercise.

HOW CAN PARENTS/PRIMARY CAREGIVERS CARE FOR THEMSELVES AND MOVE FORWARD?

There is hope for parents/primary caregivers to work through their emotions and to find ways to cope. It is important to remember to take things one step at a time. Different techniques work for various individuals and families. Identifying and practicing the best coping skills for each person is the first step.

◆ **Allow for the grief process:** There is no "right or wrong" way experience the emotions associated with grief and there is no time limit. Allowing oneself to experience feelings of sadness, anger, and/or guilt when needed, for as long as needed, is crucial. Seek therapeutic help if the grief is impacting ones' ability to function.

◆ **Find a support system:** Meet and interact with other families of children with special needs (including those with different kinds of special needs); Locate or start a support group; Seek discussion boards on the internet; Re-establish relationship with partner; Locate a therapist to address feelings; Surround self with nurturing people that are accepting of child and parenting choices; Choose a treatment team that is supportive and empowers parents/primary caregivers to make choices that are right for their family.

◆ **Find Balance:** Exercise; Enjoyable social activities; Work outside of home; Meditate; Extra-curricular activities; Fun activities as a family; "Alone time" with partner; Utilize a baby sitter.

◆ **Read:** Books by other parents/primary caregivers of children with special needs; Enjoyable books/magazines.

- **Acknowledge positive aspects of child and life:** Recognize that child is a fighter; See gains child has made; Realize own wisdom and strength; Involvement in other children's lives.

- **Love child for the person he/she is:** Identify what child has instead of what he/she does not have; Acknowledge child as an individual who may have different life goals; Learn to accept child for who he/she is.

- **Attempt to focus on the present instead of the future:** Once feelings of crisis have passed, attempt to focus on things that can be controlled instead of those that can't be controlled. "It is the journey that counts – not the destination".

- **Gain understanding that life is about change:** All parents are faced with different challenges related to their children.

- **Utilize religious/spiritual resources and beliefs.**

- **Practice assertiveness skills:** With treatment team, family, friends, and people in the community. Recognize that different treatment options work for different children/families.

- **Remember that taking care of yourself is important to you….and your child**

RESOURCES

Center for the Study and Advancement of Disability Policy- www.disabilitypolicycenter.org

Disability.gov- www.disability.gov

Institute for Community Inclusion- www.communityinclusion.org

National Institutes of Health- www.nih.gov

Sibling Support Project- www.siblingsupport.org

Social Security Administration- www.ssa.gov

The Family Center on Technology and Disability- www.fctd.info

WhatDisability.com- www.whatdisability.com

CHAPTER THIRTEEN

Caregivers of Veterans

Much has been written about the rewards and the stressors involved in family caregiving. However, little has been written about the special needs of Veterans and the specific challenges faced by their caregivers.

WHO ARE THE CAREGIVERS OF VETERANS?

In broad terms, they are informal caregivers, typically family members, such as a spouse, parent, adult child, or friend, neighbor, significant other, who provides some kind of regular, unpaid, care to a Veteran with a disabling condition. This may include the provision of hands-on physical care, or protection and supervision, or sometimes a combination of both. The caregiver may or may not live in the home with the Veteran, but contributes to the Veteran's physical and psychological well-being, often assisting him or her to live safely at home. The Department of Veterans Affairs (VA) recognizes that "Caregivers provide crucial support in caring for Veterans.[1] Not only does the home environment, enabled by the caregiver, provide a significant psychological benefit for the Veteran, it can

[1] US Dept of Veterans Affairs, "Services for Family Caregivers of Post 9/11 Caregivers," Web page 2013.

also defer or delay institutionalization and thus reduce medical costs.[2]

There are two cohorts of Veterans for whom the VA provides family caregiver support. One is the older Veteran with chronic illness, which may have developed long after returning home from the military. The other is the younger war Veteran, who was seriously injured in the line of duty on or after September 11, 2001. This includes the Veteran who may recover over time, as well as the Veteran with a chronic, disabling condition, such as spinal cord injury or paralysis, respiratory problem, Traumatic Brain Injury (TBI) and Post Traumatic Stress Disorder (PTSD).

HOW IS CARING FOR A VETERAN UNIQUE?

The universal themes involved in caring for a Veteran or Civilian include similarities as well as differences. In general, both caregivers tend to take on too much burden, thus neglecting their own physical and emotional health. Both tend to socially isolate themselves and may struggle with feelings of guilt, regret, anxiety and depression. Each group may lose wages, pension contributions and health benefits, as they leave the workforce to provide care for the care-recipient. Each group may experience caregiver burnout.

In addition to these general caregiver issues, Veteran's Caregivers are faced with additional complexities that make their role unique.

◆ The Veteran may have returned home with multiple wounds, injuries or illnesses that need care. They may have a physical injury such as loss of limb(s), coupled with a traumatic brain injury, and Post Traumatic Stress disorder. The Caregiver is faced with learning about each of these conditions and ways to effectively interact with and care for the Veteran, while also navigating through a very complex healthcare system. One role the caregiver of a Veteran provides is that of patient advocate. The caregiver will most likely interact with staff at the Department of Defense (DOD), The Veterans Health Administration, The Veterans Benefit Administration, and possibly outside governmental agencies, such as the Social Security Administration, or the Medicaid office. This can often be a daunting task so the caregiver may seek assistance from a Federal Recovery Coordinator or staff at a Veterans Service organization.

◆ Most of the Veterans returning from war are young or middle-aged and have a spouse/partner who is also young or middle-aged. Compared to the civilian caregiver, who is typically a 50 year old woman providing care for an elderly individual with a chronic illness, the caregiver of a Veteran who served in a recent conflict, like Iraq and Afghanistan, has an average age of 38.[3] They may also have young or teen-aged children in the home. All too often, the caregiver finds that there is not enough time or energy to devote to parenting, which causes worry about the

[2] C. Sheets and H. Mahoney Gleason, "Caregiver Support in the Veterans Health Administration: Caring for Those Who Care" Journal of the American Society on Aging, Vol 34, No.2, 2010 pp 92-98.
[3] National Alliance for Caregiver (NAC) study, 2010.

negative consequences this may have on the children. Some caregivers rely on other family members to assist them so that they may have time to care for the children.

At times, the caregiver/Veteran may depend on the older, adolescent child to care for the Veteran when the caregiver must step-out briefly. This occurs because the Veteran trusts the family and is uncomfortable with outside help coming into the home. The VA has a *respite program,* which can help by providing an agency caregiver to come in and assist. It may take the Veteran awhile before developing the trust necessary to accept an outside caregiver. A suggestion for the caregiver is to start the process slowly, introducing the agency person during the time of day when the Veteran is typically in the most stable and accepting mood. Stay with the agency caregiver and Veteran for several weeks before leaving them alone, *so that the Veteran becomes comfortable.

Some VA Medical Centers participate in the *Veteran-Directed Home and Community-based Care Program.* This is a program in which the Veteran may receive money in order to hire someone he or she already knows to provide care during the times when the family caregiver attends to other business. Not all VA medical centers participate in this program but it is worthwhile to inquire with the local VA social worker.

♦ Another difference that has to do with the younger age of the military Veteran, is that caregiving may extend over several decades, which is longer than the time civilian caregivers provide care. These caregivers suffer disproportionally from mental health problems and emotional stress, compared to caregivers in general.[4] It is extremely important to learn about and practice the variety of self-care techniques taught in the *Caregiver Helpbook.* Joining a face-to-face or online support group might be a healthy way to bond with other caregivers. There are a variety of support groups offered through the Veterans Healthcare System's local medical centers.

CARING FOR A VETERAN WITH TRAUMATIC BRAIN INJURY

One of the "signature" injuries of the war in Iraq and Afghanistan is traumatic brain injury (TBI). The most common causes are from explosive blasts, assaults/blows, falls, and motor vehicle accidents.

The severity ranges from mild to severe. In that a large majority of service members with TBI are between the ages of 18 and

4 Military Caregivers: Tanielian, Terri; Ramchand, Rajeev; Fisher, Michael P; Sims, Carra S; Harris, Racine; Harrell, Margaret C; Rand Corporation and the Elizabeth Dole Foundation, 2013.

24, there is a large population of parent caregivers as well as some spouses.

Common symptoms of TBI may be physical, such as dizziness, headache, difficulty with strength and or coordination, fatigue and sleep disturbance. Other symptoms affect mood and personality, specifically: anger, emotional outbursts, social insensitivity, lack of organization, memory problems, and loss of motivation. The Veteran may feel sad or seem irritable. There may be a decrease in concentration, impairment in judgment, and poor control over physical aggression. It may be difficult for the caregiver to understand the Veteran's impulsive or disruptive behavior. All these changes are new but there are some ways for the caregiver to interact that may be helpful.

The VA collaborated with the Defense and Veterans Brain Injury Center (DVBIC) and there is a free educational binder available to educate caregivers of Veterans with a moderate to severe TBI. It may be found on the website www.dvbic.org. The tab is at the top, titled Educational Materials.

CARING FOR A VETERAN WITH POST TRAUMATIC STRESS DISORDER

Post Traumatic Stress Disorder (PTSD) is a condition that may develop after someone has experienced an actual or threatened serious injury or death. It causes an emotional reaction of intense horror, or fear, with a lack of control over what is occurring. Exposure to combat is an example of an event that may cause PTSD to develop for some Veterans. When this occurs, the Veteran may re-experience the event repeatedly, unable to put it out of his or her mind.

There are treatments for this condition which involve psychotherapy conducted by a professionally trained person. There are also several medications that may help. Seek input from a VA mental health provider in order to explore treatments that might be available at the local medical center.

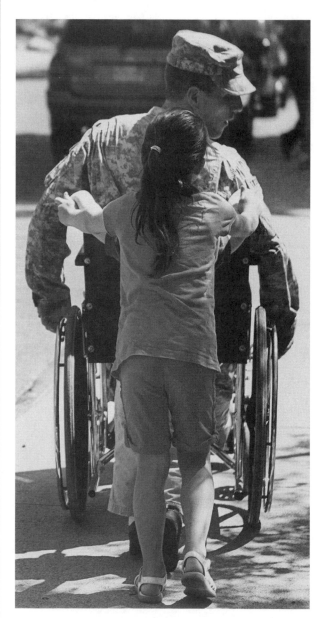

What the caregiver may do to help:

◆ Caregivers play a role in helping the Veteran to contain emotions. By anticipating cues, and using sensitivity in anticipating the Veteran's next move, the caregiver can interact with Veteran before a negative situation occurs. In one study, nearly all military caregivers reported helping their loved one cope with stressful situations, avoid "triggers" of anxiety, or thwart anti-social behavior.[5] Triggers may be: TV shows, conversation topics, disputes or anger, disrespect, and crowding.

◆ When there are nightmares or flashbacks, touch may not be helpful. Instead, use a calm voice and reassure the Veteran repeatedly.

◆ Guidelines for anger management include:

  • promotion of sleep and relaxation

  • avoidance of stimulants such as caffeine and alcohol

  • development of a list of enjoyable activities to do together

  • confrontation is NOT helpful

  • caregiver and Veteran may develop a plan of coping with impending anger ahead of time

  • allow an escape, or time-out and come back together later to discuss

◆ Formal stress management may help. Caregiver and Veteran benefit when doing them together.

  • CD's, DVD's or APP's

  • Practice daily

Reintegration into civilian life may be difficult for the Veteran. The caregiver may offer the opportunity to talk and to acknowledge the Veteran's military service, but it is best to just listen not to say, "I understand".

Caregivers must be alert to assess for risk issues. Alcohol use and depression are risk factors for aggression, and substance dependency issues may complicate family life. Rebuilding trust may be difficult as the caregiver struggles with trying to understand that the person who has returned may be very different than the person who left for war.

Sometimes, the Veteran does not acknowledge having difficulty with reintegration and may refuse to seek treatment. If the caregiver is frustrated and wants help in this particular area, he may contact someone at Coaching Into Care, a confidential and free service at 888-823-7458. Website address is: www.va.gov/coachingintocare

CARING FOR A VETERAN AT THE END OF LIFE

Over the many years of caring for a Veteran, there may come a time when the Veteran is faced with a life-limiting illness. Having been trained as a soldier, ready for combat, Veterans tend to be stoic and feel most comfortable when in control of a situation. Due to their experience with military culture, they have a "battlemind" and may view "letting go" as a defeat or weakness. In addition, they struggle against taking medication for pain, even if they are experiencing pain.

Help the Veteran to understand that dying is a natural part of living and that it is not cowardly to go comfortably and without a fight. Ask him/her if there are things about military service that they might wish to talk about. Although stoicism can keep one from sharing thoughts or emotions, for some, this may be the very time in the Veteran's life when traumatic memories surface. (PTSD at the end of life). The Veteran may need to talk about incidents pertaining to war in order to have a sense of closure. The Veteran may struggle with war-related issues such as survivor guilt, or regrets about things he did or did not do while serving the country. This may be a special time in the Veterans life, for the family caregiver to "be present" allowing these thoughts and feelings to flow.

HOW THE DEPARTMENT OF VETERANS AFFAIRS SUPPORTS THE CAREGIVER OF A VETERAN

Though providing care to our nation's Veterans may have its rewards, it may also be experienced as a daunting task for family members or friends, who find themselves unexpectedly in the role. These family or informal caregivers are a valuable resource to VA and the Veterans they care for.

On May 5, 2010, the President signed into law the Caregivers and Veterans Omnibus Health Services Act of 2010, also known as Public Law 111-163. The Department of Veterans Affairs was tasked with developing a program of Comprehensive Assistance for Family Caregivers and a Program of General Caregiver Support Services. Under the law, Primary Family Caregivers of eligible Veterans, seriously injured in the line of duty on or after September 11, 2001, may be eligible to receive a stipend, access to health care coverage and mental health counseling They may also be eligible for travel benefits when they accompany the Veteran for care or attend mandatory training.

The Program of General Caregiver Support is available for Veterans from all eras. Their caregiver may participate in a host of supportive educational opportunities, as well as the respite program. Respite is a program for the Veteran, which provides temporary relief for the caregiver. VA respite programs include adult day health care, home health aides, skilled nursing, and home based primary care. VA also has programs including home tele-health, home modifications, automobile modification and adaptive equipment. It is important to keep in mind that VA medical centers offer a menu of services and each program may not be available at every single local facility.

Many caregivers ask about long-term nursing home care. There is a program in which nursing home care may be provided in a VA or a private community nursing home for Veterans who need care, but are not in need of hospital care. This is a limited program for those Veterans who:

◆ Are eligible for VA health care.

◆ Have a Service connected rating of at least 70 %.

◆ Need nursing home care for their service connected disability.

For more information, please visit: http://www.va.gov/healthbenefits/access/geriatrics.asp

Since the Caregiver Support Program has many components, the best way to see what is available is by scrolling through the tabs and links on the caregiver website. The program provides help for the brand new caregiver as well as the more experienced caregiver. There are peer mentoring opportunities, online support groups, face- to- face support groups and telephone support. The website has a link to various caregiver stories, and a module about self-care. The address of the website is www.caregiver.va.gov

There is a Caregiver Support Coordinator, (CSC) stationed at each VA medical center. The CSC will assist the Caregiver in navigating through the VA healthcare system. The CSC is also available to provide information on the Veteran's Health Administration enrollment process. It will expedite enrollment if the Veteran has a copy of his discharge papers (DD214).

In order to locate a Caregiver Support Coordinator by area, check the caregiver website. It allows a search by zip code. One may also contact the toll free, National Caregiver Call Center at: 855 260-3274.

RESOURCES
Toll Free Veterans Telephone Numbers

Veterans Benefits Administration 1 800 827-1000 or website http://www.vba.gov/VBA/

National Veterans Crisis Hotline 1 800 273-8255

Caregiver Support Helpline 855 260-3274

Other Toll Free Telephone Numbers

Alzheimer's Helpline 1 800 272-3900

Caregiver Action Network 1 800 8896-3650

National Domestic Violence Hotline 1 800 799-SAFE

National Child Abuse Hotline 1 800 4 A CHILD

Websites

http://www.caregiver.va.gov VA Caregiver Support Program website

http://www.caregiver.va.gov/toolbox_landing.asp VA has created this Caregiver Tool Box to help you find tools that work for you. This page offers resources and information to help you stay on top of things and manage the daily stresses of family caregiving

http://www.va.gov/healthbenefits/access/geriatrics.asp

http://www.vetcenter.va.gov/

http://www.ncptsd.va.gov National Center for Post-traumatic Stress Disorder (PTSD)

http://www.mentalhealth.gov

http://www.biausa.org Brain Injury association of America

http://www.dvbic.org. Defense and Veterans Brain Injury Center

www.rorc.research.va.gov/resue Resources for Education for Stroke. Caregivers' Understanding and Empowerment (Rescue)

http://www.caregiver.org/caregiver/jsp/home.jsp National Family Caregiver Alliance

https://www.nrd.gov National Resource Directory -Connects wounded warriors, Veterans their Families and Caregivers with those who support them

http://militaryonesource.com

http://www.giveanhour.org Nonprofit organization providing free mental health services to US military personnel and their families.

http://www.afterdeployment.org

http://woundedwarriorproject.org

CHAPTER FOURTEEN

Caregiving Skills for Living at Home

The call to become a caregiver rarely comes with a book of instructions. There is much to learn, from basic care issues involving assistance with daily living to special procedures related to specific conditions. Learning how to provide care properly and sensitively will help you feel more competent and therefore less stressed. Such competency can also prevent injuries to both you and the care receiver.

LEARNING CAREGIVING SKILLS

Caregiving skills are explained, often step by step, in numerous books written specifically for caregivers. These texts can be invaluable in initiating care and as ongoing references. Home health care and hospice agencies teach nursing care and procedures for correct body mechanics for the caregiver and the care receiver. Body mechanics include rules for the caregiver to prevent back and neck injuries plus correct positioning, moving, and transferring of the care receiver.

The American Red Cross and the American Heart Association teach CPR (cardiopulmonary resuscitation), with their classes often taking place within hospital health education programs.

Hospitals often teach nursing care or therapies for specific care needs once a care receiver is discharged to home.

Some voluntary health organizations or disease-related organizations also sponsor caregiving skills classes.

In addition to teaching skills, health care providers can recommend adaptive equipment to enhance safety, convenience and independence for the care receiver.

PREPARING THE HOME ENVIRONMENT

First of all, making the home environment safe and user-friendly is imperative. Consider the following basics:

◆ Minimize clutter

◆ Provide adequate lighting. Older people need brighter lights

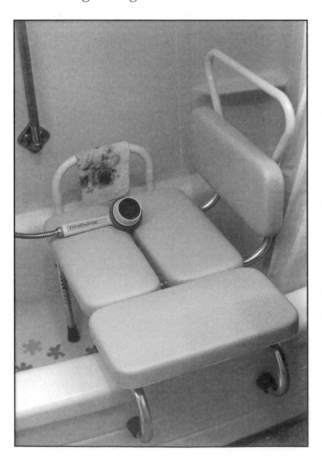

◆ Remove scatter rugs or at least put non-skid pads under them

◆ Remove dangling wires or wires under carpets

◆ Install smoke alarms that work

◆ Remove excess furniture

◆ Clear walkways throughout the house

◆ Adjust the height of chairs and bed to allow for easy access

◆ Provide bed, bath and meals on one floor

◆ Make sure there is a fire extinguisher in the kitchen

◆ Install grab bars near toilet, shower and tub

◆ Provide non-slip mats in tub and shower

◆ Install an elevated toilet seat

◆ Use an elevated bed or adjustable hospital bed to assist the caregiver in lifting

◆ Make a plan for power outages

PLANNING CARE

Establish a plan of care that includes but is not limited to:

◆ Medical history information

◆ Medications—name, dose, administration schedule and any specific instructions

◆ Diet

◆ Daily schedule of care and activities

◆ Functional disabilities—amount of assistance needed

◆ Special observations needed

◆ Names and telephone numbers of physicians and other health care providers

◆ Physicians' orders

- ◆ Telephone number of preferred hospital
- ◆ Names and telephone numbers of any services that regularly come into the home
- ◆ Names of those to call in an emergency, in addition to 911
- ◆ Health insurance plan and policy number
- ◆ Food likes and dislikes
- ◆ Special behavior management techniques

Having a plan for care is helpful for the family caregiver and any substitute caregivers who may provide respite care.

SKILLS NEEDED FOR DAILY CARE

Assisting care receivers with their basic human needs is called performing "activities of daily living." It is very important to make sure the care receiver's dignity and privacy are maintained at all times. These skills naturally include:

- ◆ Eating
  - — Special diets and good nutrition
  - — Preparing and serving food
  - — Feeding care receivers who cannot feed themselves
  - — Monitoring intake
- ◆ Personal hygiene
  - — Oral care
  - — Nail and foot care
  - — Hair care
  - — Shaving
  - — Baths
  - — Shower
  - — Tub
  - — Bed bath

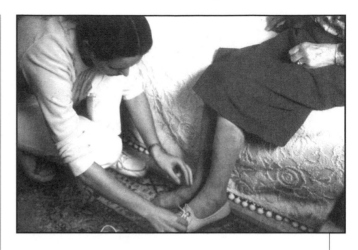

- ◆ Toileting
  - — Transfer to toilet
  - — Use of bed pans, urinals, and bedside commodes
  - — Catheter care
  - — Incontinence
- ◆ Infection control
  - — Hand washing and dish washing
  - — Cleaning methods
- ◆ Bed-making
  - — Making an occupied bed
  - — Prevention of soiling
  - — Care of soiled linen
- ◆ Dressing
- ◆ Skin care and prevention of pressure sores

CONCLUSION

Statistics and experiences prove that many family caregivers give excellent care to their loved ones. Basic skills can be learned and practiced. Even complicated procedures, such as feeding tube use, ventilator care, oxygen administration, and intravenous pump use can be handled correctly by family members. At first, the tasks appear daunting, but with proper education and support, success is achievable.

RESOURCES

American Heart Association
   7272 Greenville Avenue
   Dallas, TX 75231
   800-242-8721
   www.americanheart.org

Family Caregiver Alliance
   180 Montgomery Street, Suite 1100
   San Francisco, CA 94104
   800-445-8106

National Association for Home Care
   228 Seventh Street, SE
   Washington, DC 20003
   202-547-7424

National Hospice and Palliative Care
   Organization
   1700 Diagonal Road
   Arlington, VA 22314
   800-658-8898

McLeod, Beth Witrogen. *And Thou Shalt Honor: The Caregiver's Companion.* Rodale Inc., 2002

Meyer, Maria M. and Paula Derr. *The Comfort of Home: An Illustrated Step-by-Step Guide for Caregivers,* second ed. Care Trust, 2002

CHAPTER FIFTEEN

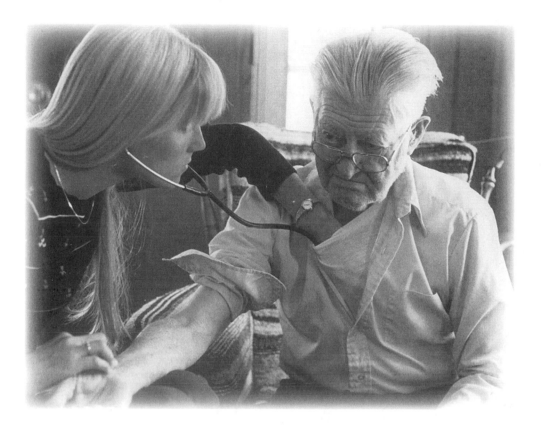

Hiring In-Home Help

Most people want to stay in their own homes for as long as possible. This is certainly reflected in the United States statistics that report more than seven million spouses, adult children, other relatives, and friends or neighbors provide unpaid help to disabled older adults living in the community. This represents 85 percent of all home care provided in America. These figures do not include care that is given to younger sick and disabled persons, so the figures are even higher. Yes indeed, home is where the heart is.

To help facilitate this desire, numerous services provided both by private and public agencies and individuals are available in most regions of the country. However, in less-populated areas service options may be limited.

RECOGNIZING AND ACCEPTING THE NEED FOR HELP

As the needs of the care receiver or the caregiver change, additional help may be necessary. Sometimes more expertise in caregiving skills is needed as the care receiver's health declines. Recognizing and accepting the need for outside help can be challenging for both the caregiver and the care receiver.

Many people do not want strangers in their homes. Caregivers can feel that they alone will give the proper care to their family member. Perhaps care receivers want help from no one but a family member. Using day care centers to relieve both the caregiver and care receiver may be viewed with skepticism. There are costs to consider, as well as availability of and access to needed services. Sometimes ethnic, cultural or language barriers exist. For a while, things as simple as home-delivered meals and medications, friendly visitor programs or life-line emergency call services will suffice. But as abilities decline, increased needs require more help within the home.

WHERE TO START

An important step is to realistically assess the home care needs. This includes both the needs of the family caregiver and the needs of the care receiver. Some general areas to consider are:

◆ Household care—cleaning, laundry, cooking, shopping

◆ Financial care — writing checks, paying bills, banking, maintaining insurance premiums, monitoring bank statements and credit cards

◆ Personal care —-bathing, dressing, eating, toileting, assisting with mobility

◆ Health care — medication management, wound dressings, catheter care, giving injections, administering oxygen or providing rehabilitation services such as physical, occupational or speech therapy

◆ Emotional care —-conversation, daily check-ins, companionship, transportation, visits to or from preferred faith communities

You can find help with these issues through word-of-mouth, personal ads, churches, senior centers, registries of workers maintained by hospitals or private registries, aging offices, hospital discharge planners, social workers, and case managers.

TYPES OF HOME CARE

There are two main types of in-home care workers: individuals who are self-employed and hired directly by a family, and people who work for home care agencies. Self-employed caregivers can be nurses, therapists, aides, homemakers, chore workers or companions. In many states, homemakers, aides, chore workers and companions are not required to be certified or to meet government standards.

Hiring Self Employed Caregivers

Be prepared:

◆ Develop a job description, listing specific care needs, such as the need for lifting, dealing with a person who is confused or incontinent, pet care, etc.

◆ Decide what qualities and experience you want in a caregiver and if you can be flexible with your desires.

Self Employed Caregiver	Home Care Agency
The family gets to choose the worker.	The agency chooses the worker.
A strong relationship can develop between care receiver and caregiver due to continuity.	A variety of caregivers can be involved
Can be less expensive for part-time care when paid out-of-pocket.	More expensive due to overhead costs.
The family and care receiver can direct and monitor the care and decide the salary.	Direction and supervision of care is performed by agency.
The family must handle screening, hiring, and firing.	Agency does recruiting and training, and manages all employee issues.
Depending on the legal work status of the caregiver (self employed or family's employee), the family may have to pay employer taxes, insurance, Worker's Compensation, plus maintaining tax and payroll reports.	The agency takes care of all employee benefits, expenses, and legal requirements.
Self employed caregivers usually do not have substitutes for days off, illness or vacations.	Agencies have multiple staff who can fill vacancies.
Less likely to be covered by insurance plans or third-party payors. In some states publicly funded programs may provide money for families to hire a family member or an individual.	Some types of care agencies are covered by Medicare, Medicaid, Veteran Services, insurance plans, and voluntary health groups like Easter Seals.

◆ Know how much money you can spend.

◆ Have a written contract.

◆ State working hours and provisions for time off for illness or vacation.

◆ Define who in the family will be directing the care.

◆ Research and know legal, financial and tax issues. Determine who will be paying taxes, workers compensation, etc.

◆ State what type of notice is required if the worker quits or the care receiver no longer needs the services.

Sample questions to ask the prospective caregiver:

◆ What is your caregiving experience?

◆ Are you bonded?

◆ Are you comfortable with me running a criminal background check on you?

◆ What are your expectations if I hire you?

◆ What classes or training have you had in caregiving?

◆ Why did you leave your last job?

◆ What do you like and dislike about home care?

◆ Can you provide three references from past or current clients?

◆ Is your license current? (as it relates to healthcare professionals)

Hiring Home Care Agencies
Homemaker agencies

These agencies provide workers who will prepare meals, assist with bathing, dressing, housekeeping, and sometimes shopping and transportation. The agency hires, trains and supervises their employees plus manages all payroll and labor law issues. Some states require these agencies to be licensed, to ensure they meet state-mandated minimum standards.

Private duty and staffing agencies

These agencies are generally nursing agencies that provide caregivers who are nurses, aides, homemakers and companions. The agency recruits these employees and is responsible for the care they give.

A few private insurance plans may pay for private duty staffing, but they are quite rare. Sometimes Medicaid and Veterans' Services will fund this type of care. Medicare does not pay for these services.

Home health care agencies

Home health care agencies provide services that include skilled nursing, physical therapy, occupational therapy, speech pathology, social workers, and home health aides for personal care. These agencies recruit, supervise and are totally responsible for their employees' salaries, benefits, and caregiving standards.

The majority of home health care organizations are Medicare-certified, so Medicare will pay for the services rendered. In addition to Medicare coverage, Medicaid, Veterans' Services and numerous other health insurance plans, plus some long-term healthcare plans, fund this type of care. Medicare-certified home health agencies have to meet strict federal and state rules and regulations to remain certified.

Home health care must be ordered by a physician and the patient must require skilled care such as injections, wound care, intravenous feedings, or certain therapies. In addition, the care must be delivered on an intermittent or part-time basis and the care receiver must be homebound during the period that the agency is under contract. As soon as the care receiver no longer requires this type of care, Medicare and most insurers will cease coverage.

Hospice care agencies

Hospice care is for terminally ill people who choose to stop aggressive, curative treatment and focus on palliative care. Designed to provide sensitivity and support, hospice care seeks to manage symptoms such as pain to provide comfort. Emphasis is on living a vital and alert life right up to the time of death.

A physician's order is needed to start and continue care and the physician must certify that there is a life expectancy of six months or less. If the person lives longer than that, the physician can recertify to continue care. Hospice follows a team approach to care including physicians, nurses, and social workers, with options as needed for therapists, bath aides, chaplains and trained volunteers. The team provides medical care and support services to the care receiver, but also assistance, direction and counseling to family. There is a nurse on call 24 hours a day in addition to the regular home visits made by nurses and other staff.

For care receivers who are Medicare-eligible, hospice care is a fully covered benefit. When hospice care is delivered by a Medicare-certified hospice organization, all medications, hospital stays and equipment needed for management of the terminal diagnosis are covered. Many private insurance plans also pay for hospice care. Within the hospice philosophy of care, services are provided to those eligible regardless of their ability to pay.

Along with providing hospice services in private homes, the hospice team can work in facilities like nursing homes, retirement communities, assisted living facilities and foster homes. Some hospitals and nursing homes have their own hospice units and teams. There are also free-standing hospices—facilities dedicated to the terminally ill who live there until they die. After the care receiver dies, hospice continues bereavement contacts with the family for at least 13 months—one month after the first anniversary of the death.

COMPARING THE CHOICES

Numerous issues emerge when considering whether to hire self-employed caregivers or work through an agency. Obviously those giving the care have to be able to meet the needs of the care receiver and family caregiver in order to create the most positive situation for all concerned.

The table on page 179 lists some of the pros and cons of each type of care (adapted from Family Caregiver Alliance's "Fact Sheet: Hiring In-Home Help").

CONCLUSION

Having additional help in the home can be a very positive experience for both the family and the hired caregiver. The success depends on proper planning, realistic expectations, and maintaining open, clear communication. Keeping these practices in place can help keep a loved one at home longer—which is almost always preferred and typically is less expensive than the alternatives.

RESOURCES

American Association of Retired Persons
  (AARP)
  601 E Street, NW
  Washington, DC 20049
  800-424-3410
  www.aarp.org

Family Caregiver Alliance
  180 Montgomery Street, Suite 1100
  San Francisco, CA 94104
  800-445-8106
  www.caregiver.org

National Association of Area Agencies on
  Aging
  1730 Rhode Island NW, Suite 1200
  Washington, DC 20036
  202-872-0888
  www.n4a.org

National Association for Home Care
  228 Seventh Street, SE
  Washington, DC 20003
  202-547-7424
  www.nahc.org

National Hospice and Palliative Care
  Organization
  1700 Diagonal Road
  Arlington, VA 22314
  800-658-8898
  www.nhpco.org

National Family Caregivers Association
  10400 Connecticut Avenue, Suite 500
  Kensington, MD 20895
  800-896-3650
  www.nfcacares.org

U.S. Administration on Aging
  One Massachusetts Avenue, Suite 4100
  Washington, DC 20201
  202-619-0724
  www.aoa.gov

U.S. Dept. of Health and Human Services
  Centers for Medicare and Medicaid
  Services
  7500 Security Boulevard
  Baltimore, MD 21244-1850
  800-633-4227
  www.medicare.gov

McLeod, Beth Witrogen. *And Thou Shalt
  Honor: The Caregiver's Companion.* Rodale
  Inc., 2002

Meyer, Maria M. and Paula Derr. *The
  Comfort of Home: An Illustrated Step-by-
  Step Guide for Caregivers*, second ed.
  Care Trust, 2002

CHAPTER SIXTEEN

Moving to a New Place

Change is hard. Leaving a home and moving to a new place is very difficult, especially if a person has lived in his or her home for a long time. The home often holds many fond memories. The house is familiar and comfortable, and the resident has it "just the way I want it." For some people, the home is completely paid for and is in an area with neighbors and friends. Gardens, flowers and trees are reminders of hard work and yet pleasant satisfaction. To leave this setting can be as difficult for the family as it is for the care receiver.

RECOGNIZING AND ACCEPTING THE NEED FOR CHANGE

As care needs multiply, often family caregivers and in-home services cannot maintain the care that is needed, so there is no other option but to move. For many people, a stay in a care facility will be short—primarily for rehabilitation from an acute illness, accident, or surgery. For others, the time in a facility will be months or even years.

WHERE TO START

Sometimes the necessity for a care facility occurs with little warning, such as after discharge from a hospital following a hip fracture or severe stroke. So, whenever

possible, planning for facility placement is best if done before the actual need arises. Check out available options and learn about different types of community-based care. This eases the decision-making process when facility care is actually required. Having a family meeting in this preplanning phase is also helpful.

The major key to success in arranging a change in housing is to realistically assess the needs of the care receiver. A constant goal should be to maintain a sense of integrity and dignity for the care receiver and to encourage any remaining independence. However, anticipating future care needs is wise, so the care receiver doesn't have to be moved often from one level of care to another.

HOUSING AND CARE OPTIONS
Shared Housing

This form of housing is for someone who is still quite able but can no longer care or pay for their own home alone.

Options include having two individuals in like circumstances share one home. In some situations, all the costs and chores are divided equally, like typical roommates. Other agreements can be made where the homeowner shares the home in exchange for cooking, laundry, maintenance, etc. Some voluntary or faith-based organizations sponsor large homes where several people share space.

Moving to a Family Member's Home

Items to consider include:

◆ How much of a disruption to the family will this be? Are there spouses, children, friends, and pets that will feel displaced?

◆ Does the care receiver have to leave his or her hometown? This will involve new physicians, dentists, pharmacists, etc. Lifelong friends and familiarity with the community could be lost.

◆ Will the care receiver require 24-hour supervision?

◆ Will relief be available so the caregiver can have time off?

◆ What is the comfort level of all concerned in regard to personal care such as bathing and toileting?

◆ Are there unresolved issues such as strained relationships, past abuse, neglect, alcoholism, or divorce?

◆ Will the care receiver be able to have some of his or her own furnishings and other familiar items?

Despite the challenges, living together can be very rewarding. The care receiver can become an integral part of the family.

Retirement Living Facilities

There are many kinds of retirement living facilities. The focus is to offer as much independent living as possible. People often reside in individual apartments or small homes, with the facility offering a variety of services such as transportation, congregate meals, weekly maid services, or planned social activities. Personal or minimal medical care often can be arranged on a temporary basis for an acute episode, but usually the resident is expected to manage personal care and medical issues. If residents are unable to do this routinely, the facility may ask them to move.

Costs vary according to dwelling size, location and level of amenities. If the retirement community offers condominiums or small homes, those prices may rise and fall like standard housing. Payment for retirement living is generally the responsibility of the resident. However, in some cases low income residents are funded by community or government sources.

Residential Care and Assisted Living Facilities

These facilities are for those who cannot completely care for themselves; they are a blend of retirement living and personal care. There is usually 24-hour supervision, assistance with personal care needs, medication monitoring, congregate meals and housekeeping services, as well as call systems in each individual residence for requesting emergency help. Consultation services by registered nurses are often available and skilled care can be provided on a temporary basis by outside home health care agencies. In most states, there are

licensure requirements for these facilities and certain standards are mandated to be met.

Payment for this care is primarily the responsibility of the resident. However, as with retirement homes, low income individuals may qualify for public assistance. There is a basic monthly rate, with additional payment required as more services are needed.

Foster Homes or Board and Care Homes

The definition of this type of care varies from state to state. Typically only a small number of care receivers (5–6) are housed. Some foster homes involve a family that takes in and cares for people; others are staffed by hired live-in caregivers. Services such as meals, laundry, and personal care are provided.

This type of care is appealing because of the home setting.

In most states, foster homes must be licensed, and there are requirements for the level of personal care they can provide. Skilled care can be brought into the homes. Some foster homes offer specialized care for complex medical conditions.

As with residential care and assisted living, third party reimbursement for care is limited to Medicaid for low income care receivers and some long term care insurance plans that include special foster care options. Veterans may receive aid and attendance benefits if eligible. Much of foster care is paid for by the individual.

Nursing Home Care

Nursing homes offer several levels of care. Nursing homes typically serve many people—often 20 or more. It is important to match individual needs with services provided. The two common levels of care are intermediate or custodial care and skilled nursing care.

Intermediate or Custodial Care

Those who need 24-hour care along with room and board, some personal care, medication management and activities are classified as custodial or intermediate care. This level of care accounts for the majority of nursing home residents.

Skilled Nursing Care

A person requiring much more complicated care and needing regular registered nurse supervision is classified as needing skilled care. Examples include:

◆ Insulin or other injections

◆ Intravenous feedings

◆ Tracheotomy care

◆ Some types of catheter care

◆ Physical, occupational or speech therapy

Nursing home care is usually the most expensive of all the housing options. Typically, there is a basic fee and then additional charges as care needs increase. Medicare, some health insurance plans and long term care insurance plans will pay for skilled care with certain limitations. Review insurance policies and their coverage.

Medicare pays for skilled care only in Medicare-certified institutions after a hospital stay. Medicare coverage is brief and short term, covering only recovery from the incident.

Alternatives to Nursing Home Care

Medicare and Medicaid currently offer limited access to nursing home alternatives. The programs are Program of All-Inclusive Care for the Elderly and Social Managed Care Plan.

Program of All-Inclusive Care for the Elderly

The Program of All-Inclusive Care for the Elderly (PACE) is a benefit under both Medicare and Medicaid for people deemed and certified to require skilled care but who wish to remain at home. PACE participants receive comprehensive medical and social services from teams of health professionals who develop an individualized care plan.

PACE receives a fixed monthly payment per enrollee from Medicare and Medicaid. The amounts are the same during the contract year, regardless of the services an enrollee may need. PACE enrollees may also have to pay a monthly premium, depending on their eligibility for Medicare and Medicaid.

Social Managed Care Plan

A Social Managed Care Plan provides the full range of Medicare benefits offered by standard managed care plans, along with additional services. These additional services include:

◆ Care coordination

◆ Prescription drugs

◆ Chronic care benefits covering short term nursing home care

◆ A range of home- or community-based services. such as:
  — Personal care services
  — Adult day care or respite care
  —-Medical transportation
  — Other services that may be provided include eyeglasses, hearing aids, and dental care

These plans offer the full range of medical benefits that are offered by standard managed care plans plus chronic care/extended care services. Membership offers other health benefits that are not provided through Medicare alone or most other senior health plans. As of late 2005, only four Social Managed Care Plans are participating in Medicare and each Social Managed Care Plan has eligibility criteria.

Each plan has different requirements for premiums. All plans have co-payments for certain services. Contact Medicare's Personal Plan Finder for details.

Continuing Care Communities

This housing option has various names, such as Life Care or Stepped Care. The philosophy of continuing care communities is to provide all levels of care from independent retirement living to nursing home or hospice care in the same facility. As the care receivers' needs progress, they move from one level of care to another, but the move is not as traumatic as having to move to a new institution. Another advantage is that the spouse of a care receiver also can live in the community.

Standard practice requires residents to buy into continuing care communities. There is an entrance fee and then monthly payments.

ASSESSING AND CHOOSING HOUSING OPTIONS

Researching and asking the right questions will facilitate the process of choosing housing.

◆ Review options before the need arises.

◆ Assess the abilities and circumstances of the care receiver.

◆ Discuss moving options with the care receiver.

Questions to Ask

There are some general concerns to explore in all cases. However, depending on the type of facility and the types of services needed, additional specific questions relating to those unique issues will be necessary.

◆ Is the license or certification current?

◆ Have there been complaints filed against the institution?

- Does the facility have a Patient Bill of Rights?

- What is the fee and what services does it cover?

- What additional services are there and do they cost extra?

- Does a contract have to be signed?

- Is transportation to outside appointments and events available?

- What is the ratio of staff to residents?

- What type of training does the staff have?

- How are complaints made and then how are they handled?

- How does the staff relate to specific behavioral issues such as wandering, angry outbursts, dementia, or non-responsiveness?

- Does the staff speak the residents' languages?

- Do physicians or registered nurses regularly visit the facility?

- Does the facility abide by State Fire Marshall rules?

- Are people on duty 24 hours, or is there an emergency call plan?

- Are medications and medical care handled professionally?

- Are door locks secure?

- Are sanitary conditions maintained throughout the facility?

- Do the call buttons work, and are they in all rooms used by residents?

- Do bathrooms have grab bars, and are showers and tubs easily accessible?

- Is the environment attractive, both indoors and outdoors?

- Are activities and hobbies available that would appeal to a variety of residents?

- Is an effort made to accommodate and relate to cultural, ethnic, and religious preferences of the residents?

- How often and when can families and friends visit? Could pets live in or make visits?

- Can the resident retain personal belongings such as pictures and small furniture?

TRANSITIONING TO THE NEW PLACE
Feelings are Strong

There's a roller coaster of ideas, choices, and feelings for both the care receiver and the family when relocating to a new home. The care receiver may feel:

- Abandoned and rejected

- A loss of privacy, freedom and space

- Angry at self and others

- Ashamed due to dependency

- A loss of financial security because of impending costs of care
- Depressed
- Confused upon entering new surroundings and routines.

These feelings should be acknowledged. The losses are monumental, especially if a person has lived in a home for many years. Stressing the positive aspects of the new place and reminders that care is no longer practical at home can help reduce the "transfer trauma."

The family and family caregiver may feel:

- Failure that they cannot continue giving the care at home
- Apprehension about care not being given properly, or not given in the way they or the care receiver prefer
- Resentment that care costs so much, especially if there is no third party reimbursement
- Relief that the burden of day to day care is lifted
- Confusion about what to do with the care receiver's home and possessions

SETTLING INTO THE NEW PLACE

- The family and family caregiver are still caregivers.
- Get acquainted with staff and volunteers. Visit at different times to become familiar with the various shift workers.
- Visit during meal times so you can observe the food, how it is being served and if the care receiver is eating.
- Pay careful attention to the care receiver's mood and behavior.

- Help the care receiver become involved with activities.
- Ask the staff what they need from you. Show appreciation for their work.
- Occasionally take gifts to the care receiver.
- Take old friends to visit.
- Take your loved one on outings, if possible.
- If the facility has a family council, get involved.

RESOURCES

For more information on PACE, visit http://www.medicare.gov/nursing/alternatives.asp for additional information on the Program of All-Inclusive Care for the Elderly (PACE) and the Social Managed Care Plan program.

American Association of Retired Persons (AARP)
601 E Street. NW
Washington. DC 20049
800-424-3410
www.aarp.org

Family Caregiver Alliance
180 Montgomery Street, Suite 1100
San Francisco, CA 94104
800-445-8106
www.caregiver.org

National Association of Area Agencies on Aging
1730 Rhode Island NW, Suite 1200
Washington, DC 20036
202-872-0888
www.n4a.org

National Family Caregivers Association
  10400 Connecticut Ave., Suite 500
  Kensington, MD 20895
  800-896-3650
  www.nfcacares.org

Senior Solutions of America Inc.
  P.O. Box 22123
  Sarasota, FL 34276

U.S. Administration on Aging
  One Massachusetts Ave., Suite 4100
  Washington, DC 20201
  202-619-0724
  www.aoa.gov

U.S. Department of Health and Human
  Services, Centers for Medicare and
  Medicaid Services
  7500 Security Blvd.
  Baltimore, MD 21244-1850
  800-633-4227
  www.medicare.gov

McLeod, Beth W., ed. *And Thou Shalt Honor:*
  The Caregiver's Companion. Rodale Inc.,
  2002

"Choosing a Nursing Home 2004" U.S.
  Department of Health and Human
  Services, Medicare and Medicaid Services.

CHAPTER SEVENTEEN

Sensory Changes

As we all discover in time, aging is an individual journey. The variations are almost as great as the number of us who make the trip. Despite the uniqueness of our paths, there are some commonalities we share along the way.

In the physical realm, there is the gradual loss of muscle mass, bone density and heart and lung capacity, for instance. Reaction time slows. While staying active and physically fit is possible, and certainly beneficial, doing so is a bit more of a chore than it was in younger years.

Research into the psychological impact of aging has led to mixed findings. Short-term memory abilities seem to show areas of slight decline, while long-term memory seems less affected, if at all. Our ability to use language seems to get better, assuming overall good health, as both our vocabulary and word fluency improve.

When it comes to aging, little, if anything, remains exactly as it has been. So it is with our senses—vision, hearing, touch, smell, and taste.

SENSORY GOOD NEWS/BAD NEWS

Each of our sensory capabilities — detection, recognition and discrimination — declines with age. But there is some good news. For starters, most individuals have more than enough sensory capacity and

Sensory changes...

- Shrink the world people see, hear, and participate in. Sensory loss can lead to embarrassment and withdrawal from family, friends, and activities.

- Restrict freedom. They create reluctance to drive, use mass transit or even to leave the house.

- Reduce self-esteem. A loss of independence, even to a small degree, can have a negative impact on one's self-esteem.

- Add to the difficulty of chronic conditions such as arthritis and high blood pressure.

- Trick people about what they hear or see. Misunderstandings, fear, anger or suspicion are common results of sensory decline.

- Negatively affect previously enjoyable activities, such as listening to music, engaging in hobbies or mealtime pleasures.

- Create a sense of clumsiness due to sight and tactile changes.

- Increase the risk of accidents and injury. Slowed reactions to hazards, falls, cuts, burns and bruises are all more likely with sensory loss.

capability to last them throughout their lives, no matter how old they live to be. Some may notice little or no decline. Additionally, changes to sensory ability most often occur gradually, which allows for successful accommodation to the change. Furthermore, at least for many, there is the opportunity to aid change or loss via corrective lenses, hearing aids, dietary adjustments, etc.

WHY SENSORY CHANGES MATTER

One goal of good caregiving is helping the care receiver stay engaged with the world in as meaningful a way as possible. Sensitivity to these changes improves the chances of better interaction. Given the role senses play in our lives, change can affect both the care receiver as well as those around her or him. Senses connect us to the outside world. Being aware of age-related sensory changes allows one to accommodate them and minimize loss.

How Sensory Changes Affect Lives

- Reduce ability to communicate and interact
- Decrease mobility and freedom
- Increase dependence on others
- Alter perception and response to environment
- Lead to social isolation and deprivation

COMMON AGE-RELATED SENSORY CHANGES
Vision Changes

The most recognized age-related vision change is presbyopia, or farsightedness, which is caused by the gradual loss of flexibility of the eye's lens, and results in a decline in the ability to focus on small objects. This change usually occurs between ages 40 and 55. Presbyopia is a normal condition, not a disease, and usually can be corrected with reading glasses or other corrective lenses.

Another normal change is the reduction in peripheral vision—the size of the perceived visual field gets smaller. This can be dramatic, decreasing from 250 degrees or more to as little as 120 degrees. An older person may not notice a pedestrian, a bicyclist, or a car approaching from the side the way he or she might have in the past.

Additionally, there is a marked decline in convergence between the eyes. This means the eyes are not able to focus together, making it more difficult to judge distance and depth. This is particularly problematic in low-lighting situations.

Light is also an issue with other changes older persons will likely experience. One is the slowing of the eye's adaptation to changes in light, which is particularly noticeable after age 70. Going from a lighted room to a darkened one, or vice versa (think about a movie theater, or a midnight trip to the bathroom), or moving into and out of shadows (walking along the sidewalk on a sunny day) can be troublesome for the older person if not given ample time to adjust. Glare becomes an increasing problem, as does an increased light threshold, or the need for more intense and direct lighting.

There is also increasing difficulty in color discrimination, especially at the cool end of the light spectrum—violet, blue and green. For an older person, distinguishing differences between darkish greens, blues and black is difficult, and interferes with color coordinating clothing or seeing the edge of the step at the top of the stairway. (Hence, the yellow tape on the edges of steps in public places.)

Diseases of the eye

It is important to realize that not all vision changes are age-related or inevitable with advancing years. Sadly, many diseases can reduce or totally rob one's sight, and their symptoms can be difficult to spot. Disease symptoms sometimes mimic the age-related changes discussed above, and thereby might go unnoticed until much damage has been done. Or, a symptom may be noticed, but mistakenly chalked up to "old age."

Some eye diseases, such as macular degeneration and glaucoma, occur most commonly among the elderly. Others, like diabetic retinopathy, are the result of an existing or chronic condition. Vigilance is key, and seeking professional eye care on a regular basis is vital, especially for those past age 65.

Vision assistance: what to do

Many things can be beneficial to those with visual limitations. Being aware of how the eye changes over time or the characteristics of a given disease or condition are good beginnings, providing a base to build on. Being alert to safety hazards in and around the home is another. Throw rugs, clutter on the floor, poorly lit areas (especially stairways) and electrical cords lying across a pathway are invitations for accidents. Balanced, even lighting reduces glare and shadows, making distance and depth easier to judge. Paying close attention to where light originates (windows or lamps), and to highly reflective surfaces (floors, woodwork and walls, mirrors, table tops, etc.) can help in managing glare.

Some additional hints:

◆ Keep corrective lenses clean and handy

◆ Use magnification tools

◆ Use direct lighting

◆ Use enlarged reading materials

◆ Use large black markers on light backgrounds for written instructions

◆ Keep surroundings predictable and relatively free of visual clutter

◆ Respect the routine of the care receiver, and provide a stable routine yourself

◆ Identify yourself when you enter the person's space, and announce when you leave

◆ Where possible, face the visually impaired person and speak directly to him or her. Not only does it improve verbal communication, it is a show of respect

Hearing Changes

Hearing difficulty is one of the most common chronic conditions affecting older adults. Technically, hearing loss may begin as early as the mid-20s, but most people

have no noticeable symptoms until much later. Approximately one-third of Americans older than 60, and as many as half of those older than 85, have significant hearing loss.

Hearing loss can come in many forms and has numerous causes. The National Institutes of Health list two general categories of hearing loss—sensorineural and conductive.

Sensorineural hearing loss is the result of damage to the inner ear or the auditory nerve. This type of loss is permanent.

Conductive hearing loss is caused by the inability of sound waves to reach the cochlea, a small bone located deep in the inner ear. The causes are many, including wax build-up, excessive fluid, eardrum damage, etc. Many times these conditions can be treated and improved.

Presbycusis, one form of hearing loss commonly associated with increasing age, can result from changes to any or all parts of the ear. It comes on gradually, generally affecting those age 50 or older. Common symptoms include a decreased ability to hear certain sound frequencies, especially those at the higher end of the frequency range, difficulty hearing low intensity ("soft") noises, an increased intolerance for loud sound, and difficulty hearing when there is background sound. Causes can include aging, loud noises, genetics, circulation problems, head injury, infection or medications.

Hearing loss indicators

The National Institute on Deafness and Other Communication Disorders recommends a hearing exam for anyone experiencing more than a couple of the following issues:

◆ Difficulty hearing on the phone

◆ Difficulty hearing with background noise

◆ Difficulty following conversations when more than one person is talking

◆ Difficulty understanding the speech of women or children

◆ Regularly misunderstanding or responding inappropriately

◆ Regularly asking others to repeat themselves

◆ Experiencing others' speech as mumbling

◆ Receiving complaints about the high volume of TV, radio, or phone

◆ Straining to hear or understand a conversation

◆ Hearing ringing, roaring, or sounds that seem too loud

While hearing loss is prevalent in our society and particularly so in the older community, not all hearing loss is normal, unpreventable or untreatable. Seek medical attention as soon as possible.

Hearing loss impact

Helen Keller made this distinction between blindness and deafness: blindness separates man from things, while deafness separates man from man. Few of us are more qualified than her to speak on this topic, yet many people say that what they fear most is losing their sight. Whatever one's opinion, no one doubts that loss of hearing has a profound impact:

◆ Safety (public and private) may be compromised

◆ Pleasurable activities, such as music, travel, or conversation, may lose their appeal

◆ One may receive insensitive treatment in social exchanges

◆ Withdrawal and social isolation may result as a way of protecting one's energy and self-esteem

◆ Hearing-impaired people must constantly work to find the energy to interact in an environment created for, and often dependent on, sound

Hearing assistance: what to do

People with hearing impairment or loss should try to surround themselves with others who are willing to understand, people with whom they can share their experiences. As a caregiver for a hearing-impaired person, you can bolster your care receiver's confidence and self-esteem, reduce the everyday stresses accompanying hearing loss and help recharge emotional batteries when necessary. Tips include:

◆ Face the person, making eye contact

◆ Speak clearly and slightly louder, but do not shout

◆ Limit other noises

◆ Be prepared to repeat, using simpler phrases

◆ Avoid chewing, smoking, or covering your mouth when speaking

◆ Use expressions and gestures to clue the person

◆ Determine if the person has one ear that hears better than the other, and speak to that side

◆ Ask family, friends, and health professionals about communication techniques to use or avoid

◆ Ask the listener if any further help is needed

◆ Include the hearing-impaired person in conversations about them

◆ In public settings, choose locations away from crowded or noisy areas

◆ Be patient, positive, and stay relaxed

Tactile Changes

With aging comes a reduction in touch sensitivity, so higher thresholds for touch sensitivity are needed. This is especially true in the fingertips, palms, and lower extremities. The ability to distinguish touches ("Am I touching one, two or three needles?") is lessened, particularly in the fingertips. Pain sensitivity also is less for external stimuli, and there is a lessening of ability to distinguish levels of perceived pain, such as discerning the difference between a cool object and a very cold object). Vibrations are also more difficult for older people to detect.

With age the skin becomes thinner, dryer, less elastic, less supple and less taut, and overall more vulnerable. Damage to the skin that occurs after many years, decreased blood flow to the touch receptors, the brain, or spinal cord, or nutritional deficiencies contribute to these changes. Diseases such as Parkinson's disease, diabetes, and conditions brought on by strokes, arthritis, or swelling can exaggerate these tactile losses.

Impact of tactile changes

When compared to vision and hearing loss, tactile changes may appear benign. Yet changes in the ability to feel one's way in the world are not without an impact. Reduced tactile sensitivity places an individual at an increased risk of sustaining serious injuries, pressure sores, skin ulcers, heat stroke, burns and hypothermia. A loss of sensitivity may result in not knowing how tightly to grasp something or someone, cause one to over-react or under-react to pain or not be able to effectively manipulate tools. People with diabetes can lose limbs because they do not realize they have hurt themselves until the wound is out of control. Alzheimer's sufferers sometimes cannot process pain as they would normally, resulting in life-threatening situations. Persons who are bedridden or spend large amounts of time sitting are at considerable risk of developing pressure sores. This can be made even more pronounced by decreased tactile awareness. In short, tactile decline is significant for many older persons, and can be a threat to their safety, social and emotional well-being.

Tactile assistance: what to do

Some useful tips to prevent or minimize touch-related problems:

◆ Be aware that skin thins with aging. Thin skin bruises and tears more easily, and may take longer to heal.

◆ Pay careful attention to wound prevention and care.

◆ Avoid exposure to extremes of hot or cold.

◆ Always wear shoes or slippers to protect less-sensitive feet.

◆ Test water with your wrist before using it for an older person.

◆ Blot rather than rub the skin when drying.

◆ Use moisturizers to help protect older skin.

◆ Limit the maximum water temperature in your house

◆ Dress for the temperature. Do not wait until you become overheated or chilled.

◆ Inspect skin, especially on the feet, regularly.

TASTE AND SMELL CHANGES

Taste and smell are separate and distinct, but they often work together. Sometimes, a problem with one may be mistaken as a problem with the other. Taste and smell can give pleasurable sensations or warn a person of danger. They play an important role in the acceptance and enjoyment of food. And though they are the only two senses whose cells are replaced regularly throughout life, their sensitivity decreases with age just like the other senses.

Taste suffers the least decline of any of the senses, but in general older people need a higher concentration of sweets to taste sweetness, a higher concentration of salt to taste saltiness and a lower concentration of sour to taste sourness.

The reasons for these changes are not fully understood, and they may or may not be caused by advancing age alone. Possible explanations for this decline include:

◆ Loss of taste buds over time

◆ Reduced production of saliva that sometimes accompanies advanced age

◆ Poor oral hygiene and resulting tooth decay or mouth sores

◆ Certain drugs and medical treatments (such as chemotherapy or radiation)

◆ Poor nutrition

Taste contributes to our ability to enjoy food. Any problems with taste can have a major impact on the lives of those individuals affected. When taste is impaired, we may eat poorly and socialize less. Loss of taste can lead to a loss of appetite, resulting in weight loss, reduced immunity, malnutrition, and worse. It can also result in eating too much of the wrong thing, in an attempt to recapture missing tastes (e.g., salt). Taste impairment may also make it more difficult to figure out if food is suitable to eat.

The olfactory sense—smell—begins a significant decline by age 60. By age 80 or so, smell sensitivity has likely been reduced by about half compared to one's youth. In addition to age, many things can affect smell, including diseases of the nose, nasal passageways or sinuses; neurological diseases; head injuries; allergies; and exposure to airborne toxic chemicals (cigarette smoke is the most common). Medications, medical treatments or complications of sinusitis can also affect smell sensitivity.

As with taste, the loss of smell can have a pronounced affect on our enjoyment of the world around us. The scents of food cooking or flowers in the garden are, for many, examples of the essence of a life worth living. But there are other aspects to the loss of smell. The sense of smell can serve as a warning signal, alerting us to smoke from a fire, the odor of a natural gas leak or spoiled food. Cooking accidents, eating or drinking spoiled foods or toxic substances and failing to detect gas leaks or fires all increase when smell is impaired. Loss of smell can also be an early indication of a more serious disease or condition such as Multiple Sclerosis or a brain tumor.

Those with a loss of smell should take extra precautions to ensure their safety and health. Be extra careful with food, making sure it is not spoiled. Ask someone to help in making an assessment, or throw it out if you are not certain. Install smoke alarms and gas detectors, and change the batteries on a regular basis. If you or the care receiver has a sudden change in the ability to smell, make an appointment with your physician.

RESOURCES

AllRefer Health, http://health.allrefer.com

American Tinnitus Association
P.O. Box 5
Portland, OR 97207-0005
800-634-8978 or 503-248-9985
http://www.ata.org

League for the Hard of Hearing
50 Broadway, 6th Floor
New York, NY 10004
917-305-7700; 917-305-7999 (TTY);
http://www.lhh.org

Lighthouse International
111 East 59th Street
New York, NY 10022-1202
212-821-9200; 800-829-0500;
212-821-9713 (TTY)
http://www.lighthouse.org

National Eye Institute
National Institutes of Health
2020 Vision Place
Bethesda, MD 20892-3655
301-496-5248
http://www.nei.nih.gov

Senior Health
National Institute on Aging
U.S. National Library of Medicine
National Institutes of Health
http://nihseniorhealth.gov

National Institute on Aging
National Institutes of Health
P.O. Box 8057
Gaithersburg, MD 20898-8057
800-222-2225; 800-222-4224 (TTY)
http://www.nia.nih.gov

National Institute on Deafness and Other Communication Disorders
National Institutes of Health
1 Communication Avenue
Bethesda, MD 20892-3456
800-241-1044; 800-241-1055 (TTY)
http://www.nidcd.nih.gov

Self Help for Hard of Hearing People
7910 Woodmont Avenue, Suite 1200
Bethesda, MD 20814
301-657-2248; 301-657-2249 (TTY)
http://www.shhh.org

CHAPTER EIGHTEEN

Caring for Memory-Impaired Elders

Caring for a memory-impaired family member or friend who has irreversible progressive dementia —such as Alzheimer's disease or a related disorder—can be particularly stressful. If a care receiver has dementia and also presents behavioral challenges, research shows that caregiver stress will be even higher than if the care receiver only has physical disabilities. Over time the person's language, reasoning ability, memory, and social behavior will decline and the person will require increasing assistance and supervision.

A recent report issued by the Federal Interagency Forum on Aging-Related Statistics (www.agingstats.gov) states that 36 percent of people 85 or older have moderate or severe memory impairment. That group is also the fastest-growing segment of the population in the U.S.

Alzheimer's disease is the most common form of dementia, but there are many other causes. Other irreversible dementias include strokes or multi-infarct dementia, Parkinson's disease, Huntington's disease, HIV-associated dementia, Pick's disease, Lewy body disease, and supranuclear palsy. Although each of these conditions has its unique features and progression, caregivers share many common issues and coping strategies.

There are many conditions that mimic serious disorders but are reversible through treatment. These conditions are often called "pseudo dementias," and are usually treatable. Some reversible conditions with symptoms that include dementia are:

- Reactions to medications
- Depression
- Stressful major life events such as divorce, death or retirement
- Electrolyte imbalances
- Nutritional deficiencies
- Infections
- Hydrocephalus
- Brain tumors

A dementia diagnosis requires a complete medical and neuro-psychological evaluation and complete patient history. Much of the diagnostic procedure is a process of elimination to rule out the many treatable causes of dementia. In most cases, a definitive diagnosis is not possible until after an autopsy. There are a variety of tests that can be an important part of the diagnostic process, such as CAT (computer assisted tomography) scans, MRI (magnetic resonance imaging) or PET (positron emission tomography) scans.

CARE AND MANAGEMENT

The amount of care, supervision, and help a memory-impaired person needs will depend upon the specific disease, e.g. Alzheimer's, Parkinson's, vascular dementia, AIDS, Pick's disease, Huntington's disease. Treatment strategies need to be individualized based on the specific diagnosis.

The following guidelines will help improve the quality of life for both the caregiver and person with dementia.

Establish a proper diagnosis—The first part of any treatment is early evaluation and correct diagnosis. An error in this initial step can have serious consequences for the affected person and the person's family.

Learn as much as you can—An educated caregiver is the best resource for the person affected by dementia. Being better prepared to manage behavior may delay the need for nursing home placement.

Minimize risks—Monitor safety issues (such as the person's ability to drive and cook) and hazards that increase risk for injury. Some states require physicians to report individuals whose ability to drive is impaired. The intent is to ensure the safety of all who are on the road. Remove firearms from the home. If the person with dementia is hospitalized, be on guard for the use of restraints, because they can increase the possibility of injury.

Correct sensory deficits—Evaluate and correct hearing and visual impairment. This can reduce social isolation, reduce depression, and lessen the effect on cognitive dysfunction.

Be prepared for medical appointments—Observe and report changes in the care receiver's sleep patterns, personality, memory, duties and tasks, ability to follow conversation, ambulation patterns, behavior in social situations, changes or additions to medications, as well as how the person with dementia reacts to and recognizes family and friends.

Outline the goals of care—Complete advance care plans at an early stage in the course of the disease, when the person still has capacity to make health care decisions. Handling legal and financial decisions, balancing a checkbook, dealing with insurance, paying bills may become frustrating and overwhelming for the person. Prior to this point, identify a surrogate—someone who could help make health care decisions in the event that the affected person is unable to do so. During this time, preferences about cardiopulmonary resuscitation (CPR) should be documented.

Monitor changes in behavior—Conditions such as agitation, purposeless motor hyperactivity or restlessness may be behavioral expressions of physical discomfort, fecal impaction, pain, medical illness, change in environment, or sensory deprivation. If you suspect any of these, an urgent evaluation is in order.

Avoid medications that can hinder cognition or level of alertness.

Utilize community resources—This includes adult day care centers, home health aides, respite programs and participating in caregiver support groups.

Focus on strengths rather than deficits. Encourage recognition rather than recall. Use reminiscence. Reassure and praise.

COMMUNICATING WITH A PERSON WITH DEMENTIA

Even if you have excellent communication skills, you are likely to be very challenged when communicating with a person with dementia. However, finding new approaches to communication is worth the time and effort. Your stress level as a caregiver can be significantly lower if you feel confident in your ability to communicate.

When communicating with a person who has dementia it's important to remember:

◆ Because of the disease's impact on the brain, learning and remembering new information is difficult.

◆ As the disease progresses, the person may lose short-term memory.

◆ A person with dementia can feel a full range of positive and negative emotions. Sometimes the condition causes mood swings and even changes in personality.

Tips for Effective Communication
Be respectful, positive and friendly

◆ Treat the person like an adult.

◆ Remember that the person with dementia is likely to pick up on your emotional "vibes" more than the words you are using.

◆ Eliminate noise and activities that might confuse or distract.

◆ Ensure that the person is physically comfortable.

◆ Call the person by name and refer to yourself by name when first entering the room.

◆ Face the person directly as you talk.

◆ Keep instructions, explanations, and responses brief.

◆ Use simple words and short sentences.

◆ Keep an even, neutral tone to your voice.

◆ Phrase questions in a way that can be answered with a simple yes or no.

◆ Ask preferences by giving choices between things that can be seen. For example: Would you like this pudding or that piece of cake?

◆ Choose what is really worth the effort and what you can just ignore or drop.

◆ Avoid correcting or arguing.

◆ When the person does not know who you are, calmly refer to yourself by name and identify your relationship through the course of your conversation.

◆ Use distraction if the person keeps repeating the same question, or keeps insisting that something is different than how it really is.

◆ Learn about the person's past, and his or her former interests, so you can talk about experiences he or she remembers accurately.

◆ Listen patiently. Give the person time to form a response. Gently provide a word if he or she gets stuck.

◆ Try to sense the feeling behind the words rather than just focusing on the words.

◆ Remember to be playful.

Use your sense of humor as an effective communication tool. Joke respectfully, do silly things, move joyfully, dance or make music together. The two of you might enjoy looking at funny pictures or watching funny movies. Remember that sometimes laughter is indeed the best medicine.

HANDLING CHALLENGING BEHAVIORS

Alzheimer's disease and related dementias often create changes in personality and behavior. This section highlights some of the most common behavioral changes that can trouble caregivers and lead to frustration between the caregiver and the person with dementia. Each topic includes some practical tips on how to respond to the situation to lessen stress and help everyone cope.

Agitation or Anxiety

◆ Check with a physician to rule out physical problems and side effects of current medications.

◆ Simplify the environment—reduce noise; avoid overstimulation from too many people, activities, or clutter.

◆ Maintain a daily routine.

◆ Validate feelings of frustration and anger over loss of independence and control.

◆ Distract and redirect with activities of interest to the person.

◆ Use a calm voice. Play soft music, read poetry, take a walk, massage or touch gently.

◆ If you feel physically threatened, stay out of reach and call for help from family, neighbors, friends, or police as a last resort.

Bathing

◆ Consider maintaining the pre-dementia bathing routine.

◆ Prepare the environment so it is comfortable, safe, and secure.

◆ If bathing in a tub or shower is extremely difficult, try a "towel bath"—no-rinse soap and a bag of warm water with warm towels and washcloths massaged over the body.

◆ When a person with dementia needs assistance bathing, this particular loss of independence can be very difficult and make the person feel extremely vulnerable. If the person refuses bathing assistance and personal care becomes a problem, consult your health care provider. There may be medication that can help reduce resistance.

Eating and Nutrition

◆ Reduce noise and distractions in the room during meals. Create a routine, so the care receiver is eating around the same time everyday. Sometimes a person with memory loss will eat better if offered smaller but more frequent meals.

◆ Play relaxing background music.

◆ To prevent chewing and swallowing problems, avoid sticky foods such as peanut butter, bread, and caramel. Serve chopped foods, offering one bite at a time if necessary.

◆ If loss of appetite becomes a problem, request an evaluation to identify possible reasons, such as depression or side effects from medication.

◆ Provide verbal cues to guide the person through the meal.

◆ Eat with the person at mealtimes. Remember that you are not only a social companion but also a model of how to behave during meals.

◆ Don't rush at mealtimes.

Incontinence

◆ To prevent accidents, establish a routine for using the toilet. Provide step-by-step verbal cues as needed.

◆ Establish a schedule for having the person take in fluids. Avoid drinks that have a diuretic effect, e.g. coffee, tea, beer or caffeinated soft drinks.

◆ Limit fluid intake prior to bedtime.

◆ Identify the bathroom door with visual cues such as signs with pictures.

◆ Use incontinence products in combination with easy to remove clothing. Limit buttons and zippers; use Velcro or elastic waistbands.

Repetitive Speech or Actions

◆ Use an activity or snack to distract or redirect.

◆ Do not remind the person that he or she just asked the question. Sometimes ignoring repetitive behavior will help to reduce its frequency.

◆ Consider whether the care receiver is expressing a physical need. For example, tugging at pants may indicate a need to go to the bathroom, asking what's for lunch means he or she is hungry, etc.

Paranoia

◆ Avoid arguing or disagreeing.

◆ Help the person look for objects that are "taken" and keep some of the objects in close reach. For example if the person believes that someone has taken his or her money, keep the money in a pocketbook or wallet and look at it together for reassurance.

◆ Respond to the feelings with reassurance and touch (if they are responsive to touch).

◆ Have vision and hearing checked. Poor vision or hearing can lead to misinterpretation of the environment.

◆ Seek a medical evaluation to determine whether there are medications that can be helpful in treating psychotic and delusional behaviors.

Sleep Difficulties or Sundowning

◆ Limit caffeine, sugar and alcohol intake, particularly late in the day.

◆ Encourage a high level of activity and physical exercise during the day. Plan quiet activities for late afternoon and evening. This is a good time for listening to soothing music, taking a walk outside, or whatever is relaxing and helps the person wind down.

◆ Try to avoid having the person nap during the day (although *you* may need one!). If the person is worn out in the early evening, a nap in the early afternoon may help.

◆ Establish relaxing bedtime rituals—a certain time, glass of milk, light snack, music, reading.

◆ If agitation happens in late afternoon or early evening—often referred to as "sundowning"—try closing curtains to shut out the darkness, and turn on bright lights. Distract with activities, but limit the number of visitors during this difficult time.

◆ If the care receiver's behavior is preventing you from getting adequate sleep, seek help. Consider asking a relative or friend, or hiring help so that you can get a good night's sleep.

◆ Talk with your health care provider about medications that might help the person sleep.

Wandering

Try to understand the care receiver's need to wander, and then address those issues.

◆ Is the person restless and needing more regular physical activity?

◆ Is the person bored, looking for ways to feel useful, and needing to become involved in meaningful activities?

◆ Is the person sleeping much of the day and then wandering at night?

◆ Are physical needs such as thirst, hunger, or bathroom need causing the person to wander?

◆ Are visual cues—such as a coat, purse or glasses—triggering exit-seeking behaviors?

◆ Create a safe place so the person can wander without worry.

◆ Consider installing locks that require a key, plastic door knob covers, or a home security system.

◆ Use visual cues like a stop sign or barrier blocking a door.

◆ Have the individual wear an identification bracelet and clothes that are labeled.

◆ Register with the Alzheimer's Association's Safe Return program.

RESPONDING TO BEHAVIORAL CHALLENGES

Chapter 7 offers a seven-step model for making caregiving decisions (see page 141):

1) Identify the problem
2) Gather information
3) Generate options
4) Evaluate options
5) Create a plan
6) Act
7) Reassess

This model can be very useful when addressing behavioral challenges related to dementia.

When using this decision-making model it is crucial to attempt to understand why the behaviors are occurring and identify some of the triggers that you may be able to change. Being as objective as possible when gathering information will help you to better understand the issues. Using some of the tips provided under each of the behavioral topics in that chapter will help you throughout the problem-solving process. Learning as much as you can from other caregivers, friends, family, health care providers, and from books and organizations will help you to generate and evaluate options. The more information you gather, the more likely it is that you will develop the best plan possible for you and your care receiver.

Even the most successful caregiving plan will need to be reassessed when there are changes in the caregiver and care receiver's needs. Using the seven-step model for making decisions will give you a valuable process to use each time you need to readdress the ever-changing challenges of caring for someone with dementia.

It is also important to recognize that a time may come when the personal care and safety needs of the impaired person exceed the resources and abilities of the family caregiver. Exploring care facility placement may be the next logical step. Chapter 15 will be a helpful resource if you are facing this difficult decision.

RESOURCES

Alzheimer's Association, www.alz.org, 800-272-3900 or 312-335-8700.

Alzheimer's Disease Education and Referral Center (ADEAR)
800-272-3900 or 301-494-3311
www.alzheimers.org
E-mail: adear@alzheimers.org

Doka, Kenneth J., ed. *Alzheimer's Disease: Living with Grief*. Washington, DC: Hospice Foundation of America, 2004. www.hospicefoundation.org

Kuhn, Daniel, *Alzheimer's Early Stages: The First Steps in Caring and Treatment*. Alameda, CA: Hunter House Publishers, 1999. P.O. Box 2914, Alameda, CA 94501-0914, 800-266-5592.

Barrick, Ann L. et. al. *Bathing without a Battle*. Springer Publishing, 2002. 877-687-7476.

Eldercare Locator, 800-677-1116, is a free service that will put you in touch with a local area agency on aging or other local support resources, including low-cost legal services.

Family Caregiver Alliance National Center on Caregiving offers help in locating information and support services, research and advocacy.
800-445-8106 or 415-434-3388
180 Montgomery Street, Suite 1100
San Francisco, CA 94104.
www.caregiver.org
E-mail: info@caregiver.org

Robinson, A. et al. *Understanding Difficult Behaviors: Some Practical Suggestions for Coping with Alzheimer's Disease and Related Illnesses*. Ypsilanti, MI: Eastern Michigan University, 1989.
734-487-2335.

CHAPTER NINETEEN

Driving Issues

Driving safely is a major issue for many older people and those with chronic conditions. It is also a very important concern for the driver's caregiver.

How do you communicate your concerns with the impaired driver? Addressing a hazardous driving situation begins with accepting the fact that the life of the care receiver — and the lives of others— may be in peril when he or she is behind the wheel. Sharing your concerns with the driver will be difficult, but it is crucial.

Driving skills generally begin to diminish at about age 55, but age is not the only cause for this decline. Age or medical conditions by themselves are not valid reasons to question

driving skills, but age-related impairments can affect a driver's competency. Age-related changes or health problems such as stroke, Multiple Sclerosis (MS), Parkinson's disease, poor hearing, failing eyesight, physical flexibility limitations, or slower reaction time also impact driving skills.

Signs of unsafe driving include:

◆ Driving well below the speed limit

◆ Disobeying traffic signals

◆ Getting lost while driving on routine local errands

◆ Slow reaction time to events while driving

◆ Inattention to other vehicles, pedestrians, or bicyclists

Most drivers don't want to stop driving and thereby lose their independence and their connection to friends and social activities.

Occasional evaluation of the impaired driver's driving abilities will be beneficial. However, the driver may become angry and resentful when his or her driving skills are questioned.

You may wish to have a family meeting with the driver to state your concerns. Be prepared with information on alternative modes of transportation so the driver understands the options for getting around.

Your state or local motor vehicles office may be willing to write a letter to the driver, stating that he or she could be breaking the law by continuing to drive. You may want to ask the driver's physician to discuss with the driver the risks of continuing to drive. Physicians may be required by law to report possible unsafe drivers to the state or local motor vehicles office.

Don't wait for an accident to happen!

When discussing driving concerns:

◆ Include the driver in the discussion.

◆ Discuss driving concerns early and often.

◆ Keep a written record of observations of unsafe driving. Share these concerns with the driver, other family members, or healthcare professionals.

◆ Begin discussions early with a person who has been diagnosed with dementia. Determine his or her wishes regarding driving as cognitive skills decline.

◆ Ask the driver to sign the "Agreement with My Family about Driving," available at www.thehartford.com/alzheimers.

TRANSPORTATION OPTIONS

If the impaired driver does stop driving, it will require an adjustment because of the loss of independence. There may be a feeling of loss of connection with friends and community. The person may fear becoming a burden to others, and become hesitant to ask for assistance. There will be an extra burden on the caregiver, who may become responsible for transportation. There may also be a strain on the relationship between the impaired driver and the person who started the discussion about the driving situation.

In urban areas, there are often services available to help non-drivers maintain community connections and ease feelings of isolation. Contact your local area agency on aging to get information on transportation options, meals-on-wheels agencies, in-home companions, etc.

RESOURCES

AARP has information concerning driver safety on their Web site at www.aarp.org/families/driver_safety

AARP and The Hartford Insurance Company have prepared a booklet "We need to talk…Family conversations with older drivers" (Booklet # 105924). It has tips on conversations about driver safety concerns with an impaired driver. Worksheets on alternate transportation modes or determining transportation costs are included. www.thehartford.com/ talkwitholderdrivers

The American Medical Association has handouts available for caregivers.
— "Am I a Safe Driver?" a questionnaire for older drivers to complete
— "Successful Aging Tips"
— "Tips for Safe Driving"
— "How to Help the Older Driver"
— "Getting By Without Driving"
These are located in the Physician's Guide to Assessing and Counseling Older Drivers at www.ama-assn.org/ama/pub/ category/10791.html

Alzheimer's Association, www.alz.org
— Driving and Dementia (fact sheet)
—About Driving (fact sheet)

National Highway Traffic Safety Administration
— "Driving Safely While Aging Gracefully"
www.nhtsa.dot.gov, select "Traffic Safety" tab, then "Older Drivers"

New York State Office for the Aging Older Driver Family Assistance Project.
— "When You Are Concerned" A handbook for families, friends and caregivers worried about the safety of an aging driver.
http://aging.state.ny.us/caring/concerned/ contents.htm

Bowman, Sally, and Vicki L. Schmall. "Older Drivers: Deciding When to Give up the Car Keys" Oregon Gerontological Association.
www.oregongero.org/resource_mtrls/ older_drivers.htm

The Hartford Fire Insurance Company— "At the Crossroads: A Guide to Alzheimer's Disease, Dementia & Driving" www.thehartford.com/alzheimers

CHAPTER TWENTY

Your Mental Health

Good self-care includes caring for your mental health as well as caring for your physical health. Often caregivers do not mention mental health concerns to their physicians, other health care providers, or family members or friends. They may not know that the symptoms they are noticing are signs of emotional stress or a potentially serious psychological condition. Many caregivers believe that if they talk about their emotional concerns that others will minimize their feelings or behavior. Or perhaps they worry that others will respond judgmentally with labels such as "weak," "complaining," "nervous" or "feeling sorry

Mental Health Services

The information in this chapter is for non-emergency situations. If you or someone you are caring for is in crisis (for example, is psychotic, suicidal, behaving strangely after taking a medicine, or having psychiatric symptoms related to a medical condition) call your doctor or 911, or get to the nearest emergency room as quickly as possible. Mental health crisis intervention requires immediate evaluation and treatment.

for yourself." It is important for caregivers to have accurate information about common emotional responses to caregiving and care receiving. It is also important to understand how to navigate the mental health system so that services can be found when needed.

In years past, it was easier to access public and private mental health services. Community mental health clinics and a strong network of private practitioners were available to provide services to people dealing with emotional stress and discomfort, mental illness, or addictions when these conditions were creating problems. Large cuts in federal and state budgets and changes in private insurance coverage have reduced or eliminated many of the mental health programs previously available. In spite of this, it is still possible to find good mental health services in your community.

GETTING STARTED

It often takes some sleuthing to find the right mental health services in your geographic area. Some suggestions:

- Ask your physician or another health care provider

- Ask friends or family members whose opinion you respect

- Contact your insurance company's Behavioral Health or Mental Health Referral Service.

- Contact your local hospital's Community Resource Office, Department of Social Work, Spiritual Services Department, or Outpatient Department of Psychiatry for resources.

- Look in the phone directory or on-line under headings such as: Psychiatrists (M.D.); Psychologists (Ph.D., Psy.D. or Ed.D.); Clinical Social Workers (LCSW); or Counselors (LPC).

- Contact professional organizations in your state, such as the Psychological Association, the Association of Social Workers, Medical Association or the State Board of Behavioral Science for local providers.

You may have to make several calls before you find someone who provides the services you are looking for, at a cost that you can cover, and at a location and time that works for you.

TYPES OF MENTAL HEALTH PROVIDERS

There are a number of professionals who receive specialized training in mental health, and most states have laws regarding the licensing of these professionals.

Psychiatrist (M.D.)—A medical doctor who has completed medical school followed by at least four additional years of advanced training in psychiatry. Board Certified psychiatrists have taken national examinations to become certified in psychiatry and neurology. Psychiatrists' services include evaluations; medication evaluations, recommendations and management; inpatient services; and outpatient psychotherapy.

Geriatric Psychiatrist (M.D.)—A psychiatrist who specializes in working with adults over 60 years of age.

Geriatrician (M.D.)—A primary care physician or internist who has advanced training in working with older adults. A geriatrician may have expertise in the mental health issues of older patients even if he or she is not trained as a geriatric psychiatrist.

Psychologist (Ph.D., Psy.D. or Ed.D.) — A mental health professional who has completed a doctoral degree, an internship, a year of post-doctoral experience and then passed a licensing exam. Psychologists provide a variety of mental health services, including psychotherapy, evaluation and assessment with written evaluation reports, and psychological testing.

A Licensed Psychologist Associate holds a master's degree in psychology, has post-degree supervised experience, and has passed a licensing exam.

Licensed Clinical Social Worker (LCSW)—A social worker who has specific

training in mental health, has completed a two year master's degree (MSW), has two years of supervised post-degree clinical training, and has passed a state and/or national licensing examination to qualify as an LCSW. LCSWs are trained to provide a variety of mental health services including individual, couples, and family counseling.

Psychiatric Mental Health Nurse Practitioner (PMHNP)—A nurse who has completed a two year master's degree, has two years of post-degree supervised experience in mental health, and has passed a licensing examination. An Advanced Nurse Practitioner has additional special training in psychopharmacology (medication) and can prescribe medication. Psychiatric Nurse Practitioners and Advanced Nurse Practitioners are trained in a variety of mental health therapy techniques and approaches.

Licensed Marriage and Family Therapist (LMFT)—A counselor who has completed a master's degree in marriage and family therapy, has post-degree supervised experience, and has passed an examination to receive a license to provide mental health services. The focus of the training for a MFT is individual, couple, and family issues.

In addition to these categories of mental health providers, there are other qualified professionals who provide counseling services such as pastoral care or physician counseling.

Many factors will affect your choice of a counselor: the type of services you are seeking, the availability of providers in your area, financial considerations, insurance benefit regulations, and personal preference. Participating in a mental health service is a personal experience and the match between you and the person you work with is very important. If the first person you contact does not seem like a good fit for you, contact someone else.

COVERING THE COST OF MENTAL HEALTH SERVICES

Some insurance plans do not require a medical referral for mental health services. Others do. If you are going to attempt to get insurance coverage for your mental health appointments, you will want to determine the rules of the policy before you contact a potential provider. There may be limits on which providers your insurance company will approve, the number of sessions or dollar amount they will cover if they accept your claim, the type of counseling or kind of medication they will cover. It will be worth your time and effort to get this information before you contact a provider for an appointment. Insurance coverage for mental health services varies greatly from policy to policy.

If you are planning to pay for all or part of your mental health services out-of-pocket, clarify with the provider if there is a sliding

fee or low fee rate, and if you can make payments or need to pay in full at the time of your appointment.

Many disease-specific organizations and hospital community education centers offer support groups for caregivers and/or care-receivers. Often there is no charge for participating in these groups.

COMMON REASONS FOR SEEKING MENTAL HEALTH SERVICES

The most common reasons caregivers and care receivers contact mental health professionals include:

Stress—Change and uncertainty are two of the main triggers for stress, so most caregivers and care receivers are going to experience elevated levels of physical and emotional stress at some point. Symptoms of stress include:

◆ Headache

◆ Digestive problems

◆ Muscle strain

◆ High blood pressure

◆ Irritability

◆ Anxiety

◆ Frustration

◆ Discontent

◆ Worry

High stress levels increase the risk for chronic illness, depression, anxiety attacks, or behavioral problems such as anger or overuse of addictive substances or activities. Learning some stress-reduction techniques is important for caregivers and care receivers.

Depression—Everyone has experienced "the blues," or periods of time when they felt down, sad, or pessimistic. When these feelings become pervasive or persistent, it is important to determine if sadness has become depression. Depression can be mild or severe. Estimates claim that nearly 20 million adults in the U.S. are affected by depression. Depression rates are highest among women, older people, people with chronic conditions, and caregivers. Caregiver-related depression is highest among those caring for a person with dementia, or a spousal caregiver whose partner has died.

Depression can be a symptom exhibited by some people with certain medical conditions, including cancer, heart attacks and other cardiac problems, stroke, diabetes, and Parkinson's disease.

Symptoms of depression include:

◆ Feelings of sadness, hopelessness or despair

◆ Loss of joy

◆ No interest in previously pleasurable activities

◆ Frequent crying

◆ Increased irritability or anger

◆ Repetitive thoughts

◆ Persistent pessimism and worry

◆ Increased or decreased appetite

◆ Significant weight loss or gain

◆ Sleep disturbances

◆ Feeling tired in spite of getting adequate sleep

◆ Loss of energy and feeling weighed down

◆ Low self esteem with feelings of worthlessness

◆ Increased negative self-talk

◆ Restlessness or agitation

◆ Ongoing anxiety and worry

◆ Guilt

◆ Difficulty thinking, concentrating or making decisions

◆ Over-use of alcohol, tobacco, tranquilizers or other addictive substances or activities

Depression is treatable, and for most people treatment is successful. Yet many people do not seek help, or wait until the condition is very serious before seeking help. Reasons for this include denial, self-blame and shame; lack of information about the condition; fear of what will happen if the depression is acknowledged; and financial or geographic barriers to treatment.

The results of untreated depression can include loss of physical health, loss of social connections, disrupted family relationships, employment problems, and a general loss of interest in life. Untreated serious depression can result in suicide. The goal in treating depression is to keep the depressive episode "short and shallow"—address the depression as quickly as possible and keep it from becoming severe or chronic. This treatment plan might include talk therapy, learning depression management skills, or medication. Research has shown that a combination of interventions is usually the most effective.

Anxiety—Increased anxiety is a given in caregiving and care receiving. For most people it would be impossible to live with the uncertainty of the future, the issues of dependency, and the fear of death that accompany caregiving and chronic illness without feeling anxious. However, sometimes the normal amount of anxiety escalates into significant, ongoing anxiousness that disrupts daily functioning. This degree of anxiety is experienced as an on-going feeling of dread or apprehension accompanied by one or more of these symptoms:

- Headache
- Rapid heart beat
- Shortness of breath
- Shakiness
- Sweating
- Intense worry
- Tingling or cold hands/feet
- Diarrhea
- Nausea
- Muscle tension, twitching or tics
- Loss of appetite or nervous eating
- Physical hyperactivity or racing thoughts
- Rapid speech
- Poor memory and difficulty making a decision
- Feeling immobilized
- Phobias

Because these symptoms mimic other serious medical conditions, people with high anxiety often fear they are having a medical crisis. For this reason, it is especially important to get an accurate diagnosis so that serious medical conditions are not mistaken for anxiety or vice versa. There are many self management skills that can be learned to handle anxiety. Talk therapy and/or medication may be recommended.

Grief—Both caregivers and care receivers experience grief. It's normal to grieve for such things as:

- The loss of mental or physical abilities
- The loss of health
- The loss of relationships
- The loss of hopes and dreams
- The loss of financial security
- The loss of a sense of self
- The loss of self-esteem
- The loss of independence

Hospice, grief, and faith-based counseling and support groups are often helpful for people experiencing normal grief. When grief does not begin to lessen over time, or turns into depression or anxiety, a mental health evaluation is recommended.

Anger—Anger is a familiar emotion for caregivers and care receivers. Anger is a natural response to sadness, fear, or feeling out of control, and caregiving is fraught with these emotions. In addition, dealing with the situation of being dependent on others, or having someone else dependent on you, can stir strong feelings of anger. If someone has an addiction or an anger control problem before the caregiver-care receiver relationship develops, anger management may be a major issue. Many chronic conditions include personality changes, and a person who has never had a problem with anger may suddenly become chronically angry or have frequent anger outbursts. Working with a counselor to learn anger management techniques and healthy ways to respond to another's anger can be helpful.

Family issues, conflict, and tension—Relationships between family caregivers, care receivers and other family members exist long before the caregiving situation develops. Prior to the caregiving period, those involved all have individual and relationship issues and dynamics. Marital problems, parenting difficulties, negative personality traits, poor problem-solving or communication skills, family relationship problems, and anger control problems are just some of the "pre-existing conditions" that have the potential to create additional stress and strain in the caregiving/

care-receiving environment. Individual, couple, and family counseling are all forums in which family conflict issues can be addressed in a safe and positive way.

Addictions and abuse—A caregiver or care receiver may have a history of abuse or addictions long before caregiving begins. It's also possible for abuse and addiction problems to develop as a result of the stress of caregiving, or as a symptom of depression or another physical problem. When addictions or abuse are problems for the caregiver, care receiver, or other family members or friends on the caregiving team, counseling is vitally important as part of the caregiving plan and should be considered a high priority, not just a possible option.

Making a plan to pay attention to your own and your care receiver's mental health is an excellent self-care tool.

Ask yourself the following questions:

◆ Do I or my care receiver have any of the mental health issues mentioned in this chapter?

◆ Am I experiencing difficulties with my marriage, job, friends, or parenting that leave me stressed, depressed, anxious or angry? Would it help to talk this over with someone and to learn skills to deal with things more effectively?

◆ Did I or my care receiver have an emotional or psychiatric condition before the current chronic condition and caregiving situation developed? Is this pre-existing condition causing difficulties in the caregiving situation?

◆ Has my personality or temperament, or that of the care receiver, changed significantly during this time of chronic illness and caregiving?

◆ Do certain medications seem to be affecting my emotions or my care receiver's emotions?

◆ Are other people who know us well commenting about changes in personality, behavior, or mood that seem to affect our ability to carry out our daily routines?

◆ Am I feeling emotionally different than before? Do I worry that "something is mentally wrong with me?." Do I sometimes feel like I can't go on like this much longer? Have I wondered if I or my care receiver could benefit from some mental health evaluation or counseling?"

If the answer to any of these questions is "yes," make an action plan to take the first step. Decide who you want to talk to about a plan to take care of your emotional health.

RESOURCES

Cade, Eleanor. *Taking Care of Parents Who Didn't Take Care of You.* Hazelden Press, 2002.

McKay, Matthew, and Peter Rogers. *The Anger Control Workbook.* Oakland, California: New Harbinger Publications, 2000.

McKay, Matthew, et. al. *When Anger Hurts.* Oakland, California: New Harbinger Publications, 2003.

Copeland, Mary Ellen, and Matthew McKay. *The Depression Workbook: A Guide for Living with Depression and Manic Depression.* Oakland, California: New Harbinger Publications, 1992.

Bourne, Edmund J. *The Anxiety and Phobia Workbook,* Oakland, California: New Harbinger Publications, 2005

National Alliance for the Mentally Ill— www.nami.org

CHAPTER TWENTY-ONE

Loss, Grief, and End-of-Life Issues

Caregiving and experiencing loss go hand-in-hand; many losses occur along the way for both caregivers and care receivers. These can include loss of time, money, body image, dreams, autonomy, friends, personhood and family roles. The ultimate loss is the death of the care receiver. But sometimes the caregiver dies before the person they have cared for. The caregiving journey may end at death, but the journey through grief continues.

WHAT IS GRIEF?

Grief comes with every loss. Grief is a normal response to loss, and has been described as "the price one pays for the ability to love." It can manifest itself in a number of ways. Physically, individuals may experience fatigue, insomnia, aches and pains. Emotionally, there can be guilt, anger, anxiety, sadness, and jealousy, just to name a few. Troubling dreams or visions, forgetfulness, and irrational behavior can occur. Many of these symptoms can be present at one time, giving the grieving person the feeling of being on a roller coaster that is out of control.

The amount, length and depth of grief depends on how much value, interest, commitment and love the grieving person had for whatever or whoever was lost.

Each person grieves in their own unique way. Underlying these differences in grieving are similarities that need attention to help reduce additional distress in the care receiver and to prevent increased fatigue and burnout in the caregiver.

DEALING WITH GRIEF

There are a variety of ways to address grief and the grieving process in the caregiving journey. The amount and type of support needed will vary during different times of the caregiving experience. It is very helpful for the caregiver and the care receiver to be able to acknowledge the losses they are experiencing. Once the losses are identified, expressions of grief can be validated as normal, and the emotional and physical reactions can be understood as normal as well.

Venting feelings and emotions can help to work through the grieving process. As the grief work continues, there are coping strategies helpful to grievers, such as:

- ◆ Sharing painful thoughts

- ◆ Identifying destructive coping strategies like substance abuse and working to eliminate them.

- ◆ Recognizing those who are truly supportive, and taking advantage of the help they offer. This would include support groups.

- ◆ Planning realistically for the future.

- ◆ Exploring new avenues for healing and growth – things not done before, such as hobbies, travel, social clubs, sports, etc.

- ◆ Examining spiritual issues and struggles that might have been brought on by the caregiving experience, and reuniting with beliefs, rituals and faith communities

END-OF-LIFE PLANNING

End-of-life planning is important. Experts say that by age 50 each of us should have a will and healthcare directive in place. If such planning has been done, it is important to review those plans when serious illness strikes. Planning not only helps the caregiver and family, it can give the care receiver who helps with the planning a sense of control and closure in the final phase of life.

Your planning should include consideration of advance directives, which are documents with medical care instructions for use especially in instances when individuals can no longer speak on their own behalf.

Advance directives include:

- ◆ Physician Orders for Life-Sustaining Treatment (POLST)—Provides detailed instructions about the end-of-life treatment the signer desires. The POLST is completed by the primary care provider or another authorized medical professional. This form should be prominently displayed; it will assist emergency health care personnel if or when they are needed.

◆ Living Will—Indicates whether medical professionals should use aggressive treatments to prolong life in the event of terminal illness.

◆ Power of Attorney for Healthcare—Designates a person to oversee medical care in the event of incapacity, including but not limited to terminal illness.

◆ Power of Attorney for Finances—Designates a person to share legal authority in financial matters.

◆ Will—A legal statement of a person's wishes concerning the disposal of his or her property and personal possessions after death.

In addition to preparing the above documents, it is important to note the location of records such as:

◆ Guardianship documents

◆ Living trusts

◆ Health care directives

◆ Marriage license

◆ Wills

◆ Divorce decrees

◆ Funeral directions

◆ Others' death certificates

◆ Home, health, and life insurance papers

◆ Armed services records, veterans records

◆ Mortgage papers and property deeds

◆ Income tax records

◆ Bank statements, bank account numbers

◆ Health records

◆ Power of attorney forms

◆ Stock, bonds, and annuities

◆ Birth certificates

◆ Safe deposit box and key

◆ Social Security cards

◆ Naturalization papers

Making funeral plans can be difficult. However, stating one's wishes can be a comfort to the dying person as well as his or her family. Funeral considerations include type and location of burial, cremation and disposition of ashes, type of final service, obituary information, and organ donation.

FINANCIAL INFORMATION

Information about income is crucial. List the sources of income and the amounts received from Social Security, pensions, and other sources. Note the identification number or account number of each source, the frequency of payments, and where the payments are received.

Any outstanding obligations, such as loans or lease agreements, should also be noted.

IMPORTANT PEOPLE

Make a list of names, addresses, and phone numbers of people to contact (relatives, lawyers, accountants, executors, financial planners or advisors, etc.).

HOSPICE CARE

Caregiving in the final stages of life can be frightening and stressful. Hospice care can provide welcome relief for caregivers, care receivers, and their families.

> What is hospice? Considered to be the model for quality compassionate care for people facing a life-limiting illness or injury, hospice and palliative care involve a team-oriented approach to medical care, pain management and emotional and spiritual support expressly tailored to the patient's loved ones as well. Hospice believes that each of us has the right to die with dignity and without pain, and that our loved ones can receive the support necessary to allow us to do so. The focus is on caring, not curing, and in most cases care is provided in your own home. Hospice can be provided in freestanding hospice facilities, hospitals, and nursing homes or other long-term care facilities. Hospice is available to people of any age, religion or race.
>
> —adapted from National Hospice and Palliative Care Organization

GRIEF THERAPY— REVIEW, CEREMONIES AND RITUALS
Review

Grief that has occurred throughout the caregiving experience, with its many facets and manifestations, continues after death. This is especially true for the caregivers and close loved ones. Even though prolonged illness allows survivors to ease into the severity of the disease, and allows for finishing business and saying goodbyes, it can still be difficult.

Prolonged illness can complicate the grieving process. The caregiver may have guilt about medical decisions, or about how long and to what extent the care receiver had to suffer. The caregiver may question whether he or she did something wrong, or whether he or she did not do enough. At the point of death, the caregiver may be exhausted, and things might be said or done that produce guilt. To continue care for the caregiver, it's important to remember that the losses need to be validated.

Kenneth J. Doka, Ph.D., in his book *Caregiving and Loss*, suggests that survivors review their caregiving experiences and the lessons they learned. Journaling may be helpful.

He also suggests that survivors review photographs or videos of the deceased as a way to regain earlier images and dispel the later painful memories.

Ceremonies and Rituals

Many people find rituals and ceremonies valuable for healing and processing grief. Almost all faith communities have spiritual practices designed to comfort, honor, and bring peace to survivors. These practices are as varied as the number of faith communities. Each has its own belief system and values concerning life and death. To the believer, these practices can provide a place of stability and focus during a difficult time.

Other rituals and practices that have been meaningful to grieving persons include:

◆ Journaling

◆ Lighting candles in honor of the deceased

◆ Releasing balloons (check local environmental regulations)

◆ Making a personal history collage

◆ Asking the person who is dying to dictate or record a review of his or her life

◆ Playing music special to those involved

◆ Making memory boxes

◆ At holidays, having each person say something about the deceased

◆ Spreading cremains (ashes) in a favorite place

◆ Visiting the cemetery on special days

◆ Planting a tree, flower, or garden in honor of the deceased

In situations where there is regret, guilt, or shame after the death, it may be helpful to write a letter to the person who has died, stating those feelings. Writing the letter, then burning it and disposing of the ashes in a special cleansing place, may bring some closure to the situation. Some have found it helpful to talk to an empty chair—perhaps the deceased person's special chair—seeking closure by asking for forgiveness.

CONCLUSION

Loss, and thus grief, is a constant companion on the caregiving journey. Acknowledging losses as they occur and validating the feelings that surround them as normal is the first step in healthy grief work. Planning for end-of-life can be extremely helpful to care receivers and caregivers and to their families. These plans prevent confusion, heartache, and legal and financial hassles. Planning ahead gives a sense of control for all concerned.

Grief work is some of the hardest work we do as caring human beings. Resources such as hospice, faith communities, and ritualistic ceremonies and practices can help us as we face the difficult tasks in the grieving process.

RESOURCES

"A Guide to Living Wills and Health Care Proxies" Harvard Medical School Special Health Reports. Harvard Health Publications.

Aging with Dignity
P.O. Box 1661
Tallahassee, FL 32302
888-594-7437 (888-5-WISHES)
http://www.agingwithdignity.org

American Association of Retired Persons
601 E Street, NW
Washington, DC 20049
888-687-2277
http://www.aarp.org

American Bar Association
321 North Clark Street
Chicago, IL 60610
312-988-5522; 800-285-2221
www.abanet.org/aging/toolkit/home.html
www.abanet.org/aging/myths.html

"Being Prepared: A Resource Guide for End-of-Life Decisions and Planning" Oregon Governor's Commission on Senior Services. 500 Summer Street, NE E02, Salem, OR 97301-1015. 800-282-8096

Caring Connections
1700 Diagonal Road, Suite 625
Alexandria, VA 22314
703-837-1500; 800-658-8898
http://www.caringinfo.org

Center for Ethics in Health Care
Oregon Health & Science University
3181 SW Sam Jackson Park Road
Portland, OR 97239-3098
503-494-4466
http://www.ohsu.edu/ethics

"Caring Conversations: A State Specific Workbook on End-Of-Life Decisions" Midwest Bioethics Center, 1999. Available from AARP.

Doka, Kenneth J., ed. *Caregiving and Loss.* Hospice Foundation of America, 2001.

Doka, Kenneth J., ed. *Living with Grief: Loss in Later Life.* Hospice Foundation of America, 2002).

Hospice Foundation of America — www.hospicefoundation.org

National Hospice & Palliative Care Organization (NHPCO)
1700 Diagonal Road, Suite 625
Alexandria, VA 22314
703-837-1500
http://www.nhpco.org

"The Dying Process: A Guide for Caregivers" Hospice Foundation of America, 2005.

U.S. Living Will Registry
P.O. Box 2789
Westfield, NJ 07091-2789
800-548-9455 (1-800-LIV-WILL)
http://www.uslivingwillregistry.com

Index